# ANATOMY OF TORTURE

# ANATOMY OF TORTURE

Ron E. Hassner

CORNELL UNIVERSITY PRESS   ITHACA AND LONDON

First published 2022 by Cornell University Press

Library of Congress Cataloging-in-Publication Data
Names: Hassner, Ron E. (Ron Eduard), author.
Title: Anatomy of torture / Ron E. Hassner.
Description: Ithaca [New York] : Cornell University Press, 2022. | Includes
    bibliographical references and index.
Identifiers: LCCN 2021033284 (print) | ISBN 9781501762031 (hardcover) | ISBN
    9781501762048 (ebook) | ISBN 9781501762055 (pdf)
Subjects: LCSH: Torture—Spain—History. | Inquisition—Spain. | Torture—
    Mexico—Mexico City—History. | Inquisition—Mexico—Mexico City.
Classification: LCC HV8599.S8 .H37 2022  (print) | LCC HV8599.S8  (ebook) |
    DDC 364.6/750946—dc23
LC record available at https://lccn.loc.gov/2021033284
LC ebook record available at https://lccn.loc.gov/2021033285

*In memory of Carolyn Paxton (1948–2020)*
*who loved truth, justice, and history,*
*and cherished human worth and dignity*

# Contents

# ANATOMY OF TORTURE

# HOW LITTLE WE KNOW
# ABOUT TORTURE

Does torture "work"? My answer will frustrate some readers and infuriate others. Those who believe that torture "doesn't work" will read that torture has, at times, forced victims to divulge crucial and truthful information that they would not otherwise have revealed. On the other hand, those readers who regard torture to be a quick and effective, if cruel, tool for addressing "ticking bomb" threats will learn that torture is slow and tends to provide fragmentary information even under optimal conditions. It also exacts a tremendous social, political, and moral cost. Bluntly put, torture "works" but not the way you think it does.

It is impossible to assess the nature of modern torture. We know too little about contemporary cases, in the United States or elsewhere. Most of the information on recent US torture is classified and is likely to remain inaccessible for decades to come. Evidence from twentieth-century cases is equally sparse. Governments that have engaged in torture have not released comprehensive data that would permit a thorough analysis. Witness accounts are no less problematic. Victims and perpetrators alike are loath to share their experiences. Social science research on confrontational interrogation methods relies on analyses of police interrogations or on laboratory experiments, neither of which involve torture.

There exists, however, an underutilized historical source that can shed significant light on the nature of torture. That source is the archives of the Spanish Inquisition. This book is the first to wield extensive data from the Inquisition in order to conduct a dispassionate empirical analysis of torture, its causes, characteristics, and effects. I analyze scores of manuscripts, drawn from key periods in the history of the Spanish Inquisition, to provide an anatomy of torture.

To analyze these findings, I bring together two research programs that have not been in conversation with one another: the historiography of the Spanish Inquisition and the study of contemporary interrogational torture. I analyze the intersection of these two literatures by means of a third field of inquiry, the scholarship on intelligence analysis, to explore how the Inquisition assessed information extracted by coercive and noncoercive means and to explain why it adopted the torture practices that it came to adopt.

This book does not purport to provide *the* anatomy of torture. Five-hundred-year-old evidence can only teach us so much about current torture practices. This is *an* anatomy of torture. It is a study of how torture has been employed in the past, in a specific period and under particular circumstances. Those circumstances are extreme: the Inquisition's target population was confined within the realms of an authoritarian state in which the Inquisition wielded absolute power and could draw on near-unlimited resources. The most important of these resources was time. The Inquisition suffered none of the pressures of a combat setting or an antiterrorism campaign. It could afford to spend decades and centuries perfecting its methods, and it could afford to dedicate years to gathering evidence against its prisoners. Thus the specific anatomy of torture presented here functions as an a fortiori argument. It showcases the strengths and weaknesses of torture under the most permissive conditions, which are unlikely to be met during future interrogation efforts in the United States or other democracies.

How best to define torture has become a matter of some contention in the context of the US counterterrorism effort post-9/11. The United Nations Convention against Torture defines torture broadly to include "any act by which severe pain and suffering, whether physical or mental, is intentionally inflicted on a person for such purposes as obtaining from him or a third person information or a confession, punishing him for an act he or a third person has committed or is suspected of having committed, or intimidating or coercing him or a third party."[1] In contrast, US advocates of "enhanced interrogation" have conceived of torture more narrowly to include only physical pain that is equivalent in intensity to serious physical injury, such as organ failure or death. They have argued that US coercive interrogation practices fall short of constituting torture.[2]

No such ambiguity clouds the Inquisition's definition of torture. As I elucidate in the next chapter, inquisitorial handbooks defined torture very clearly. It consisted of only three forms of physical coercion, applied only in the torture chamber, under strictly delimited circumstances. The Inquisition did not regard harsh confinement prior to interrogation, or the threat of torture, to be torture, nor did it regard painful sentences executed after the end of a trial, such as lashes or hard labor, to be part of that torture.

Institutions have employed torture to punish, hurt, and terrorize. My focus in this book is exclusively on interrogational torture, torture designed to extract information. Interrogational torture is analytically distinct from confessional torture, torture designed to elicit particular statements. In reality, these categories overlap, and they overlap with other forms of torture, such as torture designed to intimidate, or control a population. Often, torturers will purport to torture for one purpose while introducing other goals, intentionally or accidentally.

I divide interrogational torture into two types: exploratory torture and corroborative torture. Exploratory torture is interrogational torture that occurs early in an investigation in order to reveal novel information. As I show, this type of interrogational torture rarely yielded information that the Inquisition found significant or reliable. In the absence of parallel sources of information, detainees subjected to exploratory torture were able to provide false information, hide true information, or pretend not to know much. Indeed, given how sparse information can be at the outset of an investigation, the Inquisition often subjected detainees to exploratory torture even though they had no relevant information to share. Exploratory torture fails because it risks interrogating the wrong individuals and because it fails to uncover the right information. A second type of interrogational torture, corroborative torture, occurs toward the end of an investigation. It is used to confirm or reject prior information, not to generate new discoveries. At times, this type of interrogational torture provided the Inquisition with truthful, and useful, information. Nonetheless, the Inquisition treated its results with suspicion, as one questionable source among many in its investigations.

The next chapter will demonstrate that the primary goal of inquisitorial torture was interrogational, and not confessional as is often falsely believed. The Inquisition was not interested in unfalsifiable claims about belief, and it did not demand, let alone believe, confessions of faith. The "confessions" that the Inquisition sought were falsifiable statements of fact about heretical practices, not heretical ideas or sentiments. The Inquisition corroborated these testimonies by contrasting them with parallel sources of evidence, as any intelligence-gathering organization would. In that sense, its stated goals were not much different than the purported goals of contemporary intelligence agencies. And since the stated goal of inquisitorial torture was interrogatory, that is also the standard against which I evaluate its results. Did its suspects reveal accurate information that the Inquisition considered useful, as a result of torture, that they would not have revealed in the absence of torture?

Drawing on hundreds of cases of inquisitorial torture, I show that interrogational torture did provide the Inquisition with reliable information under very restricted conditions. Like all sources of intelligence, interrogational torture misguided and mislead much of the time. But it also yielded accurate and actionable intelligence, especially once the Inquisition developed sophisticated tools to discern truth from lies. Its tribunals used information on heretical practices, some of which was extracted by means of violence or threat of violence, to eradicate entire communities of Jews, Muslims, and non-Catholic Christians.

I also demonstrate that interrogational torture was an imperfect source of information. Unlike many of their modern counterparts, inquisitors did not regard torture as easy, quick, or cheap. Despite the immense resources and freedoms at their disposal, they treated torture cautiously, even suspiciously. Inquisitors tortured as a last resort in order to corroborate existing information, not in order to uncover new leads. They never relied exclusively on information gleaned from torture to condemn the accused.

Both of these findings have important implications for ongoing torture debates. Torture critics are unwise to base their condemnations on efficacy grounds, for two reasons, one stronger than the other. For one, torture has occasionally proven effective at extracting relevant information. This is an unfortunate reality, but it is also a fact. More important, the efficacy of torture has no bearing on morality. Critics should judge the morality of torture on moral grounds. If torture is evil, its efficacy is irrelevant.

At the same time, torture defenders are misguided in advocating for torture as a counterterrorism "silver bullet." Torture is least effective where torture proponents advocate its use most enthusiastically: when responses to urgent crises call for novel and comprehensive information. In actuality, torture proceeds in small and modest steps. Analyzing intelligence extracted by means of torture requires corroboration, and corroboration takes time. Because corroboration is crucial, intelligence analysts will always distrust information that was provided by one source at one particular moment in time compared to intelligence gradually culled from multiple independent sources. No torture has, or will ever, defuse a "ticking bomb."

## The Problem of Feeble Evidence

No form of torture has come to symbolize American torture policy more than waterboarding. But what, exactly, is waterboarding? Does it involve drowning or just the perception of drowning? Does water enter the detainee's lungs, posing a threat to life? As practiced in the Philippines under Ferdinand Marcos, or in Algeria under French occupation, waterboarding involved pouring water down a detainee's throat until he was "filled . . . up with water."[3] In contrast, as practiced on US troops during Survival, Evasion, Resistance, and Escape (SERE) training, waterboarding involved water on the face only, to "mimic" drowning.[4] Which of these variants did the CIA practice in the aftermath of September 11, 2001? Outside the CIA, nobody seems to know the answer.

Some propose that it creates the mere illusion of drowning. According to a Senate report on the treatment of detainees in US custody, waterboarding is "the use of a wet towel and dripping water to induce the *misperception* of drowning."[5] CIA officials offered a different description to *ABC News*: "Cellophane is wrapped over the prisoner's face and water is poured over him. Unavoidably, the gag reflex kicks in and a terrifying fear of drowning leads to almost instant pleas to bring the treatment to a halt."[6] An August 2002 memorandum by the Department of Justice described the procedure as involving a saturated cloth: "Once the cloth is saturated and completely covers the mouth and nose, air flow is slightly restricted for 20 to 40 seconds due to the presence of the cloth."[7] Jose Rodriguez, former director of the CIA's National Clandestine Service, claims that waterboarding involves neither drowning nor asphyxiation. Rather, it creates "the *sensation* of being on the verge of drowning."[8] Mark Fallon, director of the Criminal Investigative Task Force in Guantánamo confirms: Waterboarding "can *feel like* you're drowning . . . *as if* you're suffocating."[9]

Others have proposed that waterboarding drowns detainees outright. The *New York Times* cited an administration memorandum that authorized the CIA to use full-body dunking, tying a detainee to a board and pushing him under water "until he nearly drowns."[10] A Salon.com exposé alleged that CIA interrogators "pumped detainees full of so much water that the CIA turned to a special saline solution to minimize the risk of death."[11] A Navy instructor who oversaw hundreds of waterboarding training sessions argued that "it's not simulated anything. It's slow-motion suffocation."[12] Other critics split the difference, proposing that waterboarding manages to somehow both imitate and cause drowning. For example, one historian describes contemporary waterboarding as "pouring water down the victim's throat to simulate, with terrifying reality, the sensation of drowning."[13] He does not explain how the procedure can both simulate suffocation and suffocate at the same time. Summarizing, Darius Rejali characterizes what we know about contemporary waterboarding as "incoherent."[14]

We also do not know how often waterboarding has been employed or with what results. One CIA source claims that Abu Zubaydah (AZ) was waterboarded only once, for thirty to thirty-five seconds. A second CIA source claims that he was waterboarded about five times. AZ told the Red Cross that he was waterboarded at least ten times. But a third CIA report claims that he was waterboarded 83 times.[15] Federal Bureau of Investigation (FBI) interrogator Ali Soufan claims that Khalid Sheikh Mohammed (KSM) was waterboarded 183 times, a CIA source claims that he was waterboarded fifteen times, but KSM himself told the Red Cross that he was waterboarded five times.[16] Which of those statements is correct?

The study of interrogational torture has made significant strides in recent years.[17] But the literature on contemporary US torture continues to be riven by bitter disagreements about the causes and effects of torture. At the foundation of these disagreements lie basic uncertainties about facts. Scholars know little about torture in the twentieth century and even less about torture in the aftermath of 9/11. Much of their assessment is based on speculation, at best, or a selective reading of the historical record, at worst. The evidence available is spotty, frequently unverifiable, and often biased, intentionally or otherwise.[18] FBI and CIA accounts, for example, provide a great deal of evidence about institutional rivalry and bureaucratic animosity but little reliable evidence about the efficacy of the US torture program. As a consequence, the ongoing debate around interrogational torture suffers from a good deal of guesswork, misinformation, and prejudice.

The fault lines, dividing those who see torture as effective from those who do not, run along several predictable axes. Among US political leaders, conservatives tend to laud the utility (and legality) of torture more often than their liberal counterparts.[19] Intelligence officials tend to be split by rank and intelligence service. Low-level interrogators who have offered testimonies of their experiences have expressed disdain for torture.[20] CIA officials have affirmed the value of torture whereas their FBI counterparts have criticized the practice.[21] Jose Rodriguez, the former head of the CIA's Counterterrorism Center (CTC) in the aftermath of 9/11, has spoken most vocally in defense of torture:

> I am certain, beyond any doubt, that these techniques . . . shielded the people of the United States from harm and led to the capture and killing of Usama bin Ladin. . . . I am confident that more than ten serious mass-casualty attacks were thwarted because of information received from detainees who had been subjected to enhanced interrogation. . . . What I can swear to you, as head of CTC at the time, and what every one of the people working under me implementing the program would tell you, is that we have never in our careers ever seen such important, critical, and lifesaving intelligence come from any other program.[22]

James Mitchell, who developed the CIA's enhanced interrogation program, later argued: "I can say with confidence that in my opinion they never would have given up the information that led to bin Ladin without enhanced measures."[23] Several former CIA directors have alleged that torture provided a bulk of the knowledge about the structure and activities of al-Qaeda, assisted in thwarting al-Qaeda efforts, and facilitated the killing of Osama bin Laden.[24] Former CIA director Michael Hayden has also argued that, much as the public might object to torture, it could not object to its effectiveness.[25] His opinion was initially echoed by Deputy National Security Adviser John Brennan, who argued that torture yielded counterterrorism information that "has saved lives."[26]

But Brennan later amended his view, arguing that the Senate Select Intelligence Committee Report on CIA interrogation "raises serious questions" about the information he was given regarding torture.[27] Former FBI director Robert S. Mueller was more outspoken: he rejected the notion that interrogational torture had thwarted terror attacks. An FBI taskforce concluded in 2003 that torture tactics "have produced no intelligence of a threat neutralizing nature to date."[28] There is a divergence of opinion about torture even within the CIA. Some CIA personnel characterized torture as "bad interrogation" but others note that the topic is the subject of an ongoing debate in the organization because many members found the practice "both valid and necessary."[29] A CIA Inspector General report of May 2004 found it "difficult to determine conclusively" whether torture had helped prevent specific terror attacks.[30] When Hayden's predecessor as CIA director, Porter Goss, asked two national security experts to evaluate the effectiveness of the CIA's interrogation program that same year, one concluded that it was effective but the other offered "a more ambiguous conclusion."[31]

To validate their claims about the effectiveness of US torture, intelligence officials cite the outcome of recent interrogations, especially those of al-Qaeda related detainees. Even here testimonies conflict.[32] Officials have cited multiple cases in which detainees subjected to torture provided the names of insurgents, tactics, or planned operations.[33] Yet a 2012 report of the Senate Select Committee on Intelligence concluded that the CIA's torture "was not an effective means of acquiring intelligence," citing lack of proof that torture had prevented attacks or saved lives.[34] The Senate Select Committee on Intelligence relied on over six million pages of classified CIA documents to prepare its six-thousand-page report on CIA interrogation methods, but it only made public the five-hundred-page executive summary of that report, and that too is extensively redacted. It will remain classified until 2028. The CIA criticized the report for its alleged bias and errors, noting that the committee did not interview any CIA officials involved in the program.[35] Rebutting the report authored by their Democratic colleagues, Republican members of the Senate Select Committee on Intelligence wrote that they had "no doubt that the CIA's detention program saved lives and played a vital role in weakening al Qaeda."[36]

CIA officials claim that the torture of Khalid Sheikh Mohammed (KSM) disrupted five separate terror plots and led to the capture of Osama bin Laden.[37] After six weeks of sleep deprivation and "walling," KSM is said to have provided information about Riduan Isamuddin ("Hambali"), mastermind of the 2002 Bali bombing, who was planning a second wave of hijacked airplane attacks in LA, Seattle, and Chicago.[38] KSM's torture is also said to have helped in the arrest of Iyman Faris, tasked with attacking the Brooklyn Bridge; Jafar al-Tayyar, who plotted an attack on the New York subway; and Saifullah and Uzair Paracha, who were trying to smuggle explosives into the United States to target East Coast gas stations.[39] These claims are disputed by senators Diane Feinstein, Carl Levin, and John McCain, who argued that KSM revealed his most significant information prior to being tortured.[40]

The CIA claims that the torture of Abu Zubaydah (AZ) yielded "some of the most important intelligence collected since 9/11," because he knew bin Laden personally and could identify all major al-Qaeda leaders, including KSM and his secret alias. His torture, they argue, prompted operations that led to the capture, killing, or disruption of many other al-Qaeda operatives, including Jose Padilla, Ramzi bin al-Shibh, and Hassan Gul. They further claim that, as a result of sleep deprivation, slapping, and waterboarding, AZ agreed to work with the CIA, provided unsolicited information, and even advised the agency on how to best use torture on other detainees.[41] FBI agent Ali Soufan disputes these claim.[42] Whereas Rodriguez argues that the CIA resorted to torture because the FBI's "ham handed" approach led AZ to "clam up," Soufan claims that AZ cooperated during noncoercive interrogation by the FBI but ceased to provide information once the CIA took over.[43] Rodriguez dismisses this FBI claim as "absurd," argues that FBI agents are not privy to the intelligence obtained from AZ, and characterizes Soufan as "lying or deluded."[44] In contrast to both, James E. Mitchell, who participated in the interrogation of AZ, describes this interrogation as a "team effort" by the FBI and the CIA, combining sleep deprivation, rapport building, psychological and religious manipulation, and astute intelligence analysis.[45] These accounts cannot be squared.

## The Problem of Unreliable Sources

Given the uncertainty surrounding simple empirical questions about contemporary torture, like the nature or rate of waterboarding, the lack of consensus on the nature of torture is hardly surprising. One scholar notes: "We really have no idea how reliable torture is as a way of obtaining information."[46] Another adds: "Evaluating the efficacy of torture requires information not currently available and perhaps unknowable."[47] Initiating a rigorous research program on interrogational torture requires distinguishing myths from facts, but reliable data on contemporary torture are hard to come by.[48]

Scholars are now beginning to mine historical archives for detailed records of past torture campaigns. If information on current torture practices serves as the battleground between torture proponents and opponents inside the intelligence community, past records on torture form the arena in which historians struggle to assess the efficacy of torture. The sparsity and ambiguity of the historical record pose the most serious challenge for that assessment.

For example, French historian Lisa Silverman has analyzed 785 trials in France between 1500 and the mid-1700s in which torture was occasionally employed. She found that less than 14 percent of the cases yielded confessions.[49] Yet Silverman does not note how frequently torture was employed in these trials, does not report how high the confession rate was in the absence of torture, and does not assess the veracity of those confessions that did occur.

Accounts of torture under Communist rule in China and Russia draw on occasional survivor accounts and select trial documents that do not suffice to establish patterns of cause, use, or efficacy.[50] Statistics regarding torture during the Second World War are no easier to obtain. Anecdotal evidence suggests that the torture of Croatian, French, and Norwegian resistance fighters occasionally provided the Gestapo with important intelligence, but because German intelligence relied on a combination of threats, informants, and torture, used in parallel, it can be hard to parse which of these sources provided valuable, let alone exclusive, information.[51] Only three official documents on the Gestapo use of torture have survived the Second World War.[52] Analogous archival evidence regarding British torture of German POW's in the "London Cage" seems to show that 30 percent of German prisoners provided information.[53] Yet, this evidence is based on POW testimony alone. The data include no information on how many of the prisoners were tortured, what information they provided, or what the collaboration rate was among those who were not tortured.[54]

Albert Biderman conducted one of the most ambitious studies of torture in the postwar era based on interviews with US POWs who were tortured during the Korean War.[55] Like his predecessors, Biderman had no access to documentary evidence, let alone information from interrogators, prior to conducting his analysis. His finding, that torture intensifies rather than weakens resistance, thus relied entirely on the claims of torture survivors who, naturally, reported to their fellow Americans that they had kept silent under torture. More troubling yet, Biderman's analysis had a primary influence on the CIA's declassified manual on interrogation, the *KUBARK Counterintelligence Manual*, and shaped US torture policy after 2001.[56]

The French counterinsurgency in Algeria should have provided a robust source of empirical evidence on torture, given its massive scope. Of the twenty-four thousand Algerians detained, some 80 percent of men and 66 percent of women are said to have been tortured. Yet the French released no official figures, let alone names or transcripts, and declassified no reports that provide details on the nature of that torture campaign.[57] The most robust source of information regarding torture in the Battle of Algiers consists of a collection of affidavits and letters from torture survivors, most of whom claim to have successfully resisted torture.[58] General Paul Aussaresses and Colonel Marcel Bigeard, on the other hand, claimed that torture produced "good results" and provided the only means of extracting real-time information from insurgents.[59] More recently, Aussaresses went so far as to recommend torture to his American counterparts as "the only way" to make al-Qaeda suspects reveal their plots.[60] Yet, as Darius Rejali notes, the French have offered not a single persuasive example of a case in which torture yielded success.[61]

The US Army's experience with torture in Vietnam was codified into a series of Army Field Manuals, starting in 1967, all of which denounced torture for its "unreliable results," for discrediting the United States and for undermining its war efforts. Here too witness accounts differ, ranging from the claim that "there can be no doubt that it extracted useful information in most cases" to the claim that torture "did not provide any worthwhile intelligence and often yielded false information."[62]

The Army Field Manual of 1992 brought the military into full compliance with the Geneva Conventions by prohibiting all forms of torture.[63] Scholars cite this and prior field manuals as reliable evidence regarding the inefficacy of torture.[64] William Levi has raised doubts about the credibility of that claim, noting that the purpose of these field manuals is not to provide factual analysis but to indoctrinate. They are not works of social science but handbooks designed to convince American soldiers that they can resist torture, should they fall into enemy hands.[65]

Among Israeli interrogators, some believe that torture produces misleading information while others argue that it can save lives.[66] When Israel's Supreme Court outlawed the use of torture, members of Israel's intelligence services claimed that the ban hampered counterterrorism efforts in at least one crucial case. Observers have found that claim difficult to assess.[67] Of the two most cited cases of counterterrorism torture, one resulted in operational failure and the other may not have involved torture at all.[68]

This hodgepodge of fractional cases and unreliable evaluations is characteristic of the publicly available information on the nature of interrogational torture. In each historical instance, the data are sparse and one sided, privileging either perpetrator claims about the efficacy of torture or victim claims about the inefficacy of torture. In not one historical instance is the evidence comprehensive enough to establish conclusive patterns, nor varied enough to permit tight comparisons between cases of coercive interrogation and cases of noncoercive interrogations. The few detailed accounts of specific torture incidents that exist rely on recollections after the fact. No government has released official records offering the details of specific torture sessions, let alone transcripts of such sessions. The Spanish Inquisition offers a remarkable exception.

## The Archives of the Spanish Inquisition

How the Inquisition tortured and why it did so is the theme of the next chapter. My goal here is to note the five advantages that this archival source holds over contemporary and historical sources.

First, the archives are vast, containing tens of thousands of files spanning two continents and three hundred years. Often, comprehensive records are available for the interrogation of entire communities, allowing us to trace how information provided under torture by one detainee led to the arrest, interrogation, or torture of others in their network.

Second, the files include cases of nonviolent interrogation alongside cases that involved torture in multiple forms, yielding a range of results. This makes it possible to compare information extracted by noncoercive means with information extracted by means of torture.

Third, the cases are not merely numerous but painstakingly detailed. Each suspect's file can consist of many dozens of pages of minute notes, recorded by secretaries who not only witnessed court deliberations that preceded and followed the interrogation but were also present in the torture chamber. Frequently, their notes include verbatim transcripts of torture sessions, allowing me to identify the precise conditions under which detainees began, or refused, to collaborate.

Fourth, contrary to popular perceptions, though the Inquisition was a religious institution established with ambitious religious goals in mind, it engaged in torture for pragmatic ends. The goal of the Inquisition's interrogation program was to identify the leaders, members, and facilities of underground networks of Jews, Muslims, and Protestants who practiced their religion covertly. It did not torture to extract confessions of faith. It employed torture in order to extract information regarding heretical *practices*, and it used that evidence to confirm or overturn evidence from witness testimony.

Fifth and finally, and again contrary to common expectations, the Holy Office of the Inquisition had no particular incentive to portray the effectiveness of torture in a positive or a negative light. Its reports were intended for internal consumption. Their readers did not consider interrogational torture abhorrent or remarkable. In their documents, inquisitors openly admitted to frequent instances of failed torture, compared and contrasted alternatives to torture, and displayed evidence of institutional learning over time.

Contrast how little we know about contemporary waterboarding with the wealth of information contained in one brief but harrowing excerpt from a single trial among the thousands available for analysis. This text comes from the trail documents of Marina González, a case I analyze in detail later in this book. She was tortured on April 29, 1494, in the Spanish city of Ciudad Real, about a hundred miles south of Madrid. Her words were recorded by a scribe who sat by her side in the torture chamber:

> She was stripped of her old skirts and put on the rack, and her arms and legs were tied tightly with cords. She also had a cord tied tightly around her head. They put a hood in front of her face, with a jar that held three pints, more or less. They started to pour water down her nose and throat. Having poured up to a pint, Lord Inquisitor Mazuecos asked her if she had done anything. She said no.
>
> They continued to give her water and told her to speak the truth. She said nothing. They gave her more water and said if she would speak the truth, they would not give her any more. She said nothing. His reverence ordered her to be given water until the three-pint jar ran out; she never said a word. He said that they should take the cord off her head, and she would speak the truth; the cord was taken off, but she said nothing. They tied her up again and began to give her more water from the jar, which they had refilled. He said that they should raise her head so she would speak the truth. They raised her, and she said nothing.
>
> When they put her back down again, she asked that she might be raised up, and for Holy Mary's sake, she would tell everything. . . . They gave her more water, and she said she would tell everything, for Holy Mary's sake. She said that a neighbor woman fasted during some fasts, and [she knew this] because she was her neighbor. She said that if they would take her from that place she would tell them about it, and if they would raise her head she would speak the truth.
>
> But when she was raised up, she refused to say anything at all. They again put the cord on her head, very tightly, and told her to say everything. They gave her more water, until the jar was empty, and she never said anything at all. Their reverences ordered her removed from the torture, as they did not hold her to torment her, etc.
>
> When she was removed from the torture, she said that her neighbor, the wife of Gómez de Chinchilla, resident of Ciudad Real, fasted. Asked which fasts, those of the Jews or of Christians, she said those of the Jews. Asked why she believed this, she said because the neighbor observed Saturdays.[69]

This brief excerpt provides more information on waterboarding than any single contemporary source currently available to us. No contemporary source offers this level of detail on torture procedures because no contemporary source relies on evidence collected in the torture chamber, let alone provides verbatim quotes from torture victims. We know exactly how and why Marina González was tortured. Since her trial is one of a network of more than a hundred interrelated trials in her town in this period, it is possible to analyze the causes and consequences of her torture, including the condemnations that led to it, statements made about her in other trials, and the veracity of her statements regarding the wife of Gómez de Chinchilla.

Several historians have collected detailed empirical data on the practices of the Spanish Inquisition.[70] Their findings are important, but they do not focus on torture, and they provide sparse information about torture rates, conditions, or outcomes. I supplement their findings with data from three archival sources. In chapter 3, I analyze a medium-sized dataset, containing 124 moderately detailed cases in late-fifteenth-century Ciudad Real. Torture occurred in nine of those cases, and I investigate why. I also document how the Inquisition changed its torture practices over the course of these trials, which lasted from 1474 to 1515. In chapter 4, I analyze a large dataset, consisting of 1,046 cases, from sixteenth-century Toledo; 123 of the detainees were victims of torture. This broad range of cases, and variation between cases (of torture and nontorture) allow me to uncover broad patterns in the use and efficacy of torture in this period. In chapters 5 and 6, I explore fine-grained accounts of trials against the Jewish community in Mexico City in the same period, to trace how the Inquisition used information extracted in the torture chamber to unravel a network of Judaizers, or crypto-Jews, nominal Christians who were practicing Judaism covertly.

Why focus on these three periods and locations? The manuscripts of the Spanish Inquisition are as vast as they are unplumbed when it comes to analyzing torture. It is impossible to explore the Inquisition's three-hundred-year history of torture with any semblance of thoroughness. Instead, I selected three moments in the Inquisition's history. The trials in Ciudad Real, explored in chapter 3, occur very early in the history of the Spanish Inquisition. The court was established in 1483, one year after the Inquisition was proclaimed in the Crown of Castile. But trials against Ciudad Real residents lasted until 1515, and in those thirty-two years the court's torture practices changed in subtle and illuminating ways. They provide evidence of institutional learning. In its latter years, the Ciudad Real court was transferred to, and merged with, the Toledo court. The cases in chapter 4 take up the procedures of that same court sixty years later, in the period 1575–1610. Chapters 5 and 6 explore inquisitorial torture on the other side of the world, in Mexico City. Whereas chapters 3 and 4 share geographical continuity, chapters 4, 5 and 6 share historical continuity: the trials in Mexico City occur between 1589–1601 and showcase many of the same patterns and outcomes as the parallel trials in Toledo.

A second reason for selecting these particular sets of documents, as opposed to any of the hundreds of other archives, is the variation in the quality and quantity of the data across archives. The 124 trials from Ciudad Real are detailed and quite numerous. The 1,046 trials from Toledo are less detailed and far more numerous. The dozen trials from Mexico City that I analyze are very detailed.

Finally, I chose to focus on these three instances of torture because of the relative ease of access. Inquisition manuscripts can be difficult to decipher. They are handwritten in a five-hundred-year-old Castilian dialect. The texts display no punctuation marks and are replete with abbreviations, obscure notations, and idiosyncratic references. I am a political scientist, not a historian of the Inquisition, and I have no particular expertise in archival work for this period. So, I was glad to build on the partial transcribing and translating work initiated by eminent historians of the Inquisition.

As I detail in the chapters that follow, Chaim Beinart collected, transcribed, and annotated (but did not translate) the Ciudad Real trials. Henry Charles Lea discovered, transcribed, and translated the summary records for the trials in Toledo (though his handwriting, too, required significant deciphering). The trials of the Carvajal family and the Jewish community surrounding them have been the topic of much scholarship, particularly by Martin A. Cohen, Samuel Temkin, Stanley M. Hordes, and David M. Gitlitz. Those are some of the shoulders on which I have had had the privilege of standing. None of these scholars focused primarily on torture in their research. My efforts to analyze these cases through their work would not have been possible without a sizeable research and translation team. But the prior efforts invested by eminent historians in analyzing these documents helped point me toward fruitful resources and relieved me of the dread of diving unguided into the bottomless archives of the Inquisition in search of evidence.

## Torture in Cold Blood

What lessons does the experience of the Inquisition hold for the contemporary torture debate? I detail those lessons and contrast them with what scant evidence is available regarding US torture policy, in chapter 7. Two specific lessons deserve particular attention.

The first is that extracting reliable information from torture is a slow process. This is a crucial observation because the efficacy of torture is often lauded in crisis scenarios, so-called ticking bomb cases, in which speed is of the essence. Torture is not speedy for two reasons. One, which might be termed "the shadow of torture," is that anticipation, uncertainty, and dread play a crucial role in terrorizing torture victims. The Inquisition learned that it was not merely pain but the expectation of future pain that motivated its prisoners to divulge information. That is why Inquisition tribunals were required to threaten torture, at least three times, prior to exposing their victim to the torture chamber and the tools of torment. The Inquisition also learned, in the first years after it was established, to imprison victims for periods of months and years prior to torturing them. It found that prisoners often provided information between torture sessions, and not necessarily in the torture chamber, so it employed multiple sessions, punctuated by lengthy pauses of weeks or months, even when the initial use of torture seemed to reveal useful information. These pauses permitted prisoners to recover from torture, thus magnifying the effects of subsequent torture, but they also induced a terrifying uncertainty regarding the timing and severity of that subsequent torture.

The second reason why torture was slow has to do with the fundamentals of intelligence analysis. Information extracted from torture, like intelligence extracted from any other source, requires sorting, analysis, corroboration, and confirmation. In the case of the Inquisition, this involved contrasting evidence from the torture chamber with evidence provided by voluntary witnesses, evidence collected in the homes of suspects, evidence provided in other trials, and information revealed in other torture sessions. The files of the Inquisition are often detailed enough to allow us, the readers, to follow this process of corroboration and to see why the Inquisition recalled particular witnesses, why it distrusted some statements but not others, and when it chose to decree torture. This process of collecting and contrasting parallel evidence took a great deal of time and patience. But then again, the Inquisition was in no hurry to complete its inquiries. It was not operating under crisis conditions. It patiently gathered information about suspects for years before deciding whether to administer torture.

As one example of the complexity of the process of correlation that the Inquisition oversaw, consider that scribes were required to make multiple handwritten copies of every testimony, coerced or voluntary, so that these copies could be appended to the trial documents of every suspect who was mentioned in that testimony. Thus, identical copies of one and the same testimony that names, say, twenty suspects can be found in each of the twenty court documents of those suspects. This made it relatively easy to connect cases to one another. But it was also a laborious and time-consuming process.

A second lesson to be gleaned from the Inquisition's experience relates to the role of torture in relationship to other sources of information. The Inquisition assigned a secondary role to torture in its investigations. It treated information extracted by means of torture with suspicion. With all its authority and resources, its full and complete control over society and its members, its ability to arrest and interrogate everyone and anyone, the Inquisition did not resort to torture primarily in order to uncover new evidence. It used torture primarily as a means of confirming or disconfirming evidence extracted earlier by nonviolent means.

Inquisitorial tribunals did engage in a modicum of (what I call) "exploratory torture" at the outset of series of trials. The information it extracted from those early torture sessions was sparse and often misleading. In the absence of parallel information from alternative sources, there was no way for the tribunal to disconfirm torture statements or to know whether a victim was withholding information. The bulk of the torture executed by the Inquisition occurred at the very end of a series of trials, close to the conclusion of those trials. This "corroborative torture" served to confirm or negate information previously collected outside the torture chamber rather than collect new information.

Why did the Inquisition assign this secondary role to torture? Simply put, the Inquisition did not trust information revealed in the torture chamber. Not, as some torture critics argue, because it worried that prisoners were merely parroting back what their interrogators wanted to hear. As I show, inquisitors were scrupulous about avoiding leading questions or providing clues to victims about what the tribunal knew, did not know, or wanted to learn. The accused were not even informed of the precise nature of their alleged crime, let alone the identity of the witnesses who had testified against them. Nor did the Inquisition mistrust evidence derived from torture because victims were likely to lie under threat of pain. After all, voluntary witnesses who came before the Inquisition were no less likely to deceive, and the court had multiple means of corroborating evidence and exposing lies, regardless of the conditions under which these lies were told. As I show in chapter 3, the Inquisition even used torture to expose lies that had been told outside the torture chamber.

It is possible that inquisitors were aware of the negative impact that pain has on memory and recollection, an effect confirmed by modern psychologists who study torture. More important, the Inquisition, like any institution designed to gather and analyze information, distrusted dramatic revelations from individual sources. Intelligence analysis proceeds in cautious steps.[71] Because torture seeks to draw substantiable information from one witness, its findings defy the fundamental logic underlying intelligence analysis procedures and contradicts the basic instincts of intelligence analysts.

All new information is inherently unreliable. Some sources are more knowledgeable than others, some deceive intentionally, others unintentionally. This reality calls for a piecemeal approach to information gathering. Every new piece of information has to be evaluated based on its relationship to existing information. This comparison serves to corroborate new information, so that this information can be incorporated into the larger intelligence picture or be rejected. The burden is on the new information to prove its worth in contrast to the mass of evidence that has already been carefully accumulated. When doubts arise, because a new datum does not fit well with the already assembled picture, it is the new datum and not the picture that is put in question. As a result, analysts view with greatest suspicion information that is surprising or derives from a single source.

Inquisitors learned that multiple voluntary witnesses, contributing small snippets of information that could be assembled into a coherent image, were far more reliable than the copious statements of desperate torture victims, eager to reveal all they knew. Furthermore, since the guidelines that moderated the use of torture required that it be employed only in cases of strong but incomplete suspicion, inquisitors had to assemble sufficient information from alternative sources before torture could even be contemplated. This, combined with the desire to delay torture until the victim had been imprisoned for prolonged periods of time, meant that torture occurred at the end of long series of trials. It was used to tie up loose ends, and to corroborate evidence collected outside the torture chamber. And it was used to ensure that prisoners had provided a full and complete declaration for the salvation of their souls, even if the content of that declaration was already known to the court.

Perfecting its institutional practices over the course of decades and centuries led the Inquisition to develop an array of cruel but efficient procedures for extracting truthful statements from uncooperative suspects. The methods of the Inquisition stand in stark contrast to American torture policy. In the aftermath of 9/11, US interrogators quickly formed an interrogational torture program in order to prevent additional mass terror attacks and dismantle the al-Qaeda network. American interrogators tortured rashly, amateurishly, and haphazardly. These interrogation sessions were not carried out by professionals, they were not overseen by a bureaucracy according to strictly delimited procedures, and they did not lead to an accumulation of organizational expertise. Rather than torturing those believed to withhold crucial information, CIA personnel tortured suspected terrorist leaders who, they believed, had "blood on their hands." Culpability, not utility, determined who would be tortured. This was hot-blooded torture.

The torture practices of the Inquisition were the result of centuries of institutional learning. It came to torture the young and the old, the guilty and the innocent, those accused of severe offenses and those merely suspected of hiding information. There was nothing urgent, improvised, or ad hoc about its methods. It tortured slowly, holding prisoners in its cells for months and years before tormenting them in the torture chamber. It did not torture primarily to punish or to terrify, nor did it torture with particular enthusiasm. It tortured as part of a bureaucratic procedure designed to collect information. It tortured in cold blood.

## Lessons from the Spanish Inquisition

Analysis of the archival evidence from the Spanish Inquisition allows us to identify, for the first time, exactly how inquisitorial torture worked in the fifteenth and sixteenth centuries. Yet applying lessons from these historical cases to current concerns demands extreme caution. The following pages explore three moments in the extensive history of the Inquisition. A great deal of additional archival research would be necessary in order to establish whether the patterns that I have identified in Ciudad Real, Toledo, and Mexico City, in these particular periods, apply to the torture practices of the Inquisition elsewhere. Even institutionally and geographically affiliated tribunals, such as the Spanish Inquisitions in Lima, the Canary Islands, or Sicily, or the Inquisition in Portugal and its overseas territories, faced different realities. These challenges—availability of witnesses and suspects, legal and financial constraints, and institutional priorities—varied across time and space. Consequently, the torture practices of the Inquisition also evolved over time. I document some of that evolution in chapter 3 and show some consistency across cases in later years but this amounts to little more than an initial foray into the extensive evidence available.

More important, the historical context in which the Inquisition tortured differed drastically from the circumstances in which torture takes place today. Inquisitors used many of the methods that contemporary torturers employ, and their victims share the physiology and psychology of modern torture victims. There is no reason to assume that sixteenth-century suspects were more or less susceptible to torture than are contemporary detainees. But that is where the similarities end and key differences between the cases become apparent. Inquisitors tortured for different reasons, with different goals, based on different assumptions, and in a social, political, and religious setting that is entirely alien to that of modern interrogators. For example, inquisitors focused their interrogations on uncovering past crimes and were less concerned with the future intentions of their victims. American interrogators, on the other hand, have employed torture to uncover existing plans to commit future attacks, a far more difficult task. Carelessly translating insights from one case to the other poses real dangers to scholarship, to policy, and to professional ethics.

Why then turn to five-hundred-year-old cases for lessons on interrogational torture? Because no other historical moment comes close to providing even a fraction of the evidence that the Spanish Inquisition provides. Its archives are immense, detailed, meticulously organized, and publicly available. While scholars have labored to glean hints about contemporary torture campaigns, with only the vaguest notion of the identity of victims, why they were tortured, the information they provided, or the veracity of that information, the records of the Inquisition provide hundreds of thousands of comprehensive accounts of arrests, trials, testimonies, and verdicts, including verbatim transcripts from the torture chamber. There is no equal to this empirical wealth in the history of interrogational torture.

These data serve to disabuse us of several wrongheaded notions about the nature of torture. The Inquisition put in place a vast bureaucratic apparatus designed to collect and assess information about prohibited practices. It tortured comprehensively, inflicting suffering on large swaths of the population. It tortured systematically, willing to torment all whom it deemed to be withholding evidence, regardless of how severe their heresy was or how significant the evidence was that they were withholding. The Inquisition did not torture because there were gaps in its records that it wanted to fill by tormenting a new witness. On the contrary, it tortured because its records were comprehensive enough to indicate that a witness was withholding evidence.

This torture yielded information that was often reliable and falsifiable. Names, locations, events, and practices provided by witnesses in the torture chamber matched information provided by witnesses that were not tortured. This finding bears important implications for contemporary torture critics. These critics stand on shaky ground when they claim that "torture never works." Instead, they should rest their opposition to torture on moral grounds. They ought to reject torture because it dehumanizes its victims, treats them as instruments rather than as beings of value. Unlike killing in war, in which those attacked can defend themselves, torture is an attack on the defenseless, who cannot shield themselves, evade, or retaliate, and who cannot know when or whether the attack will ever end. Torture opponents should reject torture despite the fact that it may at times work, and despite the costs that a refusal to torture might carry. I discuss the moral implications of my argument in detail in the epilogue to this book, including the ethical implications of this research agenda for scholars of torture.

Torture advocates, in turn, should note well that the most powerful institution to have utilized torture systematically, the Spanish Inquisition, treated the results of torture with suspicion. Tribunals tortured witnesses rarely and, if necessary, only at the very end of a series of investigations. Despite the tremendous investment in time, money, and manpower that the Inquisition put into institutionalizing torture, its officials did not rely on the resulting testimony as a primary source of evidence. For example, in Mexico City, not one crypto-Jew was executed based only on evidence extracted in the torture chamber.

This systematic, dispassionate, and meticulous torture stands in stark contrast to US torture policy in the aftermath of 9/11. The torture perpetrated by US officials has been selective, vindictive, and reserved for a handful of al-Qaeda leaders presumed to have "blood on their hands." Executed under tremendous time pressure, interrogators tortured rashly, improvising methods and protocols. Whereas the victims of the Spanish Inquisition sat in prison for months and years before they were tortured, CIA interrogators hoped to extract "actionable intelligence" from terror suspects within days after they were apprehended. Most troublingly, US interrogators engaged in what I call "exploratory torture." They expected to uncover information from detainees that was groundbreaking: novel, crucial, yet somehow trustworthy. That is an unverifiable standard of intelligence that the Inquisition, despite its vast bureaucratic apparatus and centuries of institutional learning, would not have trusted. The Inquisition focused its efforts on corroborative torture, used to confirm or reject existing information, not on torture to uncover new information.

The Inquisition functioned in an extraordinary environment. Should US interrogators aspire to match the collaboration rate of the Inquisition's torture campaign, they would have to emulate the Inquisition's brutal scope, and vast resources. Our society would have to acquiesce to a massive bureaucratized torture campaign, at times of peace or war, that targeted thousands, from all walks of life, regardless of culpability, in order to extract modest intelligence that was, at best, corroborative. The archives of the Spanish Inquisition suggest that "successful" torture affords no middle ground. One cannot improvise quick, amateurish, and half-hearted torture sessions, motivated by anger and fear, and hope to extract reliable intelligence. Torture that yields reliable intelligence requires a massive social, political, and financial enterprise founded on deep ideological and political commitments. That is the cost of torture.

# THREE MYTHS ABOUT THE SPANISH INQUISITION

Can the experiences of the Spanish Inquisition teach us about contemporary interrogational torture? If popular portrayals of the Inquisition are to be believed, the answer is "no." In these depictions, sadistic leather-clad inquisitors torment their victims with a range of perverse devices, tearing at flesh, driving spikes into oozing bodies, breaking bones, and burning skin. Ruthless and relentless, the torment ceases only when the captive has screamed out the confession of faith that the inquisitor demanded all along. Or when they die on the rack.

Had this indeed been an accurate description of torture under the Spanish Inquisition, then there would be little we could learn from its archives. Its torture would have performed a confessional, rather than an interrogational function. The product of that torture would have been a meaningless (and unfalsifiable) confession of faith. And we would have been wise to treat with skepticism the self-reporting of an institution motivated by unconstrained sadism.

The reality was quite different. The Inquisition tortured ruthlessly and unhesitatingly, but it also tortured comprehensively, systematically, and meticulously. It practiced bureaucratized torture. It did not seek confessions of faith but statements of fact regarding specific religious offenses. Many of its victims provided that information. Most did not yet were released. Very few died in the torture chamber.

Why did the Inquisition torture? We can discern a mix of motives: corroboration, completeness, and salvation. Corroboration was needed because most of the information that served to identify heretical practices came from voluntary witness testimony, not from torture sessions. This witness testimony was often doubtful or contradictory. Uncoerced witnesses had reasons of their own to lie to the court: jealousy of neighbors, settling old scores, blackmail, or the wish to ingratiate oneself to the court. Evidence provided in the torture chamber could shed some light on witness testimony though, paradoxically, it raised equally serious questions of reliability, as the Inquisition admitted openly. Different forms of interrogation were used as complements, together with material evidence (such as items collected in the home or prison cell of the accused). Most often, the court used uncoerced testimony to corroborate testimony from torture, and not the other way around.

Completeness, the desire to assemble comprehensive dossiers, provided a stronger motivator for torture. Torture was reserved for witnesses who provided incomplete testimonies. In forcing all witnesses to reveal all they knew, the Inquisition could assure itself that it had exhausted all avenues of investigation prior to concluding a case. This explains why torture sessions tended to take place toward the end of individual trials and at the conclusion of networks of trials, often after years of investigations and questioning. The Inquisition did not rely on torture to uncover new evidence but to put the finishing touches on existing evidence so that a trial could end with a confident verdict, guilty or not, with no stone having been left unturned.

Underlying this pragmatic logic was a third, implicit, motivation: religion. Inquisitors were, as Edward Peters notes, "both jurists and pastors."[1] The Holy Office of the Inquisition regarded full and truthful confessions of fact (and not just faith) as a prerequisite for the salvation of souls. Concealing truth from the Holy Office was, in itself, considered a sin. If the accused were to return to the Church, in this life or the next, they had to admit fully what they did and what they saw or heard. This spiritual logic in no way undermined the pragmatic motivations for torture. The two went hand in hand. Only a truthful admission could validate reliable prior testimony, uncover deceptive testimony, complete a trial, and bring the accused back to the arms of the Church.

Because the Inquisition sought to compile exhaustive testimonies, to the exacting standards of a sacred confession, it documented its torture sessions fastidiously. A scribe in the torture chamber recorded every word spoken, every name, every accusation, every description of transgression, and every scream. Instructions circulated in 1591 by the Suprema, the Supreme Council of the Inquisition, required that the process be recorded, including the stripping naked of the prisoner, how they were tied, what devices were used, what parts of the body the torture was applied to, how it was gradually escalated, and what the victim said at each stage.[2]

A contingent of additional scribes copied the information extracted from every interrogation into files from parallel interrogations. This system allowed the inquisitors to collate and contrast names, places, and activities, as the Inquisition gradually spread its net. The same system allows us, today, to explore who was tortured and why, and to examine the nature of the information extracted during torture

**FIGURE 2.1.**   Manuscript for a single trial. This is the manuscript for the trial of Manuel de Lucena, discussed in chapter 6. It consists of 667 handwritten folios (1,334 pages). Bancroft MSS 96/95m. Image courtesy of University of California, Berkeley, Bancroft Library.

sessions. The records of the Inquisition, spanning hundreds of thousands of pages, provide scholars with a vast empirical database on the causes, nature, and consequences of the most sustained torture campaign in human history (see figure 2.1).

## Myth 1: The Inquisition Tortured Recklessly

The Inquisition tortured often, but much less often, and far less excessively, than secular courts in early modern Europe.[3] In inquisitorial courts, torture could only be employed under limited circumstances, as regulated by protocols and guarded by protections. These conditions were rigorously defined by jurists, conveyed in official proclamations, and captured in inquisitorial manuals. For example, the instructions of 1561 urged inquisitors to "take great care that the sentence of torture is justified and follows precedent."[4]

For torture to commence, three conditions had to hold. First, torture was reserved primarily for those accused of capital crimes against the Church. The Inquisition tried a wide range of offenses, including witchcraft, bigamy, false witness, and blasphemy, but with few exceptions it only tortured those accused of the most extreme forms of heresy.[5] For example, I show in chapter 4 that of the 123 individuals tortured in Toledo between 1575 and 1610, only twenty were tortured for crimes other than heresy.

The Inquisition had no authority to prosecute non-Christians. Its primary target for torture were those who pretended to be Catholics but actually practiced some other faith (usually Lutheranism, Judaism, or Islam) covertly. The persecution of Jews in early and mid-fifteenth-century Spain had led tens of thousands of Jews to convert to Christianity, some less willingly than others.[6] Even more converted in response to the expulsion edict of 1492, which forced them to adopt Christianity or leave Spain, and eventually Portugal as well. Nearly 200,000 left. A similar number stayed under the pretense of converting. The expulsion, designed specifically to empty Spain of Jews, instead created a vast underground community of Jews. This occurred even more markedly in Portugal, where Jews who had fled from Spain were forcibly baptized.

These converts were "New Christians," also known as *conversos*, as *anusim* (in Hebrew: those who were forced), or as *marranos* (in Spanish: swine, or turncoats). Many of these *converso* families came to embrace Christianity in full. Their descendants nonetheless suffered discrimination from "Old Christians" because so many "New Christians" were suspected of continuing to practice their Judaism in secret. It is that heretical subgroup, the Judaizers or "crypto-Jews," that the Inquisition sought to identify. Naturally, its primary suspicion fell on conversos and their descendants.

The second condition for torture was designed to prevent speculative torture. Torture was to take place only if proof against the accused was nearly certain. To convict the accused of a capital crime, the *consulta de fe* (the local inquisitorial court) had to obtain testimony from two eyewitnesses, catch the criminal in the act, or extract a statement of admission from the accused. All other sources of evidence constituted partial proof for the court. Only when the court was unable to obtain one or more forms of full proof but was able to assemble enough partial proofs to establish a strong circumstantial case, did its protocols allow it to try and complete its proof by means of torture.[7]

Third, torture tended to occur primarily at the conclusion of a protracted legal process. As I argue in the next chapter, the Inquisition engaged in "exploratory" torture early in its history, trying to extract information from recently arrested suspects early in the process of investigation. This form of interrogator torture proved relatively futile. In the absence of other sources of information with which it could contrast the victim's testimony, the Inquisition had no way to know whether the suspect had spoken the truth, let alone the whole truth. Over the course of several decades, the Inquisition shifted its practices to what I call "corroborative" torture, a process I document in chapter 3. Its prisoners now lingered months and years in the Inquisition prison before they were first threatened with torture. The court used that intervening period to gather information from alternative sources before it decided whether a suspect should be tortured.

Torture was not used to reveal novel information at the outset of a trial. Rather, it occurred toward the end of the trial if the court felt the accused was withholding crucial evidence that could lead to a capital conviction. Only after the prosecution and the defense had concluded their arguments would the consulta hold a vote on whether the evidence sufficed to find the defendant "semi-guilty."[8] A vote in favor of torture required consensus and could be overruled by the Suprema, which entertained and occasionally granted appeals by the accused.

Inquisitorial torture, though "extremely conservative" by medieval standards, was still widespread.[9] Generalizing over the entire course of the Inquisition's three-hundred-year reign of terror, roughly a fifth of those accused of heresy were tortured. Torture rates varied by decade and location. In the early years of the Inquisition, between 1480 and 1520, spontaneous testimonies and denunciations by neighbors and family members rendered torture relatively rare. In Ciudad Real, between 1474 and 1515, hundreds of suspects were tried for the crime of Judaizing and thousands of witnesses provided testimony, but only nine residents of the city were tortured (see chapter 3).

Over time, however, heretics and witnesses to heresy became more difficult to identify and torture came to occupy a more prominent place in the proceedings of the Inquisition. The relative calm that followed the initial persecution of Jews lasted only from 1520 to 1560, at which point the persecutions of heretics resumed with a vengeance, culminating in the late sixteenth and early seventeenth centuries.[10] In this period, torture rates rose: 7 percent suffered torture in Granada, 11 percent in Seville, 20 percent–30 percent in Valencia, and 25 percent in Toledo.[11] Almost 85 percent of the *moriscos* (former Muslims) examined by the Inquisition in Valencia between 1580 and 1610 were tortured, as were almost 79 percent in Zaragoza.[12] As the Inquisition reached its apogee, torture became ubiquitous: in Valladolid, eleven out of twelve suspects were tortured in 1624, and nine out of nine suffered torture in 1655.[13]

## Myth 2: The Inquisition Used Torture to Punish

This gradual increase in the frequency of torture supports the notion that it was the growing difficulty of obtaining reliable witnesses and suspects, not a consistent agenda of brutality for the sake of brutality, which drove torture policy. When torture occurred, it was neither penal nor, strictly speaking, sadistic.[14] Pain was not intended as a punishment but as a means to elicit information and aid the court in the very task from which it gained its moniker: inquiry.[15]

In secular European courts, a range of brutal means was used to extract evidence: whips, fire, hot irons, the rack, devices for breaking bones, tools to tear legs or distend the mouth, hot bricks for the stomach or groin, and so forth.[16] Victims of these forms of torture were likely to bleed, suffer permanent physical injury or deformity, and even succumb to their wounds. In contrast, the Inquisition relied on three forms of torture, used by the secular courts, which it considered least injurious. The *potro* was a rack on which victims were stretched or tortured by means of thick rope cords that were twisted around their arms and cut into their flesh. The *garrucha* (or *strappado, corda,* or *cordeles*) was a rope and pulley system that vertically suspended prisoners by their arms or wrists, threatening dislocation of limbs. The *toca,* or simply *agua,* was a form of waterboarding in which jar after jar would be poured into a prisoner's mouth and lungs.

Instructions issued by the Supreme Council of the Inquisition in 1591 required that the accused be given multiple opportunities to avoid torture through a series of increasingly vehement and increasingly specific warnings.[17] Prisoners would not be informed of the specific crime of which they stood accused but were warned that torture was imminent because they were suspected of not having told the whole truth. The inquisitors would then cleanse their own conscience by means of a prayer in which they stated the justification for torture and placed the responsibility for the ensuing physical harm on the prisoner. The last of these threats was issued in the torture chamber, *in conspectu tormentorum.* The prisoner would then be strapped to the instruments of torture by a masked torturer. Once again, the inquisitors, seated in the torture chamber, would urge the prisoner to tell the truth, emphasizing by means of a standard formula that they did not wish to see the suspect suffer. If this, too, was met with silence, then, and only then, could torture commence. Henry Charles Lea, the foremost American scholar of the Spanish Inquisition, concludes: "It required strong nerves to endure this threat of torture, with its terrifying formalities and adjurations, and it was frequently effective."[18]

Torture proceeded according to a strict and laborious protocol.[19] The inquisitor, a representative of the local bishop, and a doctor had to be present, along with the notary who recorded the proceedings. Usually, local executioners acted as torturers. After the sentence of torture was read, the prisoner was taken to the torture chamber, stripped of clothing, and tied to the instrument of torture. Every twist of the rope, or jar of water, was followed by a pause in which the victim was encouraged to tell the truth. Only then, depending on the responses of the victim, could the torture escalate.[20]

Torture rarely lasted very long. The condemned often survived it without providing incriminating information.[21] Torture ceased when the court deemed it to be no longer productive: when the suspect remained silent, became unresponsive, or offered information that struck the court as complete. If the accused survived the torture in silence, the court declared them innocent, or imposed minor penalties for those transgressions it could substantiate.[22] If the suspect did provide information, they were asked to repeat their statement a day or two later, outside the torture chamber, otherwise the declaration was deemed spurious.[23] Often, the victim would exploit that opportunity to recant their admission, despite the threat that torture could resume. In actuality, torture was rarely repeated. The procedures of the Inquisition prohibited torturing an individual more than once. This guideline could be circumvented by suspending a torture session, rather than ending it, but that maneuver was rarely employed.[24]

In chapter 4, I provide further evidence for the claim that inquisitorial torture was not, primarily, penal. That evidence takes two forms. First, I show that the court had far more extreme means for punishing its suspects than torture. After all, it had the authority to condemn to death. It also had the authority to decree exile, hard labor (in the form of rowing in the royal galleys), or perpetual imprisonment. In Toledo (1575–1610), suspects were three times as likely to be punished by these means as to endure torture (see chapter 4). Suspects were equally likely to be tortured as to be sentenced to fifty, one hundred, or two hundred lashes at the end of their trial, but these lashes never constituted part of the torture proceeding. The specific category of pain that the Inquisition classified as torture, then, was neither the most extreme, the most durable, nor the most frequently administered pain in its repertoire.

The second reason why it is difficult to conceive of torture as primarily penal is that those tortured were treated more leniently than those who were not tortured, if they were found to be innocent. Moreover, I show that torture victims experienced a higher acquittal rate (30 percent) than those who were not tortured (17 percent acquittal). Torture was not synonymous with harsh verdicts. Penalties imposed at the end of a trial depended not on whether torture occurred over the course of the trial but on the nature of the accusation and on the willingness of the accused to cooperate and demonstrate their guilt or innocence, either by admitting guilt prior to torture or by maintaining innocence despite torture.

## Myth 3: The Inquisition Extracted Confessions of Guilt

The notion that inquisitors sought proclamations of guilt, that they dictated the content of those proclamations to the accused, and that they eagerly accepted the resulting proclamations on face value when their victims parroted them back, is deeply misguided. In addition to requiring that all statements be affirmed outside the torture chamber, the court employed three means to ensure that testimonies were reliable.

First, the Inquisition sought statements of fact, not confessions of faith. The consulta gathered information about practices: uttering blasphemous statements, speaking forbidden prayers, or owning prohibited artifacts.[25] Witnesses rarely spoke about the piety or devotion of the accused. Instead, they provided evidence that the accused had engaged in non-Catholic burial or mourning rites, had avoided pork, or had observed the Sabbath by washing laundry on a Friday, lighting candles, abstaining from work between Friday and Saturday, and so forth. The court gathered the names of those who were present at religious gatherings, who kept unusual fasts or ate during Lent, who taught heretical beliefs to other community members, who owned books in Hebrew or Arabic, who conducted kosher or halal slaughter, or who sang prayers in foreign languages.

These were falsifiable claims that pertained to religious behavior, not unfalsifiable claims about piety. The primary accusation against conversos, for example, was not that they *believed* the Law of Moses but that they *followed* the Law of Moses, that they obeyed its precepts. Torture victims also provided concrete evidence about religious artifacts—concealed sacred scriptures, hidden prayer rooms, and forbidden ritual items—that the tribunal could verify independently.[26] The court showed little interests in beliefs, because it could not collect evidence about beliefs.

Second, inquisitors took great pains to avoid leading witnesses.[27] Torture critics often argue that torture fails because victims will tell their tormentors "what they want to hear" to put an end to torture.[28] This is a valid criticism of confessional torture, such as the torture that occurs when authoritarian rulers seek to coerce hollow statements of allegiance from torture victims. Because the Inquisition conducted interrogational torture, providing hints to suspects as to what the judges wanted to hear would have undermined the utility of the interrogation. The Inquisition was, of course, well aware of this concern and took a ruthless but simple step to avoid leading its witnesses. It did not tell them anything. The only words addressed to the suspect were an admonition to "tell the truth."[29] The prisoner was asked no specific questions and was offered no specific names. Indeed, the court went a step further and denied its victims any detailed information on the crimes of which they stood accused. Most detainees knew little beyond the fact that substantive evidence had come to the attention of the Inquisition regarding some heresy they were said to have committed. They did not know the precise nature of the accusation, or when or where it was said to have occurred.

Here, for example, is the first *monición*, the first warning, issued to Manuel de Lucena at his official arraignment on November 3, 1594. His trial is the focus of my analysis in chapter 6. This formulaic warning encapsulates all Lucena knew, formally, about the cause for his arrest:

> He was asked whether he knows or suspects the reason why he has been taken prisoner and taken to the jail of the Holy Office. He answered that he does not know, presume, nor suspect.
>
> They told him that the Holy Office of the Inquisition does not generally apprehend people without substantial information of having done or said or seen done or said to other people, something that can appear to be against the Holy Catholic faith, the Evangelical Law that is believed, preached or taught by the holy Catholic church of Rome, whether it be the law of Moses, the sects of Luther and Mohammed, or for having hidden or favored any Jews, Lutheran heretics or other people who keep the sect of Mohammed, or for having interfered with the rightful exercise of the Holy Office.
>
> And if he is imprisoned, he must know that there is preceding information against him of this sort. So they asked him, in reverence to God, that he look into himself and say the truth and free his conscience without bearing false witness against himself or others. If he does, his case will be brief and he will be treated with the mercy that the Holy Office displays toward those who are pure and clean. He said that he has nothing to say.[30]

Other than implied heresy, there was not much the accused could learn from this warning. More important, the accused did not know the identity of the witnesses testifying for the prosecution. Ostensibly, this secrecy was necessary to protect informants from danger. In reality, it served to facilitate the continuous flow of denunciations and made it difficult for suspects to issue preemptive rebuttals.[31] The accused had an opportunity, early in the trial, to name potential witnesses who should be disqualified because of personal rivalry (so-called *tachas*), but they could never know with certainty whom to disqualify. In admitting their heresies to avoid torture, they were just as likely to provide the Inquisition with new information as they were to confirm information the court already possessed. This placed victims in the unenviable position of trying to guess what the Inquisition did and did not know and then reveal just enough to satisfy the court without incriminating themselves, or others, more than was absolutely necessary.

This quandary is apparent in the following excerpt from the 1568 torture of Elvira de Campo, which Lea cites in full but which I reproduce only in part. She was tortured on the rack and waterboarded after witnesses accused her of avoiding pork and of putting out clean linens on Saturdays. Her pitiful words, spoken in the torture chamber and noted by the scribe at her side, underscore the difficulty of facing an interrogator who refuses to lead a witness:

> She was carried to the torture-chamber and told to tell the truth, when she said that she had nothing to say. She was ordered to be stripped and again admonished, but was silent. When stripped, she said "Señores, I have done all that is said of me and I bear false-witness against myself, for I do not want to see myself in such trouble; please God, I have done nothing." She was told not to bring false testimony against herself but to tell the truth.
>
> The tying of the arms was commenced; she said "I have told the truth; what have I to tell?" She was told to tell the truth and replied "I have told the truth and have nothing to tell." One cord was applied to the arms and twisted and she was admonished to tell the truth but said she had nothing to tell. Then she screamed and said "I have done all they say." Told to tell in detail what she had done she replied "I have already told the truth." Then she screamed and said "Tell me what you want for I don't know what to say."
>
> She was told to tell what she had done, for she was tortured because she had not done so, and another turn of the cord was ordered. She cried "Loosen me, Señores and tell me what I have to say: I do not know what I have done, O Lord have mercy on me, a sinner!" Another turn was given and she said "Loosen me a little that I may remember what I have to tell; I don't know what I have done; I did not eat pork for it made me sick; I have done everything; loosen me and I will tell the truth." Another turn of the cord was ordered, when she said "Loosen me and I will tell the truth; I don't know what I have to tell—loosen me for the sake of God—tell me what I have to say—I did it, I did it—they hurt me Señor—loosen me, loosen me and I will tell it." She was told to tell it and said "I don't know what I have to tell—Señor I did it—I have nothing to tell—Oh my arms! release me and I will tell it." She was asked to tell what she did and said "I don't know, I did not eat because I did not wish to."
>
> She was asked why she did not wish to and replied "Ay! loosen me, loosen me—take me from here and I will tell it when I am taken away—I say that I did not eat it." She was told to speak and said "I did not eat it, I don't know why." Another turn was ordered and she said "Señor I did not eat it because I did not wish to—release me and I will tell it." She was told to tell what she had done contrary to our holy Catholic faith. She said "Take me from here and tell me what I have to say—they hurt

me—Oh my arms, my arms!" which she repeated many times and went on "I don't remember—tell me what I have to say—O wretched me!—I will tell all that is wanted, Señores—they are breaking my arms—loosen me a little—I did everything that is said of me." She was told to tell in detail truly what she did. She said "What am I wanted to tell? I did everything—loosen me for I don't remember what I have to tell—don't you see what a weak woman I am?—Oh! Oh! my arms are breaking."

More turns were ordered and as they were given she cried "Oh! Oh! loosen me for I don't know what I have to say—Oh my arms!—I don't know what I have to say—if I did I would tell it." The cords were ordered to be tightened when she said "Señores have you no pity on a sinful woman?" She was told, yes, if she would tell the truth. She said, "Señor tell me, tell me it." The cords were tightened again, and she said "I have already said that I did it." She was ordered to tell it in detail, to which she said "I don't know how to tell it Señor, I don't know."[32]

Elvira endured this torture (and there was a great deal more than I have copied here) without collaborating. But when she was brought into the torture chamber again four days later, she admitted her Jewish practices, and denounced her mother, even before her torture resumed.[33]

A third method the court used to avoid false statements was to seek information from other witnesses, from parallel trials, and from alternative sources, prior to initiating torture. The vast majority of those burned in public autos-da-fé after 1530 were convicted on the basis of witnesses, not on the basis of torture.[34] Since many religious traditions required social gatherings, heretics were often familiar with other heretics.[35] Suspects were often tortured *in caput alienum*, regarding the behavior of others, those who participated with them in religious rituals. Indeed, when the papacy first authorized torture in 1252, it did so not to coerce suspects to testify against themselves but to uncover their accomplices and associates.[36] These were then summoned before the tribunal and questioned independently, either corroborating or contradicting the specifics provided by torture victims. As I show in chapter 6, the court also embedded informants in its prison cells, and it relied on intercepted messages between prisoners and their families to construct its cases against suspects. These methods were not substitutes for, but complements to, torture and were used to confirm, dismiss, or adjust evidence collected in the torture chamber.

The most persuasive corroboration of evidence extracted under torture came from other trials. To assemble that information into a full picture of heretical practices in a given community, the Inquisition had to be meticulous in comparing and contrasting information across cases. It did so by commissioning multiple transcriptions of trial segments in which other suspects were mentioned and appending each transcription to the relevant trial of every other suspect. This meant that every useful testimony from every trial (and there were often ten or more witness testimonies in a given trial) had to be copied, by hand, dozens of times so it could be appended to the files of all related trials.

As a consequence, trial documents are exceedingly long and detailed. They contain not only the arraignment, statements by the accused, testimony from witnesses for the prosecution and the defense (often numbering dozens each), transcripts of court sessions, transcripts of torture sessions, and summations for the prosecution and defense, all affirmed, reaffirmed, and signed but also files imported from parallel trials in which the accused was mentioned.[37] These were appended to the core documents of the trial, whereupon the entire text was bound, and a scribe numbered every page. The same scribe also highlighted the most important moments of the trial by noting them in the margins of the text: particularly damning claims against the accused, any mention of accomplices, and any occurrence of torture in all its steps (the disrobing, the final admonition, the first turn of the cord, the second turn of the cord, etc.). Finally, the scribe created cover pages that included two indexes, with page numbers. One index listed all the witnesses against the accused, the other listed those accused by the suspect. These two indexes allow any reader to link one trial manuscript to all other trial manuscripts in which the same names reappear (see figure 2.2).

A full trial manuscript of this sort can run in the many hundreds of pages, providing information about society, culture, family life, cuisine, industry, law, and faith. In the following pages, I use evidence from several collections of manuscripts to construct, as the Inquisition did, a network of denunciations and counterdenunciations that demonstrates the limited but crucial role that torture played in the Inquisition's deliberations.

In sum, the Inquisitions used goal-oriented and sophisticated methods. This is not to say that its calculus was always rational. Its magistrates believed that withholding truth was sinful, not merely criminal. It was skeptical of any and all claims made under torture, except silence, which it tended to interpret as a divinely inspired proof of innocence. Inquisitors believed in witchcraft and in blood libels. They did not hesitate to torture or burn Jews who were accused of the ritual murder of Christian children.[38]

Nor was the Inquisition free of corruption and excess. Some inquisitors were rash or careless and others had a reputation for cruelty. The guidelines I explored above were often bent in the service of expediting a trial or confiscating the wealth of the accused. At other times, they were abandoned altogether, especially in the last decades of the Inquisition, when the institution became bureaucratically inept and bloated. But it is worth noting that any information that has passed

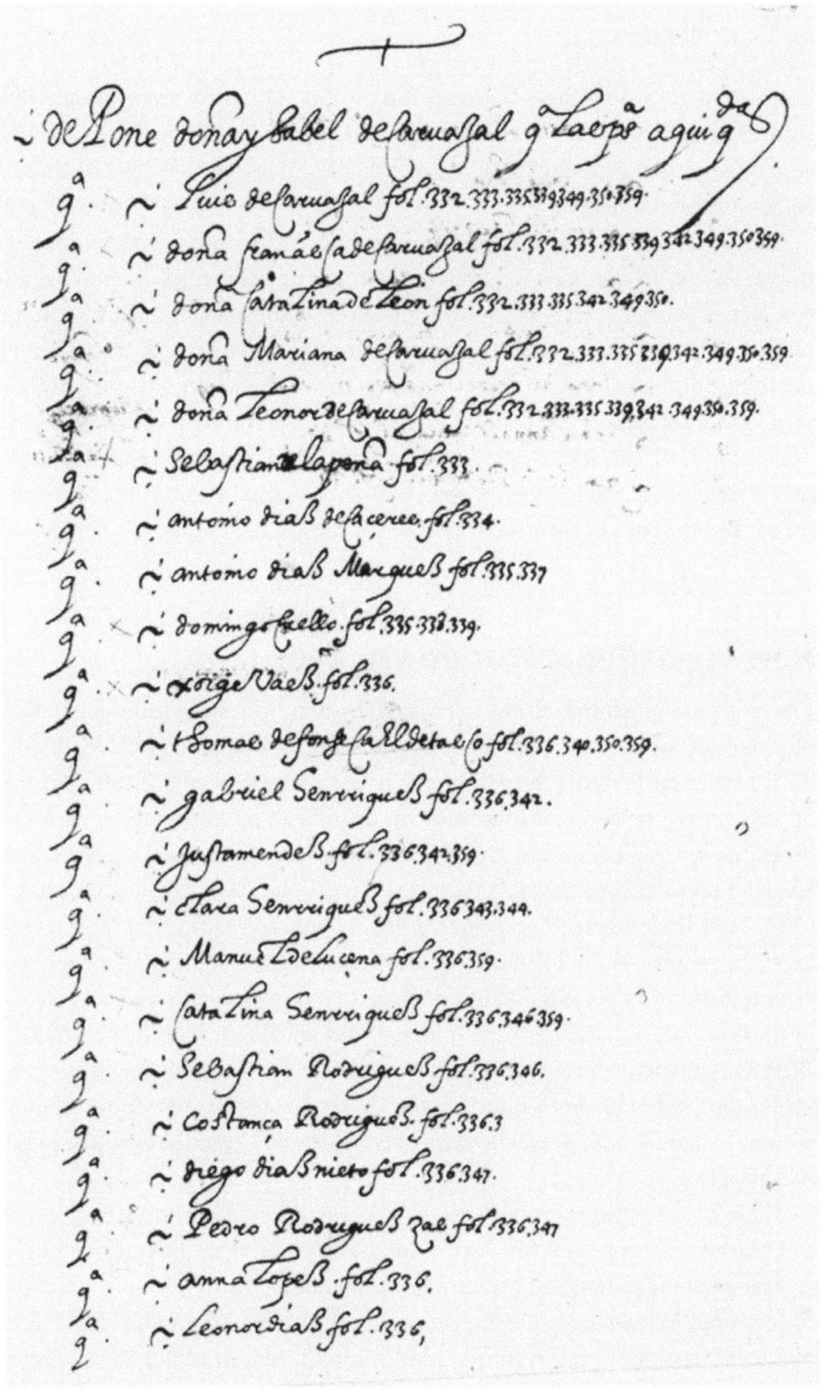
~ de Pone doña ysabel de caruajal
~ luis de caruajal fol. 332.333.335.339.349.350.359
~ doña francisca de caruajal fol. 332.333.335.339.342.349.350.359
~ doña catalina de leon fol. 332.333.335.342.349.350.
~ doña mariana de caruajal fol. 332.333.335.339.342.349.350.359
~ doña leonor de caruajal fol. 332.333.335.339.342.349.350.359.
~ sebastian de la peña fol. 333
~ antonio diaz de caceres fol. 334
~ antonio diaz marquez fol. 335.337
~ domingo cuello fol. 335.338.339
~ jorge vaez fol. 336
~ thomas de fonseca de tasco fol. 336.340.350.359.
~ gabriel henriquez fol. 336.342.
~ justa mendez fol. 336.342.359
~ clara henriquez fol. 336.343.344.
~ manuel de lucena fol. 336.359
~ catalina henriquez fol. 336.346.359
~ sebastian rodriguez fol. 336.346.
~ costança rodriguez fol. 336.3
~ diego diaz nieto fol. 336.347.
~ pedro rodriguez saz fol. 336.347
~ anna lopez fol. 336.
~ leonor diaz fol. 336,

**FIGURE 2.2.** The first index page for the trial of Isabel de Carvajal, listing key individuals mentioned in the text. For example, her brother Luis de Carvajal, the focus of chapter 6, is listed first in this index. The index shows that his name appears on ff. 332, 333, 335, 339, 349, 350, and 359. Bancroft MSS 96/95 m. Image courtesy of University of California, Berkeley, Bancroft Library.

down to us regarding these transgressions comes, primarily, from the internal records of the Inquisition itself. Inquisitors, courts, tribunals, and the Suprema, held one another to account for offenses, noted them in their official records, and sought to correct them.[39]

This was not an institution committed to indiscriminate violence. Any impression to the contrary is a function of the secrecy in which the Inquisition conducted its affairs: secret prisons, anonymous witnesses, and unknown accusations. These fostered a common perception about the unhinged fanaticism of the Inquisition, a perception that (with some encouragement from anti-Catholic propagandists) persists to this day.[40] In many ways, the reality, in which the courts of the Holy Office violently extracted information in a cold and calculating manner, is far more terrifying than the alternative, which portrays pain as both the means and the ends of torture.

## How Inquisitorial Torture Worked

The evidence presented in the following chapters will leave little doubt that inquisitorial torture "worked" to some extent: It occasionally produced truthful information that victims would not have otherwise divulged. Most of the time, torture provided scant information or misleading information. At other times, torture victims named multiple accomplices and provided evidence that was later corroborated. Several crypto-Jews in Ciudad Real named two or three fellow Jews under torture, and one named thirteen alleged community members (see chapter 3). In Toledo, of the suspects who had refused to collaborate prior to torture, 29 percent divulged information during torture (see chapter 4). In Mexico City, one leader of the underground Jewish community named 121 alleged crypto-Jews during torture (see chapter 6). Many of the details of these accusations were confirmed independently by uncoerced victims. They included not merely names but the events, places, and rituals and even the words of songs and prayers.

There is also little doubt that this torture played a role in eliminating Jewish and Muslim communities from Spain, and its colonies. Over the course of three centuries their members, their traditions, their culture, their way of life vanished. For example, in 1584 the Inquisition unraveled the Islamic community in Aguilar, the largest network of underground Muslims in sixteenth-century Spain, after a forty-year-old shoemaker, Gaspar Ozen, admitted under torture that he was the *alfaqui*, the religious leader, of that community. He identified several members of his flock, including a woman who, in turn, named 202 members of the community. The Aguilar community disintegrated. Those community members who managed to flee were caught in Aragon, where they were apprehended during prayers.[41] Given the ruthless and systematic means with which the Inquisition proceeded in the three instances I examine in this volume, it is hard to imagine that any Jews or Muslims could have survived the persecutions in Ciudad Real, Toledo, or Mexico City.

This torture campaign amounts to the most extraordinary interrogational torture campaign in recorded history, in both duration and scope. Its motivations and goals were as unique as the circumstances under which it took place. The following chapters demonstrate that the efficacy of this campaign rested on three extreme conditions: an absolute freedom to torture, the patience to torture, and a skepticism regarding the results of torture. No other torture campaign, most certainly not the US torture campaign after 2001, has met even one of these conditions.

The first condition undergirding the Inquisition's use of torture was full freedom from all political, financial, or ethical constraints. The Inquisition functioned with the approval of the two most powerful forces in Spain, the Crown and the Church. Its activities were self-funding. Confiscated goods and properties flowed into the coffers of the Inquisition and defendants had to cover the costs of their own incarceration. The courts had leave to arrest and to torture anyone at will: The young and the old; the healthy and the infirm; men, women, and children.

This was no mere whim. The logic behind the Inquisition's torture methodology required this freedom to torture. Because the Inquisition was morally and procedurally indifferent toward torture, regarding it as one tool among many for extracting information, it could apply that tool to all members of society. It did not reserve torture for the guilty or for the most significant cases. Its procedures required torture in cases of significant but incomplete evidence of heresy, regardless of how minute the missing evidence was or how inconsequential the heresy was. There was no relationship between torture and guilt. Many were tortured not because they themselves had committed heresy but because they were suspected of having withheld evidence about the heresy of others. By the same token, many of the most significant figures in underground religious networks were neither tortured nor threatened with torture. This indiscriminate purview was only possible because the Inquisition functioned as a law unto itself.

More important, the Inquisition suffered none of the time or space constraints that characterize modern torture campaigns, especially torture that occurs in counterinsurgency settings. The Inquisition had full and effective control over the population it sought to interrogate, and it had the time to collect as much evidence as it deemed fit. The persecutions in a particular town might last three years or three decades, followed by a half century of peace before a new generation of inquisitors returned to renew their efforts. There was nowhere in the Spanish dominions that suspects could flee from the long arm of the courts, not to nearby Portugal, not even to the colonies overseas. With time, the Inquisition would find them there too.

The second condition underlying the Inquisition's torture record relates to this freedom from time constraint. The Inquisition did not torture slowly merely because it operated under no particular duress. It tortured slowly because its protocols required that noncoercive measures be exhausted prior to the onset of torture. It concluded that prisoners were more amenable to the effects of torture after having spent months, even years, suffering psychological torture in its prisons.[42] In these cells, prisoners could be kept without heat or natural light, a single candle providing illumination for a proscribed number of hours per day. They were allowed no contact with the outside world: no visitors, no letters, no books, or paper. They were only permitted to leave their cell if and when they were ready to speak to the inquisitors.[43]

This isolation had a profound psychological effect on the accused. It also prevented suspects from acquiring or sharing information with others. The prisoner could receive no information from friends or relatives about who was arrested subsequently or who testified before the tribunal after their arrest. The Inquisition, meanwhile, used that time to collect, correlate, and analyze evidence from witnesses in order to establish whether there was a need for torture. If, eventually, torture was deemed necessary (because the evidence was strong but insufficient to convict), that evidence could be used to assess information produced in the torture chamber. Torture came late, not only at the end of a particular trial but in the culmination of a series of interrelated trials. Often, the few prisoners who were condemned to be tortured were tortured in quick succession, within a relatively short span of time, long after all other witnesses had offered testimony, and immediately prior to the conclusion of the court's affairs.

For example, the court in Toledo (examined in chapter 4) tortured only eighteen individuals suspected of Jewish or Muslim practices in the first fifteen years of its activity. But in the twenty years that followed, it tortured sixty suspects. In Mexico (chapter 6), most of the suspects were arrested around October 1594, yet their torture sessions occurred between January and May of 1596. The success of the Inquisition's torture, then, depended in large part on patience, taking the time to collect all other evidence prior to deciding whether and whom to torture, what evidence to expect, and how to evaluate that evidence.

Underlying these two conditions, the complete freedom to torture and the patience to torture, was a third condition: a deeply ingrained distrust of torture. Inquisitors had already recognized in the late fourteenth century that tortures were *fallaces et inefficaces*, deceptive and ineffective.[44] The Inquisition did not merely suspect torture because it perceived it as an inherently flawed means of arriving at truth. Uncoerced statements could be just as deceptive, but at least these were more numerous, quick, and effortless. They provided the bulk of intelligence against which tortured testimonies would be assessed.

Because torture occurred last and revealed, at best, the testimony of a single witness, it could perform only a corroborative function. Torture that occurred too early in the proceedings tended to mislead because there was no other evidence against which the claims of the torture victim could be measured. The function of torture was not to reveal but to complete. It was useful in ensuring that all witnesses had stated all they knew. Evidence extracted in the torture chamber was given little weight in the court's ultimate deliberations. Not once, neither in Ciudad Real nor in Mexico City, was a single converso condemned to death based on evidence from torture alone.

Those, then, are the three conditions under which torture "worked" for the Inquisition: a freedom to torture without political, financial, moral, geographical, or temporal constraints; the patience to employ torture as a last resort; and a distrust in the products of that torture. The key word is *worked*, past tense. None of these conditions hold in the recent US torture campaign and none are likely to hold in the future. Indeed, insofar as the American public is willing to endorse the use of torture at all, it would not endorse this inquisitorial manner of torture even if it could be implemented. The logic of ticking bomb arguments justifies torturing a single culpable individual, under extreme time constraints, in order to reveal new and crucial information. No inquisitor would have sanctioned such torture. No inquisitor would have expected it to succeed.

# LEARNING TO TORTURE
## Ciudad Real (1484–1515)

The Court of the Inquisition in Ciudad Real was one of the first inquisitorial courts established in the Crown of Castile. It was set up in 1483 as the central inquisitorial court of the kingdom, two years after the first courts opened in Andalusia. Because it was one of the earliest such courts, it provides evidence for a period in which the Inquisition was still "experimenting" with torture. Nine residents of Ciudad Real suffered in the torture chamber. Their interrogations reveal a great deal about how the Inquisition learned to torture. Over time, it explored new forms of torture and provided more careful documentation of torture procedures and their outcomes. Most important, the Inquisition gradually shifted its torture practices from what might be termed "exploratory" torture to what I call "corroborative" torture.

In the early years, between 1484 and 1500, the Ciudad Real court tortured to uncover new evidence, new suspects, and new converso networks. Because it began torturing as soon as it was established, prior to having initiated most of its trials or collected testimonies from most of the witnesses available, this "exploratory" torture yielded few useful leads. The Inquisition did not yet know whom to interrogate, what questions to ask, how to assess information supplied during torture, or how to estimate how much information suspects were withholding.

In these early years, inquisitors were ill-trained in legal procedures and had no clear guidelines to constrain their interrogations. One of the earliest handbooks for inquisitors, the *Directorium Inquisitorum*, authored by Nicolas Eymerich in the fourteenth century for the papal inquisition, had relieved inquisitorial judges of the obligation to follow secular judicial procedures and had sought to free inquisitors from legal formalities.[1] Procedures varied across tribunals and changed from year to year. Trials were often rushed and disorderly.[2] So great were complaints about the abuses committed by inquisitors across Spain in the early years after the Inquisition was established, that Pope Sixtus IV, who had proclaimed the Inquisition in Castile in 1478, temporarily revoked its powers in 1482.[3] In 1484, the inquisitor-general, Tomás de Torquemada, assembled all inquisitors for the first time at a council in Seville and drew up a rudimentary set of rules. He issued revised ordinances in 1485 and again in 1498. His successor, Diego de Deza, prepared a new set of regulations in 1500.[4] By then, the Ciudad Real court had completed most of its initial investigations and was moved to Toledo, only seventy-five miles away, where the last of the Ciudad Real conversos would be tried.

In the second period in which this court was active, between 1500 and 1515, its torture took on an increasingly "corroborative" form. The focus now shifted to using torture as a means for assessing prior evidence that had been provided by willing witnesses, coerced witnesses, and even prior torture victims. The tribunal had significant information about existing converso networks. Its task was to perfect its knowledge of those networks by confirming or rejecting prior testimony. Influenced by Torquemada's efforts to introduce discipline into the routines of the inquisitorial courts, scribes now provided a far more meticulous account of the procedures employed in the torture chamber and the outcomes they elicited.

The lessons from this trial-and-error approach to torture could not have been lost on the inquisitors, and I expect that they were not lost on parallel tribunals held throughout Spain. Torture revealed useful information some of the time but provided misleading information much of the time. When it was used at the outset of a series of trials it yielded little. The less inquisitors knew before entering the torture chamber the easier it was for the witness to deceive them or to withhold information. Torture yielded the most reliable informative when it occurred toward the end of a trial or series of trials to evaluate what the Inquisition already knew. It occasionally employed torture to corroborate uncoerced testimony but most often it used uncoerced testimony to corroborate torture.

My analysis in this chapter owes a great deal to the life work of Haim Beinart, the most prominent scholar of Iberian Judaism at the Hebrew University in Jerusalem. Beinart was not particularly interested in the question of torture. His goal was to use these trial documents to conjure up the life of an underground Jewish community in late-fifteenth-century Spain in all its vibrant details: its religious practices, kinship ties, commerce, culture, cuisine, etc. To accomplish this task, he dedicated much of his academic career to assembling all manuscripts related to the trials of the residents of Ciudad Real, both those who were tried in the town and those who were tried in Toledo when the court was moved there.

He transcribed the files and published them in several volumes with annotations and indexes. In all, Beinart was able to recover and transcribe eighty-one Ciudad Real trials and to reconstruct forty-three other trials that were lost.

By Beinart's count, these 124 cases represent an important but incomplete record of how the Inquisition annihilated the flourishing converso community in Ciudad Real. They involve 145 accused individuals (married couples often appeared together in the same trial). It is clear, from references in these files and from the list of 272 individuals condemned to death in Ciudad Real, that many more trials took place there and that an unknown number of court cases, perhaps as many as 300, has gone missing.[5] The surviving records are not numerous enough to permit the identification of statistical patterns in the use of torture along the lines I propose in the next chapter (focusing on late-sixteenth-century Toledo), nor are they detailed enough to provide firm conclusions about the efficacy of torture as I do in chapters 5 and 6 (focusing on the Mexico City tribunal). The Ciudad Real trials offer a compromise between these two datasets. They are a sizeable collection of relatively detailed cases that allows for a modicum of in-depth analysis and comparisons across cases.

In the following pages, I reach conclusions about the reasons for torture in three ways. First, the tribunal itself often stated its deliberations for the record in some detail. I supplement those statements with a comparison between the suspect's testimony prior to torture and the testimonies provided by witnesses for the prosecution. Third, I compare the names of hostile witnesses to the suspect's tachas because suspects were often tortured when they failed to identify and exclude key witnesses. The trial of Juan González Daza, the second trial I analyze below, offers one such example.

To evaluate the evidence provided in the torture chamber, I compare the names, events, and facts revealed by tortured suspects to information provided by their accusers and by witnesses in other trials. Here, excluded information can be as instructive as included information. For example, in the trial of María González, below, the Inquisition treated claims she made under threat of torture with suspicion, despite the fact that several of the individuals accused by González had also accused one another, because they failed to mention her in their accusations.

I draw conclusions about the impact of coerced testimony by exploring the fortunes of those accused by the torture victim. Were they tried and, if so, were they found guilty? Where possible, I examine their trials to see whether coerced evidence was cited in their trials and whether it corresponded to evidence provided by others. In the case of missing trials, I consult the lists of participants in autos-da-fé to see whether those named in the torture chamber were put to death. These lists should be consulted with caution, since the Inquisition might have deemed a suspect to be a heretic regardless of, or despite, coerced information.

Few residents of Ciudad Real were tortured in this thirty-one-year period. Conversos were so numerous, and witnesses so eager to provide leads, that torture was rarely deemed necessary.[6] Nonetheless, the modest selection of torture cases referenced in these documents provides sobering insight into why and how this tribunal tortured, what it discovered, and how it changed its torture practices over time.

# Exploratory Torture: 1484–1500

Approximately fifty converso families resided in Ciudad Real, 120 miles south of Madrid and only 75 miles south of Toledo. In the War of the Castilian Succession (1475–79), Ciudad Real had been a center of a rebellion against the Crown, with participation by conversos on both sides of the conflict.[7] This sparked subsequent investigations into the Judaizing of the community that preceded the Inquisition. When Torquemada established the court in Ciudad Real in 1483, he did so in part to settle the score with those conversos who had participated in the 1475 uprising. He also chose Ciudad Real as the initial location of the court in order to send a threatening signal to the influential converso community in nearby Toledo, whence the court would soon relocate.[8]

Once the court was established in Ciudad Real, on September 14, 1483, the inquisitors declared a thirty-day period of grace.[9] Those who provided complete information to the court regarding sins they committed, or witnessed others committing, were offered absolution. Having heard of the ruthless tactics of the Inquisition in Andalusia in the prior year, witnesses in Ciudad Real overwhelmed the court with testimonies. The court was located in the heart of the town, providing visible evidence of who was entering the offices of the Inquisition to denounce others. This prompted their acquaintances to come before the court with counterstatements and accusations of their own. The resulting stream of testimonies led the overwhelmed court to extend the period of grace for another month, starting on October 14. Clerks and scribes spent the additional month assembling all the pretrial materials that would later appear in the opening pages of the trial documents. On November 14, 1483, the court held its first trial.

## Sancho Díaz, 1474

The first incident of torture recorded in the Ciudad Real manuscripts occurred before the arrival of the Inquisition in the town. Díaz's torture is mentioned in the trial of María González, nicknamed "La Panpana" (her husband was Juan González Panpán) on November 26, 1483, the first converso to be tried in person by the Inquisition in Ciudad Real.[10] Two witnesses at González's trial, Alonso de la Serna and Diego de Poblete, recounted that Sancho Díaz had been tortured six years earlier. Under torture, he accused González's husband of Judaizing. This happened "when the city was robbed" and Sancho Díaz "was burned," likely a reference to fierce anticonverso riots that occurred in 1474.[11]

The record of Díaz's torture is brief but informative since it provides insight into the nature of torture prior to the Inquisition. According to these two witnesses, Sancho Díaz, a dyer, was arrested and tortured in the archbishop's jail. It is unclear why or how Díaz was tortured, nor is it known what became of him after his torture. According to Serna and Poblete, under torture Díaz identified three conversos. He named Juan González Panpán, husband of María González, as "butcher of the conversos," presumably the man in charge of kosher slaughter for the community.[12] And he claimed that "all the Jews of this city were conversos," who "confessed to" Alonso Escogido and Gonzalo Podrido, presumably religious leaders among the conversos.

The three accusations that Díaz is reported to have made in the torture chamber received some corroboration in subsequent trials. The butcher Juan González Panpán had fled in 1474 but eleven other community members testified against him during his trial in absentia in January 1484.[13] They reported that Panpán observed the Sabbath by wearing clean clothes and lighting candles on Friday nights. He ate kosher meat and celebrated the Passover and did not observe Christian celebrations. His home functioned as a gathering place where conversos worshipped and observed Jewish customs together. His wife, "La Panpana," at whose trial we learn of Díaz's torture, was among those who testified against Panpán, accusing her husband of teaching her Jewish practices. He was burned in effigy on February 23. His wife, in turn, stood accused of the same crimes, as well as circumcising their children and teaching them the Law of Moses. Seven witnesses testified against her and she was burned alongside her husband's effigy.

We do not know what became of Alonso Escogido, the second converso identified by Díaz. The records of the Ciudad Real trials mention only a Juan González Escogido, also identified as confessor to the conversos, also associated with Podrido. It is unclear whether they are one and the same. This Escogido was tried posthumously in March 1485 and condemned. His bones were exhumed and burned.[14] The trial record for Podrido, the last person named by Díaz in the torture chamber, has not survived.[15] We know only that he was tried and found guilty because his name appears among those burned at the stake at an auto-da-fé on February 22, 1484.

In sum, based on available documentation, the torture of Sancho Díaz provided authorities with few clues about the sizeable converso community in Ciudad Real and its members. Díaz named only three people, of whom one escaped, another may have died prior to trial, and a third was found guilty of heresy. Two of the three may have been influential members of the converso community—its rabbi and its kosher butcher—suggesting that Díaz might have known many of the hundreds of conversos who were active while he was under interrogation. But at this exploratory stage, the archbishop who tried him had no means to pursue further leads.

## Juan González Daza, 1484

As neighbors and family members flocked to the Ciudad Real court to denounce one another, conversos fled the city en masse.[16] Those that did not flee to Portugal were hunted by the Inquisition across Spain in the following months and years. For example, Sancho and María de Ciudad, both leading figures in the Ciudad Real Jewish community, fled to Valencia in the hopes of sailing from there to Italy. After five days at sea, winds drove their ship back to Spain. They were arrested, sent back to Ciudad Real, and burned at the stake at the auto-da-fé of February 6, 1484.

Juan González Daza, a notary public, did not flee. He was the third individual to be tried in person by the Inquisition in Ciudad Real.[17] His trial began on December 1, 1483, two and a half months after the Inquisition began its investigations in the city. In that period, the court had gathered testimony against him from eight witnesses. Most notable among them was Fernán Falcón, a converso and "familiar" of the court, who would go on to provide significant evidence in dozens of trials.[18]

Daza was invited to disqualify some of these witnesses but he was unsure of their identities. He named eleven persons who, he argued, bore him personal grudges but only two of those were witnesses for the prosecution. Six others testified against him, and there was a good deal of agreement between their testimonies. Three testified that Daza and his wife observed the Sabbath. Two testified that he worked on Sundays. Two others testified that he ate meat on Saturday that he had grilled on Friday because of the prohibition on cooking on the Sabbath. Another saw Álvaro, the linen merchant, pray on a Friday night with a pointed cap on his head, surrounded by a group of conversos that included Daza.

Most troubling were the independent testimonies of Antonia Martínez de Valenzuela and Elvira González, both of whom claimed to have been physically present when Daza and his family prayed with Fernando de Teva. This was damning testimony, since Teva had already admitted to following Jewish practices during the period of grace and had been condemned to death. The Inquisition knew that Teva had been a core member of the converso community, acting in the capacity of a rabbi. Martínez reported that she had stayed in the house of Teva on Yom Kippur when Daza, his wife, and his children made atonement and prayed with Teva. González saw Daza's wife and her mother pray with Teva.

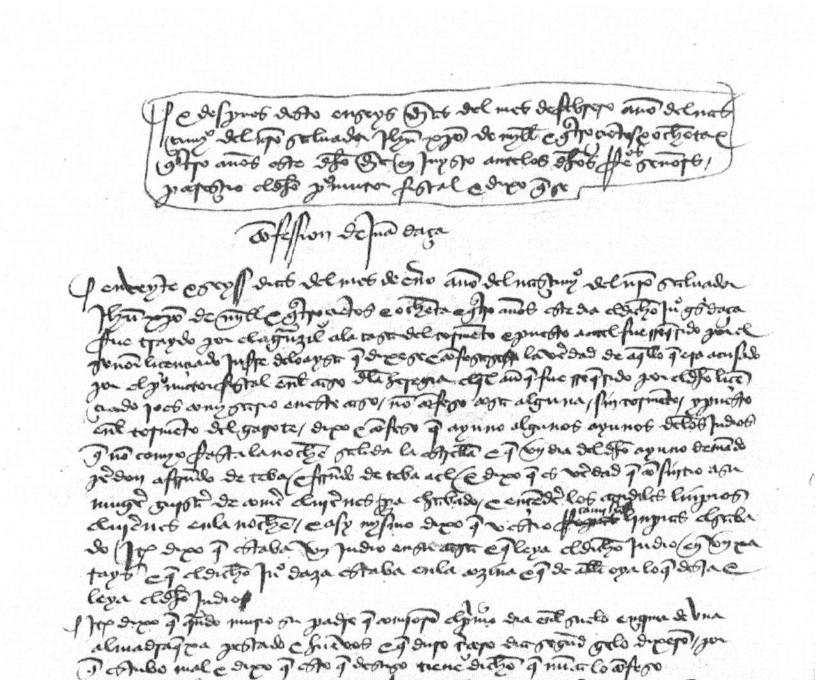

**FIGURE 3.1.** The torture of Juan González Daza: "Non confeso cosa alguna sin tormento, y puesto en el tormento del garrote, dixo y confeso." Madrid, Archivo Histórico Nacional, Inquisición, Legajo 154, Exp.9, f. 14v.

Daza repeatedly denied any and all claims that he was a converso. "I am innocent of the charges against me . . . it is clear that I have been a faithful Catholic Christian and that I never performed the ceremonies which are according to the law and custom of the Jews." Other suspects who were tried that month were quick to collaborate and quick to name fellow Jews. Daza maintained his silence over the course of two months' imprisonment, a period in which the evidence against him mounted. "Seeing the [failed] attempts by Daza to disqualify the prosecutor's witnesses, and how he persisted and continued to deny," the court decreed torture, the first performed by the Inquisition in Ciudad Real, on January 26, 1484.

In the torture chamber, Daza was offered a last chance to reveal the truth about his heresies but he refused to collaborate. He was tortured with twists of rope and the garrote. He then confessed. He had fasted on Yom Kippur, he had repented with Fernando de Teva, he had asked his wife to grill meat on Fridays, and he had worn clean shirts on Saturdays. He also admitted to sitting *shiva* for his father, eating fish and eggs while sitting on the floor for three days. His Christian prayers had been insincere, he stated, since he did not believe that the Messiah had already come. He had only attended mass to appear Christian. The court condemned Daza as a heretic and apostate, pronounced excommunication, confiscated his properties, and sentenced him to death. He was burned at the stake, together with Teva, at the great auto-da-fé of February 23, 1484.

Daza's torture confirmed much of what the witnesses for the prosecution had said about him. But it yielded little useful information regarding other conversos, beyond Teva, who had already been declared guilty earlier. Other suspects tried that month, who were not tortured, provided much more information. Juan González Pintado, tried two days before Daza, named nine fellow conversos. Juan de Chinchilla, tried two weeks after Teva, named nine others, including his own mother, stepfather, and sisters. Daza named only Teva, and the Inquisition, barely three months into its activities in Ciudad Real, had insufficient grounds for pressing him to reveal more names.

## Juan de Fez, 1484

Juan de Fez was put to torture on the same day as Daza. He was a tax collector and his wife, Catalina Gómez, was a seamstress.[19] Juan was stepbrother to Fernando de Teva, the rabbi who was executed with Daza. Catalina was niece to Juan Falcón the elder, who took over as community butcher after Panpán fled the city.

During the period of grace, in October 1483, de Fez had provided testimony against other conversos, such as Sancho de Ciudad, María Díaz, and his own stepfather, Alonso Martínez. De Fez also admitted that he himself had practiced Judaism with his mother at a young age but claimed that he had long since ceased

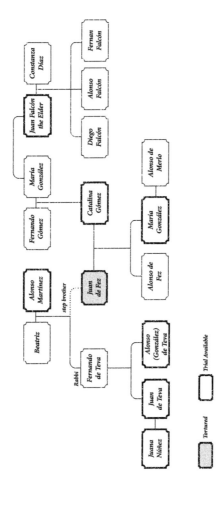

**FIGURE 3.2.** Juan de Fez and related community members.

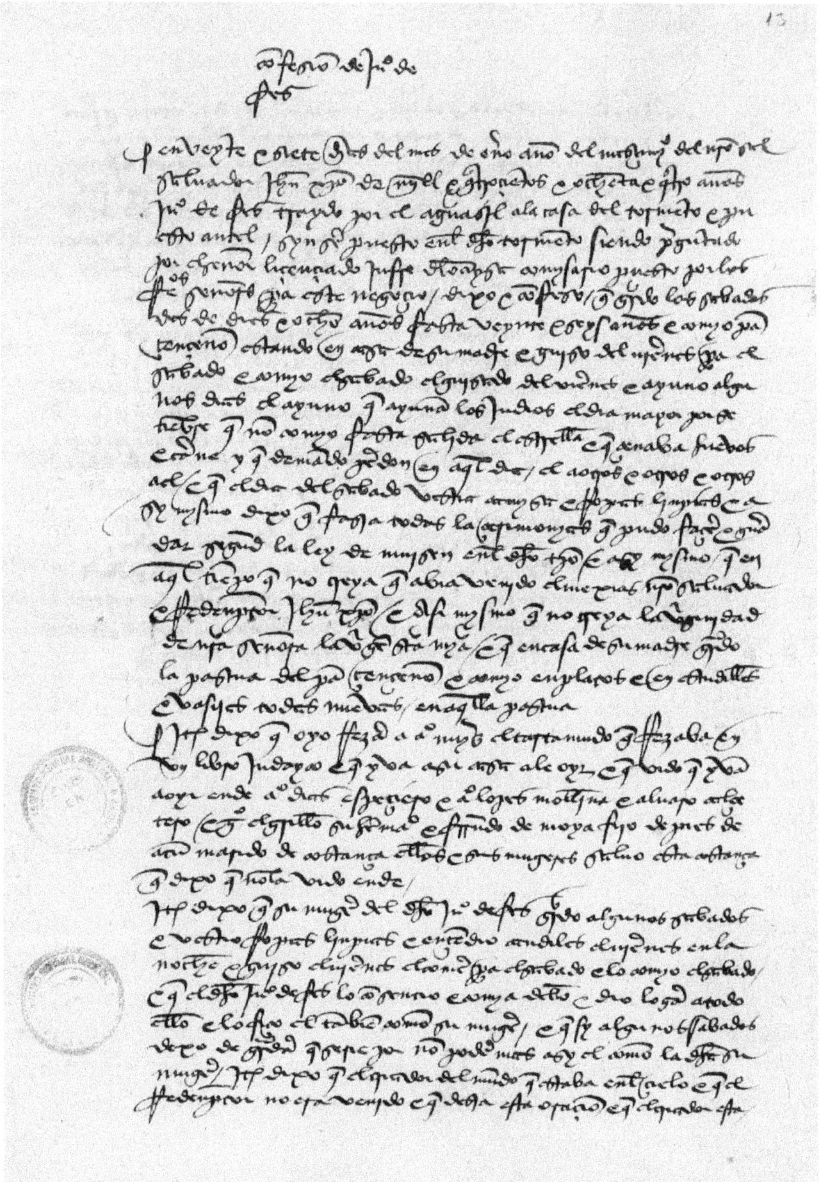

**FIGURE 3.3.** The torture of Juan de Fez: "Traydo por el alguasjl a la casa del tormento e puesto antel, syn ser puesto en el dicho tormento." Madrid, Archivo Histórico Nacional, Inquisición, Legajo 148, Exp.6, F. 13r.

to do so. He knew that Catalina, his wife, conducted Jewish ceremonies, but he had pleaded with her to stop, though she may have continued without his knowledge. He had witnessed her observing the Sabbath with his stepbrother, Fernando de Teva, and Teva's son, Alonso. Catalina Gómez, in turn, admitted that her uncle, Juan Falcón, had persuaded her to perform several minor Jewish practices.

The Inquisition suspected that there was more to their Judaizing than they had revealed during the period of grace. On December 19, several weeks after the start of Daza's trial, de Fez and Gómez were called before the court. Eleven witnesses spoke against them, including their own daughter, María. The couple were only able to correctly guess the identity, and disqualify, one of those witnesses. The others levied a long series of allegations against them. They stood accused of observing the Sabbath, eating meat on Lent, observing kosher restrictions, and working on Sundays. One witness testified to a secret passage between their home and the house of Gómez's mother, María González. The witness had seen Gómez and her mother wash the couple's children with hot water after their baptism, to remove the holy water from their skin. Another testified that many conversos acquired their kosher meat from the de Fez household. Most damning of all was the testimony of their daughter, who reported that Gómez ate unleavened bread during Passover and observed the Sabbath.

On January 26, 1484, de Fez was brought into the torture chamber. He was not physically tortured. The mere sight of the chamber led him to admit his own Jewish practices and to implicate thirteen others, including his wife, his son, and his brother. He acknowledged that he kept the Sabbath, fasted and repented on Yom Kippur, observed the Passover, and kept the Laws of Moses.

The information de Fez provided about other conversos is considerable but difficult to assess. The trials of most of the individuals he accused are missing. Two of the accused were deceased when de Fez was tried but they were tried posthumously, found guilty, and burned in effigy.[20] A third, Alonso Díaz, suffered an unknown fate but is mentioned as a converso in two subsequent trials.[21] The fourth, his wife, Catalina Gómez, was burned at the stake with de Fez on February 23, 1484. The fifth, their son Alonso, was also condemned and burned at the stake.[22] No information survives about the five others whom de Fez accused.

## Marina González, 1494

By 1494, the Ciudad Real court had moved to Toledo but was still trying residents of Ciudad Real. The second such person to be tried in Toledo was Marina González, wife of the spice merchant Francisco de Toledo.[23] Her voluntary statements during the period of grace in 1484, back in Ciudad Real, had been extensive. She admitted to observing Jewish dietary laws and the Sabbath, the feasts and fasts, the prayers and funerary practices. Her admission was long and detailed enough, and her repentance sincere enough, that she was reconciled to the Church and received mild penances. Now, in 1494, the prosecutor claimed that she had relapsed into heresy: "Postponing the fear of God, in condemnation of her soul, she returned, like a dog to its vomit, to commit the very errors she abjured."[24]

González's attorney introduced eight defense witnesses, including her husband, Francisco de Toledo. The prosecutor, in turn, presented five witnesses including, painfully, the same Francisco de Toledo. González succeeded in disqualifying three of these witnesses. But she did not envision that her own husband would testify against her, witnessing her refusal to eat pork or do her chores in the house on Saturdays, despite his admonition that she "was thumbing her nose at God." His testimony was corroborated by Pedro de Teva, a close friend of the husband. He had observed González's behavior closely and had witnessed her quarreling with her husband over Jewish practices.[25]

Having heard all testimonies, the tribunal concluded that she was withholding information about other heretics and voted (three against two) to put her to torture. She was brought to the torture chamber on April 29, 1494, but persisted in denying all heresy. The scribe recorded the torture procedure in greater detail than before, as I cited in chapter 1. Having suffered more than three pints of water while tied to the rack, González finally hinted that she knew a neighbor who fasted. Despite continued torture she revealed nothing more until she was released from the rack. She then revealed that the neighbor was the wife of Gómez de Chinchilla. That is all the information that the torture of Marina González yielded. At no point in her torture did González admit her own heresies.

González's trial provides no further information about this neighbor. A prior trial mentions a witness by the name of Juana González, wife of Gómez de Chinchilla.[26] Her fate is unknown. Gómez de Chincilla had undergone trial earlier and had been burned at the stake.[27] As for González, because she did not admit to heresy during her torture, she was offered the opportunity to undergo "compurgation," proof of innocence by testimony from eight pious witnesses. González was unable to provide eight such names, in part because she did not know who had or had not testified against her. She attempted to commit suicide by refusing all food in the Inquisition jail, actions that further strengthened the court's conviction that she was guilty. On June 30, 1494, at the Plaza de Zocodover in the heart of Toledo, she was "relaxed to justice and the secular arm." The Inquisition condemned the accused, but it was the state, the secular arm, that carried out the execution. Immediately after the auto-da-fé, González was burned at the stake.

# Corroborative Torture: 1500–1515

The torture cases in this second period took place under very different circumstances. Seventeen years had passed since the torture of Marina González. In the intervening years, the Inquisition had completed well over a hundred trials, involving many hundreds of witnesses, and had amassed significant information regarding surviving members of the converso community in Ciudad Real. Its primary concern was no longer with uncovering new networks of conversos but with completing its knowledge of existing networks and with confirming or disconfirming prior testimony.

The Inquisition had also significantly refined its torture practices. As the cases below demonstrate, the scribes now provided a far more meticulous accounts of the procedures employed in the torture chamber and the outcomes they elicited. And it prolonged the time its victims spent in jail prior to their torture from weeks, to months, and even sometimes to years.

In parallel, the torture cases that occurred after 1500 demonstrate a gradual shift away from torture used to generate new testimony and toward torture used to corroborate prior testimony. Exploratory torture still occurred after 1500 but it was increasingly used in conjunction with corroborative torture. Half of the torture victims in this period were tortured twice because exploratory torture provided fragmentary information that was later contradicted by other witnesses and by the victim's own retractions. They were tortured a second time to assess whether their initial claims or their later retractions were the more reliable.

This new mode of corroborative torture provided more extensive and reliable evidence than the older exploratory torture. But it required corroborative information from alternative witnesses, voluntary or coerced, that had not been available to the Inquisition in the 1480s and 1490s. Now, with many hundreds of witness testimonies at its disposal, the Inquisition could rely on torture to complete the picture rather than provide futile stabs in the dark.

## Elvira González, 1511

The full trial documents for Elvira González have not survived. We do not know why she was tried, who testified for or against her, or why she was threatened with torture. We only know of her torture because the relevant pages of her trial were copied and appended to the trial of three of her family members who were tried together in absentia. Nonetheless, brief as this documentation is, it provides insight into the corroborative role that torture began to play in this period. In the torture chamber, González was asked to confirm, and elaborate on, evidence provided by a prior witness. In so doing, the court breached one of its fundamental rules, the prohibition against leading witnesses by asking loaded questions. In more ways than one, then, this trial is evidence of the Inquisition's learning process.

The trial in which the torture of González is mentioned is the trial of her sister-in-law, Beatriz González, Beatriz's daughter, Leonor, and Beatriz's sister, Isabel.[28] Beatriz and Isabel had admitted to several Jewish practices during the period of grace. Now the three had fled the Inquisition to Portugal, an act that all but established their guilt. Beatriz and her family were already familiar to the court. Her husband, Juan de la Sierra, had achieved prominence when he traveled to Portugal to convince his mother, Leonor González, to return to Spain and to stand trial before the Inquisition.[29] Though de la Sierra was reconciled to the Church for this extraordinary display of penitence, his mother was burned at the stake. Ultimately, de la Sierra would return to Judaism, flee to Portugal, suffer excommunication, and be burned in effigy. Now, his wife, their daughter, and his sister-in-law were on trial, and Elvira González, another sister-in-law, was one of eight witnesses for the prosecution.

For reasons unknown to us, González was brought into the torture chamber, stripped of her clothes, and admonished to speak the truth regarding the heresies she had participated in and those she had witnessed others committing. González defied the judges to "do what they needed to do." It is here that the inquisitors chose to share evidence from a prior witness with González, though they did not reveal the name of that witness, a woman by the name of Olalla. The scribe explained: "Because they wanted to accelerate the process, because Elvira González was reluctant, because she was sickly and slim, and to help her remember what she knew about other people, your Highnesses read to her from the first witness."

This was a deviation from the Inquisition's standard practice, presumably excused by the fact that this was a trial of no great significance. The accused were absent, there were no witnesses for the defense, and the verdict was a foregone conclusion. This also explains why, in another deviation from the norm, the three women were tried together. The court was willing to threaten González with torture but, given her frailty, it was also willing to go to great lengths to avoid acting on its threat. These deviations from the Inquisition's guidelines are evidence of the fact that the rules guiding the Inquisition were still evolving. The inquisitor's need to justify their deviation in the official record suggest that the rules were also undergoing gradual standardization.

Threatened with torture, González obliged them and affirmed some of the claims made by López. She added further that the home of Juan de la Sierra was a meeting place for her circle of crypto-Jews. De la Sierra, his wife Beatriz, their daughter Leonor, and his sister-in-law Isabel observed the Jewish Sabbath by refraining from work and reading Jewish prayers. She was able to describe the book they read and the place in the house where they prayed together.

It is unknown what became of González after her testimony. She appeared as a witness in several related trials. In all cases, defendants who suspected her collaboration with the court succeeded in disqualifying her as a witness.[30] As for the three González women, they were never apprehended. Their effigies were burned in September 1511. Their children were prohibited from holding public office, or ecclesiastic positions, and were stripped of their wealth, a standard penalty, given the severe alternatives available to the court.

## Alonso Sánchez, 1512

As with Elvira González, the trial documents for Alonso Sánchez have not survived. We know about his torture because copies of his testimony were appended to the trials of his sister-in-law, Isabel de los Olivos y López, and his brother-in-law, Juan Ramírez.[31] He was tortured twice, once to elicit accusations, and a second time because he disavowed most of his accusations after the first torture.

The elements of Sánchez's testimony that survive relate to those accusations but do not include an explanation for his initial torture; however, it is easy to surmise why he was tortured. His trial in September 1511 followed promptly after one of the most significant trials to occur in Toledo, the trial of his brother in-law, Juan Ramírez. That trial began in July 1511 and ended eleven years later, long after Ramírez had died. It was significant because Ramírez was a central member of the converso community and steward to the cardinal of Cordova. His trial involved eighty-five defense witnesses, twenty-nine witnesses for the prosecution, and twenty-six disqualified witnesses. A key witness in this, and in three related trials, was Isabel, the black slave of Ramírez, who observed the comings and goings in his home but bore no particular allegiance to the converso community. One of the members of that community, she reported, was Alonso Sánchez. It stands to reason that Sánchez's voluntary testimony (which has not survived) did not line up with the copious information revealed in the Ramírez trial by Isabel and the other witnesses.

Sánchez was first tortured on March 10, 1512. Initially, he refused to answer questions and attempted instead to extract clues from his tormentors, presumably in order to avoid providing the inquisitors with new leads:

> Your Highnesses ordered for his clothes to be taken off and then for him to be put on the rack. After being asked to say the truth again, he was tied with ropes while he was again ordered to name his accomplices. He asked for the demands of Your Highnesses to be more specific. They told him that he knew what he had done against the Holy Catholic Faith, and that he should say and confess. Alonso Sánchez continued

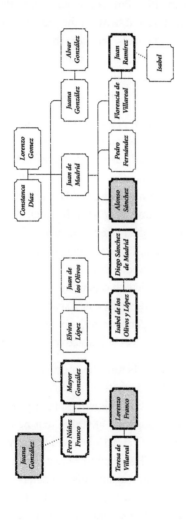

**FIGURE 3.4.** Alonso Sánchez, Juana González, Lorenzo Franco, and related community members.

to ask them to be given more clarity in the demands. Your Highnesses ordered for water to be thrown to his face from a jug of about one pint while he was tied with a rope. As they threw water to his face, Alonso Sánchez screamed that they should stop and that he would say any truth that he knew.[32]

Sánchez now proceeded to name his fellow conversos, two or three at a time, punctuated by additional water torture and twists of the rope. By the time he was untied, he had accused nineteen individuals, most of whom were family members or neighbors. They included his brother and sister, his brother-in-law, his sister-in-law, and his aunt. He provided not only names but locations and dates, details about ceremonies, and ritual implements. For example,

He was asked which book they prayed from and how it started. He answered that it was written in Romance, that it was the size of less than a quarter of a sheet, and that he had burnt it. He was asked about where the book was kept when they weren't using it. He answered that it was kept in a hole in the ground. . . . Sometimes they prayed using the big book, which was the Bribia, and at other times they used the small book which contained Jewish prayers.[33] He was then asked about which days they gathered to pray and he answered that on Fridays at one or two at night. He added that at the place where they prayed, they always placed two clean candlesticks with new candles for the Jewish ceremony. Then, after they prayed, each one went home and sometimes they ate a snack together. Sometimes they gathered on Saturdays at Juan Ramírez's home to pray before eating, and the attendees wore clean clothes and fasted on that day.[34]

Ten days later, Sánchez was brought before the court to affirm the accusations he had made under torture. Asked whether he remembered what he had said during his torture, he recalled most of the names, then promptly asserted that "he had not seen any of these people do anything that he had said while being tortured." Interestingly, his list of retractions includes only fourteen out of the nineteen names he had named. He failed to retract the other five. More suspiciously yet, he retracted an accusation against his brother, Diego Sánchez de Madrid, which he had never made.[35] Indeed, he had insisted in the torture chamber, repeatedly, that Diego Sánchez had never prayed with the rest of the group. Threatened with more torture, Sánchez begged for an opportunity to provide a written list of heretics. When he provided that list, on April 1, he refused to affirm that it was truthful and recanted again: "He had not seen any of the people whose names he had written do any of the listed crimes. He had only provided the list for fear of being tortured."

Why did Sánchez retract his testimony? The witness García de Argüello provided the answer. He was a guard in the prisons of the Inquisition and a repeat witness in this series of trials. Argüello had overheard Alonso Sánchez speaking to his brother Diego in their prison cells. Alonso admitted to Diego that he had betrayed Diego and his wife. Diego, in turn, begged his brother to recant his testimony.

The court reconvened on April 3 in the torture chamber. As his clothes were ordered removed, Sánchez affirmed twelve of the names he had mentioned during his first torture, all names he had retracted previously, and added the name of his brother, Diego Sánchez, to the list. Nonetheless, the inquisitor asked that his clothes be removed and he be tied to the rack. Sánchez pled repeatedly that he was now speaking the truth and that what he had claimed during his first torture was true. Yet the ropes were tightened, and water was poured on him, as Sánchez continued to insist that he had provided a full and accurate account.

> He was asked why he had vacillated so many times, why he had revoked his confessions. He said that because he had mentioned his siblings and family, he thought they would all die and he didn't want that to happen to them. So he revoked his confessions in order to save them, but even though he had rejected his confessions, now all he says is the truth. He said that he would confess two, three, seventy times, that it was all the truth.[36]

Despite his heartfelt pleading, Sánchez had to endure two more rounds of water torture before the inquisitors could be persuaded that he would not revoke his statement again. Two days later, when Sánchez was asked to ratify his last testimony in the torture chamber, he did so immediately.

Judging by the surviving evidence, much of the information provided by Sánchez was borne out in later trials. Four of the individuals he accused were later tried and found guilty. A fifth died in prison prior to his trial, and two, whose fate is unknown, were identified as conversos by María González and by Juan de Fez. Only three individuals named by Sánchez are known to have been cleared of heresy.

The list of people that Sánchez accused during his torture sessions received further confirmation in subsequent trials. Six months after Sánchez's torture, his sister-in-law, Isabel de los Olivos, was brought to trial.[37] She accused Sánchez of teaching her about various Jewish ceremonies and how to keep the Sabbath by wearing clean clothes, preparing kosher meat, and lighting Sabbath candles, among other things. Los Olivos also identified five other conversos, all of whom had also been named by Sánchez. Isabel, the slave of Juan Ramírez, confirmed Sánchez's claim that the Ramírez home was a central gathering place for this tightly knit group of conversos. Isabel identified Sánchez as a regular visitor to the house and named three others, also identified by Sánchez during his torture. Her condemnation of Sánchez, joined by Sánchez's brother and sister-in-law, sealed his fate. Sánchez was burned at the stake on September 7, 1513.

## María González, 1512

This trial, more than any other in the archives of Ciudad Real, provides insights into the deliberations of the inquisitors and the motivations that prompted the court to torture its suspects. González was threatened with torture because her voluntary testimony was deemed incomplete. This "exploratory" torture yielded thirty-seven accusations. Upon further investigation, however, many of her accusations were found to be without merit. Brought to the torture chamber a second time, to corroborate her prior claims, she retracted some of her voluntary testimonies, disavowed some of her claims under threat of torture, but also affirmed other statements, both those made inside the torture chamber and those made outside the torture chamber. The interrogations of María González entail clear lessons about the fallibility of torture as a source of information.

María González, wife of Pedro de Villarreal, was arrested on June 4, 1511. Upon her arrest, she testified against twenty-one conversos.[38] She then languished in prison for almost a year while the tribunal corroborated the information she had provided. By February 1512, it concluded, based on the evidence of new witnesses, that she had withheld names: "They once more required and admonished her to tell the truth about these other people, because information existed that she had committed her crimes with others, and had seen people commit other heresies."[39] González insisted that she had declared everything she knew.

A full month later, on March 30, 1512, she was sentenced to be tortured. The inquisitors documented their motivation: "Given the circumstantial evidence and suspicions that result from the trial against María González, and the fact that she has been silent about the people who participated with her in the crimes of heresy which she has confessed, we find that we must order her put to the question of torture. The torture shall be given according to our will until such time as she declares the truth about accomplices and participants in said crimes."

As with Juan de Fez, the sight of the torture chamber sufficed to coerce María González. Having been ordered to undress, she begged the lord inquisitor not to torture her and provided the names of thirty-seven additional conversos, including her own mother, five of her aunts, and her cousin. She also testified to following Jewish practices, including preparing kosher meat, cleaning her house on Fridays, wearing festive clothes on Saturdays, and blessing her children. She named the women who lit Sabbath candles with her, and the women who observed the Sabbath with her. The centers of activities for these rituals, she claimed, were the

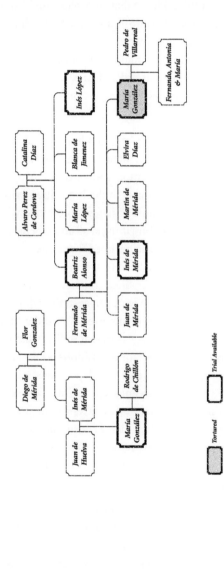

**FIGURE 3.5.** María González and related community members.

houses of Diego de Teva and his wife, Hernando de Córdoba and his wife, and Rodrigo de Chillón and his wife.

González was sentenced to excommunication, her belongings were seized, and she was condemned to perpetual prison. The Inquisition did not, however, cease investigating her claims. One by one, those she accused were arrested and brought before the court. It then correlated data from testimonies at these trials and contrasted them with the evidence that González provided before and after her time in the torture chamber. The prosecutor, Martín Jiménez, was now determined to show that she had perjured herself and that her testimony was false and contradictory. On July 19, 1513, a year and four months after her first exposure to the torture chamber, González was ordered back to the chamber, this time in order to assess her prior testimonies. The inquisitors' official deliberations offer insight into their calculus:

> She spoke against other people with whom she did not commit said crimes according to what is contained at greater length in her confessions, statements, and depositions. Some of the people against whom she testified have been prisoners in the Inquisition prison and some of them have confessed to crimes of heresy committed with other people, but they have not confessed anything at all about being an accomplice of María González. It should also be noted that some of the prisoners, who revealed that they committed heretical crimes with certain people, with whom they were very much allied, confessed nothing at all like what María González says they did with her, even though some of them have been put to the question of torture over it. And the character of María González has been taken into account, as well as what is proven against her in various trials; her style of depositions, as well as her vacillation and hesitation in her statements and depositions, has been noted. She has said some things that do not seem reasonable, and though investigations were carried out, no eyewitness testimony supports what María González herself declared in her depositions and statements. And because of other reasons that move us to ascertain the truth, as we are obliged to do for God and our consciences, we find that we must order María González put to the question of torture.[40]

Archival evidence from the trials that took place between her two interrogations makes apparent who "some of the people" were that raised questions about González's testimonies. Several of these witnesses corroborated González's claims. For example, González had accused Leonor Álvarez, who was brought to trial in July 1512.[41] Five others testified against her and she ultimately admitted to Judaizing. Álvarez also confirmed several of González's accusations, such as her claims about Juana Rodríguez, who was tried in August, found guilty of heresy, and condemned to death. Gracia de Teva, whom González had accused prior to torture, was tried and condemned to death. So was Beatriz Alonso, whom González had accused in the torture chamber.[42]

But other trials in this intervening period undermined González's claims. Under torture, González had accused the wife of Rodrigo de Chillón, also named María González, of hosting Jewish ceremonies in her home. This María González was brought to trial in November.[43] Ten witnesses testified in her defense but only one witness, in addition to González, testified against her. She was able to disqualify both witnesses and was absolved of all crimes.

González had also accused María González, wife of Alonso de Merlo (and daughter of Juan de Fez) in the torture chamber (see figure 3.2). On the one hand, this María González admitted to practicing certain Jewish customs, as had her parents, and professed to have spent a Sabbath at the house of Rodrigo de Chillón.[44] But at the same time she claimed that none of the others in the house observed the Sabbath with her, thus contradicting González's claims about Chillón. She also identified and disqualified González as an unreliable witness at the outset of her trial. Most damning of all were witnesses at the trial of Leonor Álvarez, who argued that María González was known to be a drunkard, a thief, and an unreliable witness.

As trial followed trial among those accused by María González, the Inquisition gradually formed a clearer picture of her unreliability as a witness. Of the twenty-one persons she accused *prior* to torture, the trials of five survive, all of whom were later found guilty of heresy. Of the thirty-seven persons she accused *in the torture chamber*, the trials of six individuals survive, four of whom were later found to be guilty. But even among those who would later be declared heretics, many discredited the claims that González made outside and inside the torture chamber. Since her testimonies absent the threat of torture had proved as doubtful as those made under threat of torture, and since she refused to revise her claims outside the torture chamber, the inquisitors decided to subject her to torture a second time.

Stripped of her clothes and placed on the rack, González met the inquisitor's questions with defiance: "Even if they tore her into a thousand pieces in the torture chamber and in the cart on the way to the stake she would say nothing else. . . . Tighten them and kill me, I will say no more than what I have already said." But once the ropes were tied around her arms, before the torture began, she admitted: "She had made it all up, she made it all up because she detested them. She couldn't stand those wives of Rodrigo de Chillón and Fernando de Córdoba. They treated her badly and wrecked her marriage." The inquisitors warned her to recant her lies and affirm the truth. She promised to do so if she was untied. The inquisitors refused to do so and began inquiring about her accusations, one by one.

Any hopes that this third interrogation would provide clarity were soon dashed. She affirmed her claims about Francisco Ruiz, Alonso Ruiz, Juana Núñez and Inés López. The inquisitors ordered half a jar of water to be poured into her nose and mouth. She stood by her claims. The other half of the jar was poured on her face. She revoked nothing. A second jar was poured on her. She affirmed her claims about Gracia de Teva. A third jar was poured on her. She called out in despair, captured in ghastly detail by the scribe at her side: "I speak the truth, I have spoken the truth, I have already spoken the truth, I speak the truth, what I have said is true, I am telling the truth, I do not tell any lies, I have not lied, I have spoken the truth, I have spoken the truth."[45] As the judges ordered a fourth jar to be poured, she recanted. She could not stand Lorenzo Franco's wife, a wicked and vain woman, against whom she spoke because of the great hatred she had for her. She wanted to see her ground into dust. She recanted what she had said about Rodrigo de Chillón's wife. Everything she said about Fernando de Córdoba's wife was a lie. She wanted to see them all burn.

By the time she left the torture chamber for the second time, González had affirmed eight of her prior claims, retracted twelve others, and in one case first retracted and then affirmed her prior claim. Most of her retractions pertained to names she had mentioned in the torture chamber, but some pertained to claims she had made voluntarily during her initial arrest and some of her affirmations pertained to claims that she had made under threat of torture. Confusing matters further, when she was asked, days later, to reaffirm the statements she had made under torture, a new round of thirty-two retractions and ten affirmations ensued. Some of these would have aligned with the court's expectations. For example, the court had cleared the wife of Rodrigo Chillón of all charges, even though González had accused her, under threat of torture.[46] González now retracted that statement. The court deemed Gracia de Teva guilty. González had named her prior to torture and confirmed that accusation under torture.

Yet other retractions that González made obscured matters further. She had identified Juana Núñez and Teresa de los Olivos as conversos soon after her arrest, repeated those accusations during her torture, but now retracted them. She had accused Beatriz Alonso, under threat of torture, had retracted that claim during torture, but now changed her mind again and repeated the accusation. She had testified against the wife of Alonso de Merlo when threatened with torture, and recanted that accusation when she was tortured, yet the court eventually found her guilty.

What might we conclude from the chaotic interrogations of María González, other than the fact that she was a thoroughly unreliable witness? Too few of the trials prompted by González's testimonies survive to make a confident assessment possible. Insofar as a correlation between González's accusation and the court's ultimate ruling can tell us anything at all, such correlations occurred slightly more often regarding claims she made outside the torture chamber. The judgment of the court corresponded to González's voluntary claims prior to torture five times out of five and it corresponded to her retractions and affirmations after torture four times out of six. As for torture, the court's ultimate ruling corresponded to her testimony under threat of torture five times out of six. It corresponded to her statements during physical torture four times out of six.

Subsequent trials provide further evidence that González's claims in the torture chamber were treated with suspicion. The court cited her uncoerced testimony in five subsequent trials.[47] It referenced her coerced testimony only once, in the trial of the wife of Alonso de Merlo, alongside two other witnesses.[48] Repeatedly, the court excluded her coerced testimony even when her accusations lined up with testimonies by other witnesses. For example, González's coerced testimony regarding her half-sister, Inés de Mérida, is suspiciously absent given the fact that Inés de Mérida admitted to praying with González.[49] González's coerced testimony was also excluded from the trial of Isabel de los Olivos, a significant trial in which ten other witnesses offered damning testimony.[50]

On August 22, 1513, the court assembled for a final hearing regarding María González. González attested that her initial claims had been false and insisted that her final revocations were trustworthy. She conceded that "they well knew that she deserved death on account of all those people" but she begged the inquisitors to spare her life, so that she could raise her children, lest they go astray. The court showed no such mercy. In light of her false claims, her retractions and counter-retractions, and her impenitent attitude, the court ruled that she be "relaxed to the secular arm." She was burned at the stake on September 7, 1513, together with her mother.

## Juana González, 1511

Juana González was a housekeeper in the home of Pero Núñez Franco and his wife Mayor González. Mayor was aunt to Alonso and Diego Sánchez, mentioned above (see figure 3.4). Juana's trial does not survive, but her testimony is appended to the trial of Mayor González in which Juana served as witness for the prosecution.[51] Arrested on June 4, 1511, Juana accused her employers of Judaizing, then vacillated, and ultimately refused to testify altogether. On the day after her arrest, Juana was threatened with torture. Brought to the torture chamber and undressed, she admitted, before the torture began, that Franco and González did not eat the fatty parts of the meat, lit candles, and went to bed early on Fridays, wore clean clothes on Saturdays, and abstained from work that day.[52]

A week later, when she was asked to confirm her testimony, she partially withdrew her accusations. She now denied that her masters sang Jewish prayers and blessed their children during the Friday evening Sabbath ceremony. They only sang ballads. Two days later, she withdrew her testimony entirely. None of what she had accused Franco and González of doing was true. She had only accused them out of fear of being tortured. Juana was released. It seems that the court had insufficient evidence to hold her, let alone to torture her.

Two years later, on July 2, 1513, the tribunal concluded its investigation and arrested Juana's mistress, Mayor González. Her trial was lengthy. Fourteen witnesses testified in her defense and twelve others testified for the prosecution. They revealed sufficient information to justify arresting Juana once again. She was imprisoned on August 18 and insisted that her initial accusations against Franco and González had been false, a sin, provoked by the devil. Now, two years after her initial vacillation, the court did have the evidence it needed to torture her "in light of the variations . . . until she tells the truth." Juana maintained that torture was futile: "Even if they killed her" she would not repeat the false accusations against her masters. She was shown the torture chamber, was undressed, and tied to the rack but persisted in her claim. Then the water torture began:

> They ordered a jar of water to be thrown at her and she said that she wanted to tell the truth, and that she swore on her soul that it was the truth. They continued with the water and she said that she wanted to tell the truth. Then they stopped throwing water at her. She stopped talking but didn't want to speak so your Highnesses ordered the water to continue. So she started saying that she would tell the truth, "Si si si." She asked to be given some space and then started talking.
>
> "Sirs, do not kill me. It is the truth what I said, it's the truth." She was asked what was the truth. She said that the truth was what she had said in Ciudad Real before [the inquisitor Alonso de] Maríana and that that was the truth even if she revoked it afterwards. That the truth was her first testimony. That is, that she saw Pero Núñez Franco and Mayor González, his wife, rest on some Saturdays. She had spent with them four or five Saturdays when she lived with them, and she noticed that they would wear clean clothes on Saturdays. She mentioned that her deceased sister Elena García and Aldonza [the prior housekeepers] would give them clean clothes on Saturdays and that this went on for about six to seven years.[53]

Juana now provided exhaustive details about the religious practices of her employers. She described how Franco and González passed the time on Saturdays, what parts of the lamb they would not eat, how fish, carrot, and eggs cooked on Fridays would be eaten cold on Saturdays, and how they would bless their children.

Why had she recanted her testimony, two years prior? Juana revealed that she had shared with Franco all she had initially told the Inquisition, whereupon Franco fled the city to the mountains, taking his belongings with him. Franco's son, Lorenzo Franco, summoned Juana and proposed that they "make amends," that they would arrange for Juana's daughter to marry into the family, give her everything they owned, and she would be well off for the rest of her days. That is why she changed her initial testimony. At this point in her testimony, her ropes were loosened.

Juana lingered in prison for another year before she was finally released in June 1514. She was tortured again, in September the following year. No transcript exists for that torture but it seems clear that the court used this torture, as it did with the repeated torture of Alonso Sánchez and María González, to remove all doubt as to which of her statements was valid. Juana insisted that her initial accusation was true: Franco and González were Judaizers. Only on her deathbed, in 1516, did she retract her accusations.

Amazingly, the court treated Mayor González with relative leniency. Whereas her husband, Pero Franco, was finally apprehended and burned at the stake in 1516, Mayor González affirmed her heresies. Initially condemned to life imprisonment and to wearing the sanbenito, her sentence was later commuted to penances. The torture of a minor witness such as Juana was indicative neither of the severity of a crime nor did it correlate to the ultimate punishment imposed on the accused. As far as the Inquisition was concerned, torture was no more than a tool, a fallible tool, for extracting information.

## Lorenzo Franco, 1513

Lorenzo was the son of Pero Núñez Franco and Mayor González (see figure 3.4). Not only had Juana González identified him and his parents as practicing Jews, she had also claimed that Franco had successfully bribed her to recant her testimony. Alonso Sánchez had also accused Franco, and Lorenzo Franco's wife and mother, of being members of his circle of conversos who prayed together in the house of Juan Ramírez. So had Isabel de los Olivos and so had Juan Ramírez's slave, Isabel.

It is clear, then, why Franco was brought to trial.[54] It is less clear why he was tortured, since his trial documents have not survived. Only a brief excerpt regarding his torture appears in the trial of his cousin, Juan Ramírez, but it includes no justification for the torture. As with the torture of Alonso Sánchez, it is reasonable to conclude that Franco's willing statement did not align with the significant body of evidence amassed in the lengthy Ramírez trial.

Franco was tortured on July 14, 1513. "Although he was tortured, he did not confess or say anything about himself or other people." He was absolved of all guilt and reconciled to the Church. His wife, Teresa de Villareal, who was tried with him, was not tortured. She was also cleared of all guilt.

There is not much we can learn from that brief reference. We learn only, as did the inquisitors, that torture often provided no leads at all. We further learn that the Inquisition was willing to declare silent torture victims to be innocent and to reconcile them to the faith. Indeed, as I show in the next chapter, those who survived torture while maintaining their innocence were often treated more leniently than witnesses who were not tortured at all.

## Lessons from Ciudad Real

Torture did not prove a particularly promising, let alone a particularly plentiful, source of information on heresy in Ciudad Real. At times, as with Lorenzo Franco, it provided no information at all beyond, perhaps, affirming that the accused had no information to provide and was, possibly, innocent. At other times, torture provided misleading information that would ultimately be disconfirmed, as the torture of María González demonstrated. But then again, her trial also demonstrated that uncoerced testimony was often unreliable.

In other cases, torture provided fragments of reliable information, as evidenced by the trials of Sancho Díaz, Juan González Daza, Marina González, Elvira González, and Juana González. All five made accusations against other community members that were corroborated by witnesses outside the torture chamber, including the very individuals they had exposed. They divulged more information than they had been willing to provide prior to torture, but not much more. These fragments of information were still useful to the Inquisition, which was meticulously assembling those accusations into an image of the Ciudad Real converso network.

No single testimony under torture provided an earth-shattering revelation that could unravel that network. The most revealing torture session, that of Alonso Sánchez, provided a mere thirteen accusations. The Inquisition treated even those accusations with suspicion. It decided to arrest some of Sánchez's alleged collaborators but not others. It convicted some of those identified by

Sánchez and not others. Not one converso in Ciudad Real was condemned, let alone executed, on the basis of tortured evidence alone.

The nearly three-decades-long experience with torture during these trials would have provided the Inquisition with a range of cruel insights into the nature of torture. For example, inquisitors tended to extend torture beyond the point at which the victim expressed a desire to speak. Presumably, the Inquisition had learned that torture victims often feigned a wish to cooperate with their tormentors in the torture chamber in order to gain a temporary reprieve from pain. Torture victims were also likely to retract their evidence after leaving the torture chamber, particularly if they had only been threatened with torture. They lied not only by making false claims against the innocent but also by recanting true claims against the guilty. Threats of torture in the early stages of a trial often led to painful torture sessions in the later stages of a trial.

The Inquisition also learned to wait longer before torturing the prisoners in its cells. Over the course of the Ciudad Real trials, this interval grew from months to years. The court used prolonged incarceration to isolate and weaken their suspects but also to gather further evidence so that torture could perform a corroborative rather than an exploratory function. Juan González Daza and Juan de Fez lingered for about one month in their cells before they were tortured. Marina González waited three and a half months. Alonso Sánchez spent more than half a year in prison before he was brought to the torture chamber. María González suffered in prison a whole year before she was tortured and another sixteen months before she was tortured a second time, with far more reliable results. Juana González was first tortured two full years after her initial arrest. Her second torture followed another two years later.

Torture that occurred later, both later in the course of a given trial and later in the course of the entire Ciudad Real proceedings, yielded more credible results. The more time the Inquisition had to interrogate witnesses and collect evidence, the greater was its ability to evaluate testimonies from the torture chamber. Torture after 1500 did not necessarily provide more names, but it did provide more reliable names. There was no easy way to evaluate what Daza or de Fez claimed under duress in 1484. In contrast, assessing the various testimonies of Alonso Sánchez and María González in 1512 was a straightforward matter of comparing their claims, coerced and uncoerced, to accusations made in dozens of other trials, coerced and uncoerced. Even the silence of Lorenzo Franco in 1513 was easier to interpret than it would have been three decades earlier.

The torture cases in Ciudad Real also offer two important lessons for scholars of inquisitorial torture. The first is that the Inquisition did not display a particular bias for or against torture as a means of acquiring evidence. It used torture to coerce victims who would not otherwise collaborate, knowing all too well that torture might yield misleading or confusing information, but, paradoxically, it also used torture to correct for lies told in other torture sessions. Where testimony seemed suspect, the Inquisition deemed torture a legitimate means of arriving at truth, even if the initially suspect testimony was itself the product of torture. The Inquisition tortured rarely in Ciudad Real, but it was not averse to torturing the same individual multiple times, regardless of the significance of the information at stake or the magnitude of the heresy on trial. In sum, the Inquisition regarded torture with indifference. Sometimes it revealed the truth, sometimes it did not, sometimes it had to recur multiple times before it revealed the truth, or failed to do so.

A second lesson has to do with the credibility of these archival sources. It is worth noting that our only source of information about the unexceptional torture record in Ciudad Real is the Inquisition itself. Its scribes were impartial in reporting cases of failure alongside cases of success. Indeed, in Ciudad Real the scribes of the Inquisition recorded primarily failure. They did not seek to bias the evidence since the documents they were creating were intended for internal use only. The decision to record torture in detail, regardless of outcome, provides the most persuasive evidence for the Inquisition's desire to learn from its mistakes. It had all the time and resources it needed to perfect its torture methods.

# CORRELATES OF TORTURE
## Toledo (1575–1610)

In 1902, Henry Charles Lea came across a remarkable manuscript in the Royal Library of the University of Halle, Germany.[1] It consists of 381 handwritten folios (762 pages) and documents 1,046 cases tried by the Inquisition in Toledo between 1575 and 1610, in chronological order. The provenance of the Halle manuscript is unknown. Nor is it known how Lea discovered it, a hundred miles southwest of Berlin, but it is clear that he recognized its significance. At the time, he was completing the research for his magnum opus, a four-volume *History of the Inquisition of Spain*. He summarized the manuscript page by page, reorganizing the cases by accusation, and added occasional commentary on the text. Lea's summary consists of 176 pages of notes jotted down in dense, but faint, penciled script.[2]

Several years after his death, in 1925, Lea's descendants bequeathed his personal library to the University of Pennsylvania, including not only his books and papers but his furniture, fixtures, and art. The entire library, furnished as it was in Lea's home, was transferred to the sixth floor of the university's Van Pelt-Dietrich Library, where it is kept behind lock and key, as if frozen in time. That is where, thanks to a particularly helpful archivist, I found Lea's handwritten notes. His notes, in turn, led me to the original sixteenth-century manuscript, still held at the library in Halle, now known as the Universitäts und Landesbibliothek Sachsen-Anhalt.

There is no shortage of trial documents from the Spanish Inquisition. They are available by the tens of thousands. The Archivo Histórico Nacional in Madrid alone holds information on 44,674 trials recorded by the Suprema.[3] Nonetheless, most of these documents provide a fragmented picture because so many more have been lost to fire, war, and looting and many (like the Halle manuscript) have been dispersed around the world. While it is sometimes possible to assemble several related files from one era and location in order to reach broader conclusions about the activities of the Inquisition, it is hard to do so systematically, as my attempts in the prior chapter demonstrate. The Halle manuscript is remarkable not merely because it comprises so many cases but because it does so comprehensively. It captures almost all of the trials conducted by one of the most important courts in Spain over a period of thirty-five years, at a pace of about thirty trials a year. These are *relaciones de causa*, trial summaries sent to the archives of the Suprema in Madrid, and they allow us to discern patterns regarding accusations, penalties, and torture.[4]

The Halle manuscript provides only a handful of sentences for each trial, gathered two to three per page. The information is terse. The scribes listed the year of the trial, the name and any necessary identifying details for the accused, the charges, a summary of remarkable trial highlights (irregularities regarding witnesses, whether and when the accused testified, whether the accused was tortured and with what results), and the verdict (see figure 4.1).

**FIGURE 4.1.**  Summaries of the 1575 trials of Juan Bajo, the slave Úrsula, Lorenzo de Collar, Felipe Alguazil, and Diego Martín. De Collar and Martín were tortured. Halle manuscript, MSS Yc 2° 20 (1), ff. 5v and 6r. Martin-Luther-Universität Halle-Wittenberg.

**TABLE 4.1**   Testimonies without and with torture at the Toledo Tribunal, 1575–1610

| CATEGORY | CASES | TESTIMONIES WITHOUT TORTURE | TORTURED | TESTIMONIES WITH TORTURE |
|---|---|---|---|---|
| Sorcery | 17 | 3 (18%) | 4 (24%) | 1 (25%) |
| Bigamy | 51 | 35 (69%) | 0 | 0 |
| Propositions | 161 | 66 (41%) | 12 (7%) | 3 (25%) |
| False orders | 25 | 14 (56%) | 1 (4%) | 0 |
| Lutherans | 47 | 10 (21%) | 13 (28%) | 2 (15%) |
| Jews | 163 | 83 (51%) | 32 (20%) | 8 (25%) |
| Miscellaneous | 77 | 19 (25%) | 2 (3%) | 0 |
| Fornication | 253 | 115 (45%) | 0 | 0 |
| False witness | 8 | 2 (25%) | 1 (12%) | 1 (100%) |
| Blasphemy | 46 | 28 (61%) | 0 | 0 |
| Alumbrados | 11 | 1 (9%) | 0 | 0 |
| Moors | 187 | 66 (35%) | 58 (31%) | 21 (36%) |
| Total | 1046 | 442 (42%) | 123 (12%) | 36 (29%) |

*Note:* The categories were assigned to the cases by Lea. Where information on testimonies was absent, I treated the case as if no testimony had been offered. For testimonies without torture, percentages refer to the ratio of testimonies to all cases. For testimonies with torture, percentages refer to the ratio of testimonies to torture cases. For example, the calculation of 20 percent for Jews tortured refers to 32 individuals out of 163, but the calculation of 25 percent for Jews who testified under torture refers to 8 individuals out of the 32 who were tortured. Similarly, the calculation for the total percentage of testimonies with torture, 29 percent, refers to 36 individuals out of the 123 who were tortured.

What these listings lack in detail, they make up for in quantity. The Halle manuscript documents more than a thousand trials across twelve categories of accusation. Of these trials, 397 focused on heretics, an offense permitting of torture; 47 were Lutherans, 163 Jews, and 187 Muslims (see table 4.1).

The Toledo trials reported to the Suprema display a fascinating variety of accusations, claims, testimonies, and penalties. Isabel de Soto was tried for sorcery because she distributed love potions and practiced divination. She denied this but the court, without subjecting her to torture, ruled against her and exiled her from Toledo for six years. Seven witnesses accused Luis Aquen, a Morisco, of making heretical statements. He rejected this accusation but offered no defense, so he was tortured with nine twists of the rope around his arms. He maintained his silence, so he was strangled with four turns of the garrote. Because he endured these without testifying, he received a hundred lashes and was set free. A slave by the name of Torenco Piritado was accused of saying that the law of the Moors was better than the law of the Christians. He was not tortured and did not collaborate but was condemned to death. Juan González, who was married to a woman in Guadalajara, stood accused of having another wife in Castel Rodrigo. He denied bigamy, insisting that the woman in Castel Rodrigo was not a second wife but merely his concubine. He was acquitted. Alonso and Mari López, both seventy years old, and their children Juan (twenty-eight), Catalina (thirty), and Isabel (twenty-eight), all came before the court to admit their Jewish practices and provided damning testimony against one another. The parents were condemned to life imprisonment and confiscation of property whereas the children were imprisoned for two or three years each.[5] As with all Inquisition documents, these manuscripts overflow with information about contemporary life: community, family, business, trade, crime, customs, culture, cuisine, fashion, and religion. Occasionally, Lea peppers his translations with wry commentary. When Alonso Rebellan ultimately admits under torture that he did indeed deny the Day of Judgment, Lea adds a sarcastic note in the margins: "Worth torturing him for."[6]

This chapter provides a description of patterns in these data. I show that 12 percent of suspects were tortured, mostly heretics. Torture victims tended to be somewhat older (forty years old on average) than most of the accused (thirty-six years old on average). Men were as likely to be tortured as women. Torture was directed at those who maintained their innocence despite overwhelming evidence and at those who provided suspect testimony. The Toledo tribunal did not use torture as a form of punishment: it condemned suspects to far harsher punishments (including life imprisonment and death at the stake) at the end of their trial regardless of torture. Indeed, torture victims were less likely to receive harsh punishments than other suspects if they were able to prove their innocence. Those who did not, and testified under torture what the Inquisition felt they should have testified prior to torture, received the harshest penalties of all.

Torture yielded testimonies from at least 29 percent of victims. Tortured women collaborated at a higher rate than men. Those suspected of Muslim practices collaborated at a higher rate than those suspected of Jewish or Protestant practices. Most important, in the period 1590–1610, torture tended to occur late in the activities of this tribunal, and later torture sessions tended to yield testimonies at a higher rate. I conclude with an assessment of this source and the reliability of the evidence contained in it.

## Who Was Tortured?

Of the 1,046 individuals tried by the Toledo court, 123 (or 12 percent) were tortured. This amounts to an average of three or four cases of torture per year. What commonalities do these instances of torture display?

The court focused its torture on heretics: 84 percent of those tortured stood accused of the most severe crimes tried by the Inquisition: Lutheranism (thirteen tortured), Judaism (thirty-two tortured), and Islam (fifty-eight tortured). Over the course of thirty-five years, the court only tortured twenty individuals for other religious offenses. But even though heretics were the most likely among the accused to be tortured, torture was constrained even in those cases. Of the 397 heretics examined by the court, a quarter were put to torture. The rest were not.

The Inquisition in Toledo tended to torture slightly older suspects, but it does not seem to have discriminated by sex. The data on age are slim. The manuscript records the ages of only 158 of the individuals tried by the tribunal, 15 percent of the total. Their age averages thirty-six years. The average age for heretics, who were the most likely to be tortured, was thirty-five but the average age of torture victims was forty. The youngest, Ysabel Fernández, who professed to Moorish practices under torture, was sixteen years old. The oldest, Ysabel de Faen, was eighty: she fainted during torture and took so long to resuscitate that her torture was discontinued.[7]

The slightly elevated age of torture victims is of note, because the Inquisition regularly excused individuals from torture because they were too old. For example, Gonçalo el Gordo was voted to be tortured but was spared because he was "muy viejo y enfermo." Justa Febos received "light torture" because she was old and infirm. Dominique Rael was not tortured "on account of his age" (he was eighty) and Manuel de Acosta was spared torture "on account of his infirmities."[8] Given the exclusion of some elderly suspects from torture, the elevated average age of those who were nonetheless tortured may indicate that the Inquisition in Toledo gravitated somewhat toward torturing older suspects.

The data on sex are more robust. 79 percent of the suspects tried in Toledo were men, 21 percent were women. The percentage of women among heretics was higher: Here, only 61 percent were men, 39 percent were women. This difference is attributable to offenses that were tried by the Inquisition in which men were naturally overrepresented but which did not qualify as heresy, such as bigamy or functioning under false (priestly) orders. On the other hand, a significant percentage of those accused of Lutheranism were men (91 percent), perhaps because they tended to be visitors to Spain. This would also explain the higher than average age of those accused of Lutheranism (thirty-nine years old, on average).

The sex distribution among torture victims is identical to its distribution among heretics: 68 percent men, 32 percent women. This correspondence in the distribution of sexes across the two categories, tortured and not tortured, was also apparent in Ciudad Real. There, 55 percent of heretics and 54 percent of torture victims were men.

# When Was Torture Employed?

Many of the heretics who were tortured were selected because they maintained their innocence despite overwhelming evidence. Estéfano Grillín was accused of making blasphemous statements to a group of travelers who had shared a carriage with him on the road from Játiva to Illescas. Their accounts were detailed, and in accord with one another, yet he persisted in his denial. María de Villares provided an incomplete statement even though sixteen witnesses testified against her, including her own daughters; so she was tortured. Similarly, Antonio López Duarte was tortured when he refused to collaborate even after eleven witnesses testified against him, including his sister-in-law. María Rodríguez attempted to present disqualifying evidence against her accusers but failed. Manuel Sánchez stood accused by several witnesses but was able to disqualify only some of these. Francisco Báez Pinto was tortured because he claimed innocence, even though spies in the prison provided evidence that he was persisting in heretical practices in his cell.[9]

Several of the accused were tortured because their testimony was unpersuasive or otherwise suspect. Seven witnesses heard Claudio Langier, a Frenchmen, make insulting statements about the Inquisition at the Royal Court in Escorial, but he only admitted to the court some of these statements and not others. Confronted with evidence of Lutheranism, Hernando Valiente equivocated until, under torture, he admitted that he had indeed been Lutheran until he learned about the Catholic faith four years ago. The court heard rumors that Juan del Bosque had consorted with the famous Swiss reformer Theodore Beza. During his arrest, he had removed a letter from his pocket, torn it up, and swallowed the pieces. This, despite his denials, aroused enough suspicion to torture him. Pedro Lorenço confessed "partially and extenuatingly." Guido de Armenderría, accused of blasphemy, tried to excuse and reinterpret his statements, but his statements were inconsistent and raised doubts. Isabel Pérez was accused of burying her husband according to Muslim rites. These suspicions were confirmed when his body was exhumed and found to be clad in a new shirt, his arms uncrossed. Pérez argued, in vain, that she had buried him in a clean shirt because his shirt was stained with blood and she loved him too much to bury him in soiled clothes.[10]

The trial of David de la Chinalohe presents an archetypal example for the type of uncertainty most likely to lead to torture.[11] Two Englishmen, who knew Chinalohe from France, happened to recognize him in the streets of Madrid and informed the Inquisition that he was a covert Lutheran. Once arrested, his cellmates in the Inquisition prison reported that he openly praised Lutheranism and had tried to escape through a hole in wall. Chinalohe claimed that he had once been an apostate but that he had long since converted: He had only pretended to be a Lutheran because he had fallen in love with a Lutheran girl in France. He managed to disqualify the two Englishmen as witnesses, demonstrating that they bore ill will against him. Confusing matters further, one of his cellmates retracted his testimony, arguing that the other prisoner had persuaded him to lie. The court was unable to reach a decision on how to proceed and appealed to the Suprema, which ordered torture. It yielded nothing: the case was dismissed.

# Was Torture a Form of Political Terrorism?

The Toledo Inquisition directed brutal, callous violence at helpless victims. The bureaucratic nature of its procedures does not detract from their viciousness. On the contrary, it lends the torture an almost inhuman cruelty. Yet it is hard to look at these 123 cases and walk away with the impression that the Toledo court was eager to torture. Sessions in the torture chamber ceased at the moment of full collaboration, often before torture had even begun. In two consecutive trials, Simón Fernández (aged eighteen) and Antonio Fernández (aged seventeen) both testified after the court had voted to torture them but before the torture began, so no torture took place. Alonso el Gordo falsely accused others of heresy, was taken to the torture chamber, but recanted everything before being strapped to the rack, ending the session. Lorenço López was ordered to be tortured but when he learned that his wife, Isabel, had already admitted under torture everything they had done together, he too collaborated, and his torture was not carried out. The court voted to put María de Avana to torture, but before her sentence was read to her, she testified, so no torture took place.[12] These accounts cannot be squared with the popular image of sadistic inquisitors eager to induce pain.

Did the court torture primarily in order to instill fear in the population? Modern authoritarian regimes, in Chile, Argentina, Iran, Iraq, North Korea, China and elsewhere have used torture to intimidate populations by leaking evidence and rumors about the terrors of their torture facilities. There are two reasons to doubt that torture was designed primarily to serve this function in Toledo. The first is that the Toledo court had far more extreme means for threatening those under its shadow. It tortured 12 percent of the accused (123 individuals) but it subjected 27 percent of the accused (313 individuals) to severe penalties after their trials, independent of torture. These individuals suffered exile, hard labor (in the form of service on the oars of the royal galleys), or perpetual imprisonment. Another 3 percent, or thirty-one individuals, were sentenced to death. Suspects were more likely to dread the very real chance of perpetual exile, hard labor, lifelong imprisonment, or death (30 percent) than they were to fear the odds of torture (12 percent). Yet another 12 percent of the accused received sentences of fifty, one hundred, or two hundred lashes at the end of their trial, but these never constituted part of the torture proceeding. They occurred after the trial and in a separate location as a punishment imposed on the guilty, not in order to extract information. The specific category of pain that the Inquisition classified as torture, then, was neither the most extreme, the most durable, nor the most frequently administered pain in its repertoire.

The second reason why it is difficult to conceive of torture as a form of political terrorism in this instance is that those tortured were not judged more harshly than others at the conclusion of their trial. Indeed, they were treated more leniently, if found to be innocent, than those who admitted their crimes without being tortured. Of the individuals who were not tortured, about 30 percent received harsh punishments at the end of their trials, regardless of whether they testified or were found guilty for some other reason. This is true regardless of the level of offense suspected: heretics were just as likely to receive severe penalties (29 percent) as the average suspect (30 percent), or as the suspect who was not tortured and collaborated (30 percent), or who was not tortured and refused to collaborate (28 percent). However, among those who maintained their innocence throughout the torture ordeal only 23 percent received severe sentences. Conversely, 30 percent of individuals tortured were acquitted, a much higher rate than the 17 percent chance of acquittal among those who were not tortured.

Thus torture was not synonymous with harsh verdicts. Penalties depended not on whether torture occurred over the course of the trial but on the nature of the accusation and on the willingness of the accused to cooperate and demonstrate their innocence, either by admitting their own guilt prior to torture or by maintaining innocence despite torture. For example, the court tried four individuals for the crime of denying purgatory.[13] One of the four, Mateo de Atiença, collaborated when confronted with the initial accusation and was sentenced to perpetual imprisonment. Three others refused to cooperate but, because of the presence of strong evidence against them, were sentenced to torture. Two maintained their innocence throughout their torture session: at the end of their trial, Juan Francés was sentenced to one hundred lashes, and Antón Martín Duay received a mere reprimand. The fourth, Melchior Florín, testified under torture and was imprisoned for life, with three years of hard labor in the galleys. The difference between the punishments received by Atiença and Florín can be attributed to the latter's obstinacy. Had he, like Atiença, collaborated at the beginning rather than waiting for the Inquisition to torture him, he might have avoided three years of hard labor. The variations in penalty cannot, however, be attributed to torture itself. Francés and Duay, accused of the same crime and similarly tortured, but without testifying, walked away with relatively light penalties.

Another illuminating comparison involves the three individuals who were tried for "following the law of Mohammed" (as opposed to those accused of specific Muslim practices).[14] Inés, a slave, admitted the accusation and received a reprimand. Juan Gonçález denied the claim, was tortured, but successfully maintained his innocence throughout his torture. He was required to perform a public renunciation and to receive instruction in the faith. Gaspar de Guzmán also denied the claim and was tortured but he testified as the torture was about to begin, admitting his own guilt and naming "many other" collaborators. He was punished with life imprisonment, confiscation of goods, and four years of hard labor.

In fact, one gets the impression that, at least some of the time, the Inquisition in Toledo viewed torture as a time-consuming nuisance. Torture required lengthy deliberations, significant expenses, and physical relocation of the court to the torture chamber. The court expressed its frustration by imposing particularly harsh penalties on those who only testified during torture what they ought to have testified earlier. Those who were tortured and only then collaborated stood a 59 percent chance of facing a heavy penalty, including death, compared to the 30 percent rate of harsh penalties among all other cases. The subgroup of individuals who cooperated during torture is the only group for which the number of heavy penalties exceeded by far the number of light penalties (see figure 4.2).

The Inquisition's occasional frustration with the torture process is exemplified in the trials of Manuel Enríquez and Susarte López.[15] In 1585, the court tried these two Judaizers who had studied, prayed, and fasted together. Both denied the accusation and both were tortured. López refused to testify and was sentenced

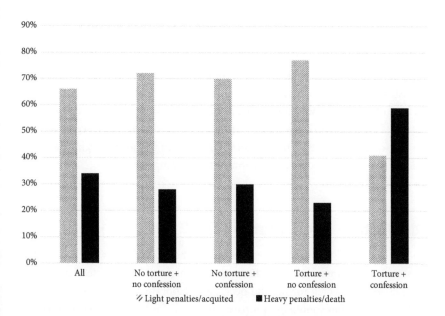

**FIGURE 4.2.**  Ratios of light to heavy penalties in Toledo, 1575–1610.

to three years hard labor. But Enríquez testified under torture, then revoked his statement, was tortured two more times, and revoked his statement each time. He received a much harsher sentence: One hundred lashes and six years of hard labor. In marginal notes on his translation, Lea comments, in typical sardonic manner: "To punish him I suppose for the trouble he gave."

It seems, then, that the Inquisition did not use torture vindictively. It did not use torture to punish, for it had a wide range of far more severe penalties that it could impose, and it did not associate torture with guilt. Instead, the Inquisition viewed torture dispassionately, as a procedural tool to resolve uncertainty and arrive at (what it considered to be) the truth. To wit, those who "proved" their innocence under torture received light sentences or no sentences at all. For example, a sixteen-year-old girl accused Domingo Pereira of teaching Judaism, leading Jewish services in his home, and helping persecuted Jews escape to France. He successfully identified and disqualified the key witness and provided the court with character witnesses, but presumably because of the presence of other reliable witnesses, he was ordered to be tortured. He did not cooperate and was set free. Five witnesses accused Bartólome López of Jewish practices, but he denied the accusation, was tortured without collaborating, and was set free. Miguel Canete stood accused of performing Islamic ablutions, but the only witness soon revoked his testimony. Canete initially testified, then claimed that he was an unlettered man, and partially deaf, and might have misunderstood the court's questions. Uncertain of his guilt, he was put to torture, withstood four turns of the cord, and was set free.[16] This pattern recurs in nearly one-third of the instances of torture ordered by this court.

In all these instances, the Inquisition viewed the ability to withstand torture without declaration of guilt as strong proof of innocence. Not once did the court punish with death those who withstood torture in silence. Indeed, less than a quarter of those who withstood torture in silence received harsh penalties. This betrays a deep irrationality on the part of the Inquisition, which seems to have viewed torture as a test of endurance, a trial by fire, a means of purging damning evidence by enduring pain proportionate to its strength.[17]

## Did Torture Elicit Testimonies?

The Halle manuscript lists 442 testimonies in the 922 trials in which no torture occurred, a collaboration rate of 42 percent (or higher). It lists 36 testimonies for the 123 trials in which torture did occur, a collaboration rate of 29 percent (or higher). These rates should be compared with caution since they do not relate to the same overall population. The 42 percent collaboration rate without torture represents a fraction of all interrogations in Toledo in this period. The 29 percent collaboration rate under torture refers only to those 123 trials in which torture did take place.

It is reasonable to measure the testimony rate under torture as a percentage of all torture cases, and not as a percentage of all cases tried, since the Inquisition did not employ torture and nontorture in parallel but in sequence. The accused were only put to torture *after* they had been given three opportunities to cooperate. Thus the 123 who were tortured were not chosen at random from among the 1,046 cases but were a subset of the cases in which a nonviolent interrogation failed and in which the Inquisition chose to pursue torture.

This has two implications. In absolute terms, torture yielded far fewer testimonies than noncoercive interrogation. Of the 478 testimonies extracted by the Toledo tribunal, only 7.5 percent (36 statements) were the result of torture. But in relative terms, these 7.5 percent are remarkable because they were extracted from the "hardest" cases: suspects who were offered multiple opportunities to collaborate outside the torture chamber but had refused to do so. Of those 123 unyielding suspects, 29 percent were willing to provide information under torture that they would not previously provide.

In actuality, the collaboration rates may have been somewhat higher for both coercive and noncoercive interrogations. The Halle manuscript lists success or failure to elicit testimonies for most but not all cases. Some 20 percent of cases make no reference to testimonies, perhaps because there was no testimony to record. Where this occurred, I treated the case as a nonconfession, even though this risks undercounting cases of testimonies. That said, there is no reason to assume that scribes were biased in mentioning or omitting testimonies when they summarized torture sessions as opposed to when they summarized nontorture sessions.

At the same time, a 29 percent collaboration rate also implies a 71 percent failure of collaboration; more than two-thirds of the torture sessions ended without a testimony. This flies in the face of the notion that the Inquisition tortured relentlessly until it obtained evidence. We do not know how inquisitors decided on the type or duration of torture. But it is clear that, more often than not, they chose to cease torturing for reasons other than a much-awaited statement. For the Inquisition, the purpose of torture was not a confession, let alone pain for the sake of pain. The purpose of torture was information.

Consequently, the Halle manuscript provides a dispassionate account of those torture sessions that resulted in collaboration alongside a majority of cases that yielded silence or inconclusive results. Luis Hernández was seen praying according to Muslim practice and keeping snakes and lizards, but his torture yielded no information. The case was suspended, and he was released, whereupon two of his cell mates testified that he had conducted Muslim prayers in prison and had fasted during Ramadan. He was arrested again and denied the accusation, leading the court to *discordia*. The Suprema ordered torture, which he endured without cooperating. Sixteen-year-old Ysabel Fernández denied being a Muslim, despite strong evidence against her. She was tortured, testified, then revoked her claim, but presumably because of the realization that torture would resume, she ultimately testified fully, denouncing several others. Susarte López was accused of keeping the Sabbath and hosting Jewish fasts and feasts at his home. He denied this and was tortured without collaborating. Ana de Castro admitted to Jewish practices and named other Jews after the court confronted her with evidence from seven witnesses. Because she subsequently revoked some of her accusations, she was tortured, but she insisted on her revocation, despite torture. Twenty-eight-year-old Isavel Franco endured seven turns of the cord and ten turns of the garrote "without an indication of suffering and without confession."[18] Accounts like these suggest that the Toledo tribunal revealed instances of effective torture alongside instances in which torture provided misleading information or no information at all.

The accounts of testimonies under torture in this manuscript also underscore the fact that witnesses provided statements of fact, not confessions of faith. Torture victims admitted to particular practices or named others who had performed heretical practices. There is no reference in this manuscript to belief. Indeed, there are few references to prohibited speech. The court tried forty-five individuals for blasphemy, but these were not tortured. Torture was reserved for those who committed heretical *acts*. Duarte Díaz stood accused of Judaism by two witnesses, one of whom was his daughter. At the second turn of the cord he testified fully regarding his own practices, his wife's, and daughter's, and many others. Ángela Pérez, a slave, was accused of refusing lard and of saying that Mohammed is in heaven and next to God. During torture, she admitted not only to the accusation but admitted that she fasted during Ramadan and that she performed prayers to Allah, morning, afternoon, and night. Gabriel de Haro, a thief, was accused of possessing a book in Arabic. His torture revealed that he was the owner of the book and that he used it for his daily prayers. Under torture, Lorenço Pérez accused Luis de Guzmán of Muslim practices. Guzmán denied this but, threatened with torture, admitted to having been a Muslim in the past. After four twists of the rope, he testified to continued Muslim practices and accused Pérez and several others. Guzmán later revoked these statements and attempted to escape the prison, was tortured again, and affirmed his prior statements. Isabel de Aguilar, mentioned above, admitted to Moorish practices under torture and named other secret Muslims, including her husband. Alonso de Mondíxar admitted to Muslim practices but denied participating in group rituals until he was tortured, whereupon he admitted to being at the assembly and named those who attended with him.[19] In these and other instances, testimonies included falsifiable claims that the court could have independently verified in subsequent trials. The Toledo manuscript is not detailed enough to permit us to do likewise. This leaves us with no easy way to assess whether these confessions were truthful, short of wading even deeper into the archives of the Inquisition in order to identify references to these individuals in subsequent documents.

## Who Testified and When?

Under torture, men testified at a lower rate than women: 79 percent of the torture victims were men but only 61 percent of the statements were made by men. Women, who accounted for 21 percent of the victims, provided 39 percent of the testimonies. The data provide no obvious explanation for this pattern. The average age of torture victims who collaborated was thirty-eight years old, compared to an average age of forty among all torture victims, a marginal difference given how sparse the available data are on the age of torture victims.

About a quarter of those accused of Jewish practices testified during torture. Fewer of those accused of Protestantism testified under torture (15 percent). The largest percentage of testimonies under torture came from those accused of Muslim practices: 36 percent collaborated under torture. We can only speculate that more Muslims were tortured, and more collaborated, because more had survived the first century of the Inquisition. Most Jews were expelled or killed prior to the late sixteenth century, at which point the Inquisition started shifting its attention to Muslims and Protestants.[20]

The pace of torture and testimonies across these thirty-five years examined here confirms a pattern that I identified in the previous chapter: the court conducted most of its torture toward the end of its trials in Toledo. When torture occurred early in the tenure of the court, it yielded far fewer statements than when torture occurred ten or fifteen years into its activities. At that point, the court had assembled sufficient information to evaluate statements, coerced or uncoerced.

During its first fifteen years of activity, the Toledo court tortured only nine individuals suspected of Jewish practices: two in 1579 and another seven in 1585. These efforts yielded only one testimony (in 1585). In contrast, between 1590 and 1610, the Toledo court tortured twenty individuals and collected seven testimonies.

The delayed pacing of tortures and testimonies is even more apparent in the case of those suspected of Muslim practices. Nine were tortured in the first year

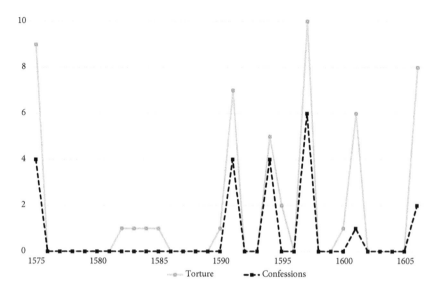

**FIGURE 4.3.**   Torture and testimonies of those accused of Muslim practices in Toledo, 1575–1610.

(1575) yielding four testimonies, but then torture trickled to a halt and testimonies ceased altogether for the next fifteen years. Only four others suspected of being Muslim were tortured between 1575 and 1590 and none collaborated. But between 1591 and 1610, forty more suspects were tortured and seventeen of those testified (see figure 4.3).

Though the files do not contain enough information to identify confidently the purpose of torture, it stands to reason that the torture that occurred late in the activities of the tribunal was more corroborative than exploratory. By 1591, when it began torturing suspected Muslims at an increased pace, it had already interrogated fifty-four of them (29 percent of the total). By 1594, when its torture of suspected Jews accelerated, it had already interrogated an identical number of suspected Jews (fifty-four suspects, 33 percent of the total). It was thus able to rely on significant information in order to determine who ought to be tortured, and how reliable the testimonies were that it had obtained in the torture chamber. Such was not the case with torture in the 1570s and 1580s, yielding few testimonies. The same pattern will become apparent in the next chapters. In Mexico, much of the torture was confined to the last four months of the court's activities, where it served to confirm information that the Inquisition already possessed.

# Can We Trust These Data?

Why should we give any credence at all to the court's claims regarding testimony rates? I can think of five reasons. For one, if the court sought to inflate collaboration rates it would not have disclosed the 71 percent noncollaboration rate. Second, it is not obvious that the court considered testimonies to be an indicator of "success" worth inflating. Its stated goal was to uncover innocence or guilt, not to force confessions. This is evidenced by the relatively lenient penalties imposed on those who endured torture in silence and by its willingness to report, frequently, on cases in which trials were discontinued for lack of evidence and on cases in which defendants were declared innocent. Third, there is no reason to assume that the court would have inflated the 29 percent collaboration rate for torture any more, or less, than it would have inflated the 42 percent collaboration rate for trials without torture. Thus, regardless of how reliable its reports might be, the relatively high ratio of testimonies from torture compared to testimonies without torture remains remarkable. Fourth, the Halle manuscript was not compiled to serve as a public document but to act as an internal report, to be read exclusively by the Suprema. Given the Suprema's frequent involvement in the Toledo court's decision making regarding torture, overruling some decisions to torture while demanding torture at other times, it seems unlikely that the Toledo court would have wanted to, or could have, manipulated collaboration statistics. Fifth, the Toledo court would have seen no need to persuade its readers of the efficacy or legitimacy of torture. Both the inquisitors in Toledo and the inquisitors in Madrid agreed that torture was a legitimate and effective legal procedure, as did all European courts in this period. There was no utility in spinning the facts to lionize torture.

The data in the Halle manuscript are not detailed enough to conclude whether statements made in the torture chamber were objectively truthful or whether they provided information that the Inquisition considered useful in subsequent prosecutions. The files do not tell us how the Inquisition decided whether a testimony was honest, or complete, or mere lip service. Determining whether torture can elicit reliable information requires access to detailed trial manuscripts, so that specific facts provided by torture victims can be compared with testimony provided by other witnesses who were not tortured. The archives of the Inquisition in Mexico City, examined in the next two chapters, offer one opportunity to perform such an analysis.

# EXPLORATORY TORTURE
## Mexico City (1589–1591)

The first name that escaped the lips of Luis de Carvajal, when the torturer tightened the cords around his arms for the second time, was that of his seventeen-
year-old sister, Anica.[1] At the fourth turn of the cord, he named his mother, Doña
Francisca, and four other sisters, Doña Isabel, Doña Catalina, Doña Maríana, and
Doña Leonor. After the sixth turn of the cord, he began naming 113 family members, friends, and acquaintances who were practicing Judaism in secret. His testimony laid bare before the Inquisition the structure of Mexico City's underground
Jewish community, a community of which Carvajal was the de facto leader.

Ten months later, in December 1596, and again in 1601, the Inquisition staged
two of the most elaborate autos-da-fé to be performed in the New World. It
paraded heretics on the Zócalo, the central square of Mexico City, publicly pronounced their sentences, performed rituals of penitence, and then "relaxed" into
the hands of the civil authorities those condemned to be burned at the stake.
Eighty-six Judaizers were condemned at the Great autos of 1596 and 1601. Carvajal had named fifty-seven of them during his torture. Of the condemned, eleven
were burned at the stake. Ten of these were garroted prior to burning, an act of
"mercy" that spared the condemned the agony of a slow death by fire. Carvajal
had named all ten under torture. The eleventh, burned alive without garroting,
was Carvajal himself.

According to traditional accounts, the torture of Luis de Carvajal, like the torture of ten other members of his circle, doomed the nascent Jewish community
in sixteenth-century Mexico.[2] The evidence I present in this chapter dispels that
notion. Torture played a far more subtle role in eradicating Judaism from New

Spain than was hitherto assumed. Much of the information that Carvajal and others provided in the torture chamber was accurate, but none of it was new. The Inquisition had already assembled this information prior to torture. It did not use torture to reveal new information but instead to corroborate information that had been disclosed outside the torture chamber. Not one converso was condemned, exclusively or even primarily, because of what Luis de Carvajal said in the torture chamber.

My account of the destruction of Mexico City's Jewish community diverges from the conventional history for two reasons. First, I compile a network of witness testimonies across dozens of trials from this period, organized chronologically, to assess what the Inquisition knew and did not know prior to the torture of Luis de Carvajal and his associates. Overlaps and discrepancies between witness accounts provide some insight into the court's decisions to torture some suspects but not others. It also permits us to understand, from the court's perspective, why some testimonies were deemed reliable while others were deemed suspect.

Second, I was fortunate to have gained access to a crucial manuscript that has only recently become available to scholars: the trial of Manuel de Lucena. Lucena, a close friend of Luis de Carvajal and a crypto-Jew, was held in the prisons of the Inquisition for two years. Though he was never formally tortured, he volunteered more information to the court than any other witness in this series of trials. The purpose of the tortures performed by the Inquisition, months after Lucena had testified, was to corroborate Lucena's testimony and to force reluctant witnesses to admit what the Inquisition already knew to be true.

The manuscript for the trial of Manuel de Lucena was considered missing until 1996, when curators from U.C. Berkeley's Bancroft Library discovered it at the California International Antiquarian Book Fair in Los Angeles.[3] It had been in the possession of a Mexican family since the nineteenth century, together with a trove of sixty other manuscripts related to the Inquisition in Mexico City, including the trials of Isabel Rodríguez and Leonor de Andrada, Carvajal's sisters. All four—Manuel, Luis, and the two sisters—were executed together at the auto-da-fé on December 10, 1596. The following chapters constitute a first effort to reanalyze the role of torture in these events using these previously inaccessible manuscripts.

The trial documents for Manuel de Lucena are fascinating for several reasons. Lucena and his wife, Catalina Henríquez, were among the most important conversos in Mexico in this period. It was in their house that many of the Judaizers met regularly to study and celebrate the holy days together. Key figures in the community often ate, sang, and prayed together in Lucena's house, accompanied by Lucena on the harp. David Gitlitz, among the first to explore these documents in detail, was able to reconstruct the names of sixty-five conversos who attended Yom Kippur, Passover, and Purim on various occasions in the home of Manuel de Lucena between 1587 and 1594.[4] Lucena and his wife knew most of the other conversos, taught them Jewish law and ritual, and introduced them to one another in their home.

As a result, once Lucena began collaborating with the Inquisition, he was able to provide more information on this community to his captors than any other witness. It is because of Lucena's damning testimony that his close friend Luis de Carvajal was arrested. This, in turn, soon led to the arrest of the entire Carvajal family and their acquaintances. The detailed Lucena manuscript lays bare the order in which these suspects were arrested, tried, and interrogated, resulting in their untimely deaths and the dissolution of the crypto-Jewish community in Mexico.

In terms of the volume of pages alone, his trial manuscript overshadows all other trial texts available for Mexico City in this period. The average converso trial in Mexico contains roughly 100 pages. The manuscript for Luis de Carvajal's seven-year trial runs 700 pages. But the leather-bound manuscript containing the trial documents of Manuel de Lucena amounts to 1,334 handwritten pages. Fifty-two witnesses appeared in Lucena's trial. Their names are listed, in order of their appearance in the manuscript, on the first three pages of the text. The next six pages list the 116 individuals whom Lucena identified as fellow Jews.

This is a remarkable source for knowledge of his community, its relationships, livelihoods, economic and kinship ties, its customs and culture, its language and its religion. Yet because the Lucena manuscript has only recently become accessible to scholars, it has yet to be analyzed extensively. It has never been transcribed or translated. When I first opened it, in the reading room of the rare books collection of Berkeley's Bancroft Library, its folios crisp from refrigeration, fine white sand trickled from between the pages onto my lap. This was the sand that the scribe had used to dry the ink on the page, four-hundred years earlier.

Given the focus of this book, the Lucena manuscript is of particular interest because Lucena was never tortured. This begs three questions: Why was so important a figure as Lucena never put to torture? Why did he nonetheless collaborate extensively? And how does the information he provided, in the absence of physical coercion, compare to the information provided by Carvajal and others who were tortured? The following two chapters provide some answers to these questions.

## The Carvajal Family

That Luis de Carvajal, his family, and his closest friends practiced Judaism secretly is beyond doubt. Carvajal wrote an autobiography and a last will and testament, both attesting to his fervent religious beliefs. He also left behind other Jewish texts, such as his personal handwritten copy of Maimonides's "Principles of Faith," his own translation of the Ten Commandments into Spanish in verse, and a Jewish prayer manual that he composed.[5] We know a great deal about his Judaism: how he adopted the pseudonym José Lumbroso ("Joseph the Enlightened"), how he circumcised himself with an old pair of scissors, how he celebrated his holidays and fasts, and what prayers he uttered. We even know how he prayed: How he fell to his knees when uttering the name of God, or how he recited the Shema prayer by lowering his head, placing his left hand on the forehead, and his right hand on his heart.

Carvajal is now recognized as the very first Jewish author in the Americas whose written work has survived to our time. Historians have used his writings, letters, and trial manuscripts to piece together information about his family, their travels, livelihoods, relationships, and tragic deaths. These documents reveal how he came to assume a position of influence in a sizeable secret Jewish community that had fled the Inquisition from Spain and Portugal to Mexico in the mid-sixteenth century.[6]

Young Luis was nephew to a conquistador, Luis de Carvajal y de la Cueva, who had arrived in New Spain in 1567 to sell wine, engage in mining, and traffic in slaves. Old Luis soon rose to prominence in both the civil and the military leadership of the colony. In 1579, he received a royal charter to conquer and administer a sizeable new region on the northeastern frontier of New Spain. He was appointed governor for life of this new territory, Nuevo León, and was charged with settling one hundred soldiers, and sixty laborers and artisans on the land.

By royal decree, no investigation into the backgrounds of these settlers was to be conducted prior to their journey from Spain to Mexico. This provided an opportunity for dozens of crypto-Jews to join Governor Carvajal on his return trip to the Indies, a noteworthy opportunity since travel to New Spain was prohibited to non-Christians after 1522, and all Jews and Muslims were banished from the colonies later that year. The Inquisition, which had driven so many Jews from Spain to Portugal and from Portugal to the colonies arrived in Mexico in 1535 and was fully established in 1571.[7] At a ceremony in the Cathedral of Mexico City that winter, which all residents older than twelve years of age were obligated to attend, the community took a public oath of persecute all heretics "as wolves and rabid dogs" or suffer excommunication.[8]

The governor and his colonists sailed to Mexico in January 1580, where they were joined by other settlers. Of the original 259 who settled in Nuevo León under Governor Carvajal, two-thirds may have been New Christians, though not necessarily Judaizers. Among the settlers who joined Governor Carvajal were his cousin, Catalina de León, and her husband, Gonzalo Pérez Ferro. Also on board

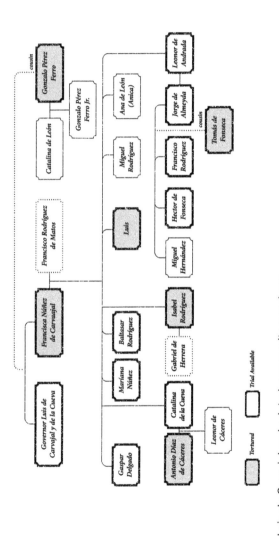

**FIGURE 5.1.** Luis de Carvajal and related community members.

were the governor's sister, Francisca Núñez de Carvajal, her husband, Francisco Rodríguez de Matos, and their eight children, including their fifteen-year-old son, Luis (see figure 5.1).

The governor soon gained powerful enemies among the ruling classes in the colonies because of his political ambitions and his reliance on the slave trade as a primary source of funding for the colony. Prime among these rivals was the viceroy, Álvaro Manrique de Zúñiga, who sought to centralize political power in Mexico City. The family's Judaizing was to become a crucial tool in discrediting the governor. The governor, for his part, knew of his sister's Jewish practices but insisted that he and his relatives were "Old Christians."

Young Luis, nicknamed "El Mozo" (the younger), to distinguish him from his illustrious uncle, was an active member of the new colony. His uncle, who had no male descendants and who recognized Luis's charisma, named him as his heir and successor to the governorship. Luis assisted the governor in his duties and traversed the mining towns of New Spain selling household articles with his older brother, Baltasar. Luis used his travels to proselytize to conversos who lived outside of Mexico City. As one scholar of the period phrased it: "The road functioned as their synagogue."[9] Baltasar had revealed the secret of their Jewish ancestry to Luis on his thirteenth birthday, and Luis had learned more about Jewish customs and beliefs from older relatives in Mexico City. He decided not only to practice Judaism openly but to try and convert New Christians back to Judaism. Luis and Baltasar were now saving money to emigrate to the Ottoman Empire or Italy where they hoped to live peacefully as members of a local Jewish community.

First among the Carvajals to be arrested by the Holy Office was Luis's older sister, Isabel. When Luis and Baltasar heard of her arrest, on March 13, 1589, they sought refuge in the home of their friend Manuel de Lucena, a safe haven for Judaizers. Suspecting correctly that an arrest warrant had been issued for them as well, Luis began secretly making his way back to the family residence in Mexico City while Baltasar went into hiding. On April 13, Luis learned that Governor Carvajal had been arrested. On May 9, the bailiffs and constables of the Inquisition came to arrest Luis's mother, Doña Francisca, and found Luis hiding in her kitchen.

# The Trials Begin

The persecution of crypto-Jews in New Spain occurred in two stages: the first in 1589, the second in 1594. The first wave involved the arrest of a small group of suspects, primarily members of the Carvajal family. Five of these individuals were tortured but their interrogations failed to uncover the magnitude of the secretive

Jewish community in Mexico City. The Inquisition exposed ten of its members, all closely related to the Carvajal family, but remained ignorant of the hundred or more other crypto-Jews in their network. Why were these individuals tortured but not other Judaizers who were far more influential in that community, such as Luis de Carvajal and Manuel de Lucena? What did these tortures reveal or fail to reveal?

Isabel, the first member of the family to be arrested, had learned the secrets of Judaism in Spain from her late husband, Gabriel de Herrera, and after his untimely death, from her aunt Doña Guiomar, wife of Governor Carvajal. Widowed at age twenty-one, Isabel found great solace in her faith. This devotion seems to have clouded Isabel's judgment for, soon after arriving in New Spain, she attempted to convert her uncle, the governor. "If you are so wise, why are you travelling along the wrong road of the law of Jesus rather than that of the Law of Moses?" she asked. And, oblivious to his seething anger, she added: "There is no Christ, and there is no Virgin Mary either."[10] The governor struck his niece across the face and knocked her to the ground. Yet he did not denounce Isabel to the authorities, as was his obligation. Instead, at the risk of abetting heresy, he informed his nephew, Fray Gaspar de Carvajal, of the incident in a detailed letter. Gaspar had entered holy orders in Spain and, like his uncle, rejected the family's Jewish roots. The governor expressed the hope that Brother Gaspar could save his sister's soul.[11]

He could not. Isabel made yet another foolhardy attempt at conversion, this time targeting her uncle's adjutant, Captain Felipe Núñez. She accosted him with statements about the "true religion" and the coming of the Messiah but quickly realized her mistake. "Why, I was just joking. I said what I did to see how steadfast your faith was . . . but don't say a word about our conversation to anyone."[12] Captain Núñez did not share his commander's sense of discretion nor his loyalty to the Carvajal family. On March 7, 1589, he approached the Inquisition to denounce Isabel. Six days later, she was arrested.

Captain Núñez made every effort to clear the governor's name in court, attesting to his commander's Christian piety. Isabel, on the other hand, suspected that it was her uncle, and her brother Gaspar, who had informed the Inquisition of her heresies. In an effort to divert the court's attention away from her mother and from young Luis, Isabel denounced the governor and Gaspar to the court. The two had known of her Judaizing, she claimed, and the governor's wife had encouraged it, whereas the rest of her family knew nothing. The Inquisition arrested both Gaspar and Governor Carvajal on April 13.

Whereas the governor feigned ignorance about his family's Judaizing, Gaspar offered detailed testimony about the Carvajals' religious practices. He had seen Isabel observing Jewish fasts. He noted how she started her work on the Sabbath after ten o'clock at night. In the spring, she once fed him flat and tasteless bread which, he later realized, was matzo. By the time the Inquisition apprehended young Luis and his mother, it had heard from Gaspar of the family's intimate conversations and beliefs, had learned about the Jewish funerary practices that accompanied the recent death of Luis's father Francisco, and had precise information about the scriptures possessed and read by the family. All these were listed in detail in the indictment preceding Luis's trial.[13]

After three months in solitary confinement, Luis requested an audience with the court. He explained that it was the devil who had prevented him from confessing earlier. He had now prevailed in his struggle against the devil and was ready to confess. His testimony began on August 7 and lasted five days. Seeking to protect his younger siblings as much as possible, he admitted his own heresies and shared damning information about family members whom he knew to have already been arrested. These included his older sister Isabel; his brother Baltasar; his mother; and his uncle, the governor. Luis remained silent about his siblings Catalina, Leonor, Maríana, Miguel, and Anica, though all had participated in the family's rituals. He claimed to know no other Judaizers in the community.

## The Torture of Francisca de Carvajal

Luis's mother, Doña Francisca, refused to cooperate with the proceedings altogether. In May she had named her daughter Isabel, whom she knew to have been imprisoned, as a fellow Judaizer and she had identified a lawyer by the name of Manuel de Morales, who had fled Mexico, as her teacher in matters of Jewish law. She refused to incriminate other family members, let alone members of her larger community.

The Inquisition had learned enough from the overlapping testimonies of Gaspar, Luis, Captain Núñez, and Governor Carvajal to conclude that Francisca was withholding information. On November 10, a full six months after her arrest, she was led from her cell into the torture chamber. The inquisitors explained why she was about to be tortured:

> She had shared a lot of clear information in line with other witnesses. However, even if she pretends to have confessed the truth and even if she asks for mercy now, she is warned that she will not deserve mercy because there are inconsistencies regarding her confession. She is withholding information about the people that taught her Jewish Law and about those with whom she shared such beliefs and traditions. It appears that she had practiced these traditions for a longer time than

she is willing to admit. In other parts of her confession she withheld information regarding her actions and her intentions.[14]

The scribe proceeded to record the particulars of her harrowing ordeal in the torture chamber in great detail. Centuries later, it would be the fifty-year-old matriarch's tragic suffering and pitiful appeals, more than those of any other member of the Carvajal family, that would move modern Mexican historians to denounce the Inquisition's cruelty.[15] The scribe quoted her at length:

> They should see that she is a woman and so she should not be tortured or undressed because she will die right here, and her children will become orphans. She would die here as a martyr and her soul would enjoy itself next to God, because she is not getting out of there alive. . . . She should be killed rather than be undressed, even if she had to die a thousand times. She cried on her knees as she said that she was an honest widow and she did not deserve this. She said that she already confessed that she believed in Mosaic Law and not that of Jesus Christ. She knew nothing else nor and had nothing to add other than that she was inconsolable, sad, and a widow with children.[16]

There followed five twists of the ropes. The scribe recorded her screaming and pleading. Luis later told the court that he could hear his mother's tortured screams from his jail cell. She was then taken to the *potro* and tied up. Before this torture could begin, Francisca revealed that her deceased husband had taught her Jewish law and custom: not to eat the food of dirty animals, such as pigs, fish without scales, or drowned fowl, and how to behead a chicken with a knife in the manner of kosher slaughter. Nobody but her husband was present when he taught her. He did so while they were alone, in the intimacy of their bedroom. But Francisca also admitted that "her widowed daughter who is also a prisoner" practiced with her. For example, she and Isabel celebrated Passover in Taxco together in 1588.

The Inquisition knew then, as do we now, that Francisca and Isabel did not celebrate that Passover alone in Taxco. It knew that her children Catalina, Baltasar, Leonor, Luis, and Maríana had celebrated with Francisca and Isabel. All this was information that the Inquisition already possessed, and that it knew Francisca to be withholding.

When the inquisitors ordered the torture to resume, Francisca struggled against her captors and tried to sit up. She then revealed that Luis (whom she knew to have been arrested with her) had prayed with them from time to time. The torturers attempted to push her onto the rack. She then admitted that her son Baltasar (who she knew to have fled) had also prayed with her, Luis, and

Isabel. She described how and when they prayed together. Three hours after it began, the interrogation ceased:

> Because Doña Francisca was exhausted, afflicted with stomach pains, and complained about being naked and cold, the torture was stopped. They told her that they might not be done with the torture and that they could continue until she told the whole truth. They undid the ropes in her arms and treated her wounds. She was then taken to a prison cell close to the torture chamber and laid on a bed with someone to take care of her arms. Once this was done, she was brought back to the audience chamber.[17]

On December 4, her daughters Maríana and Catalina were called to testify before the tribunal. The court confronted Francisca with their anonymized testimony starting on January 10, 1590, omitting names and details but warning her that they knew more than she had admitted. Francisca relented: "God has illuminated her to confess what is left." Kneeling, and pleading for mercy, she added the names of her daughters Catalina, Maríana, and Leonor to the list of fellow Jews. Several days later, she identified her cousin, Catalina de León, as a Judaizer.[18]

## The Torture of Isabel de Carvajal

Two weeks after her mother was tortured, Isabel was brought into the torture chamber. She had shared no information with the court since her arrest. In the intervening eight months, significant evidence had accumulated against her. Felipe López testified against her in March. Her brother Gaspar, the governor, and her mother testified against her in April. Her brother Luis condemned her and several of her siblings in August, and her mother accused her and her siblings again under torture.

Given Isabel's persistent silence, she was now threatened with torture. This threat yielded little beyond accusations against several of Isabel's deceased relatives: Her late father, Francisco Rodríguez de Matos, her late husband, Gabriel de Herrera, and her late aunt (the governor's wife) who had lived in Seville.[19] The Inquisition declared this "negative response" to be insufficient and pronounced a torture sentence on November 27. Once undressed, she was threatened with torture again but replied that "there is no greater torture than having to undress and show her flesh" (see figure 5.2).

> They ordered one turn of the rope. But before this could be done, she said that the truth was that her mother Doña Francisca, and Baltazar

**FIGURE 5.2.**   The torture of Isabel de Carvajal, as imagined by Primitivo Miranda. From Vicente Riva Palacio, *El Libro Rojo*, 1870, 57.

Rodríguez, and Luis de Carvajal (her siblings) taught her all that she knew about Jewish Law and they affirmed it here in Mexico. Her mother would curse her if she revealed this. They all taught her Jewish Law and she confesses that she observed it with them. She doesn't know anything else, nor does she remember when she was taught it. . . .

She was admonished to tell the truth and the rope was turned once. She screamed that she had told the truth and that she was being tortured. God was her witness that she had said the truth and she was being unfairly punished. They demanded that she tell the truth and the rope was turned once more. She screamed and told them to stop because they were killing her. She said that it's been three years since she observed Jewish Law in Mexico with her mother Doña Francisca and her brothers. She did not know of others in Taxco. The ropes were tightened again. She said that her sister Maríana also observed it with her and sister Doña Catalina, wife of Antonio Díaz de Cáceres.[20]

Still on the rack, but with ropes loosened, she detailed the family's travels and religious practices. She (falsely) claimed that Felipe Núñez, who had denounced her, was a practicing Jew. Finally, she accused two servants (Francisco Jorge and Francisco Díaz) of being Jewish. Both had indeed practiced Jewish rites with the Carvajal family, but both had also long since fled Mexico.

In sum, Doña Francisca and Doña Isabel's extensive tortures revealed little beyond the names of three immediate family members: Isabel's sisters, Maríana and Catalina, and Francisca's cousin, Catalina de León, all information that the Inquisition had already heard from Luis and Governor Carvajal. The three were soon arrested and confirmed that they had been practicing Judaism in secret with their family. Other than those three, Francisca and Isabel only named community members who had fled or who were already dead.

# Aftermath

This was the Carvajal family's first encounter with the Inquisition but not their last. Because they had all repented of their sins and pled for mercy, they were forgiven their sins and were reconciled to the Church. However, the court demanded that they abjure their sins *de vehementi*, a penance reserved for serious crimes against the Church. This meant that any future relapse would doom them to death at the stake.

Governor Carvajal continued to maintain his innocence. Since his sister, Doña Francisca, had admitted to being Jewish, and since his niece, Isabel, had accused his wife of being Jewish, his religious identity was now called into serious question.[21] And since he had failed to report the family's Judaizing to the tribunal, he was stripped of his position as governor and was sentenced to six years of exile. He died in prison before that sentence could be implemented.

The auto-da-fé took place in Mexico City's Great Cathedral on February 24, 1590. The penitents included all members of the Carvajal family except Gaspar and Anica. Also present among the accused was Hernán Rodríguez de Herrera, an acquaintance of Luis's, and Francisca's cousin Catalina de León with her husband, Gonzalo Pérez Ferro, and their son. All were reconciled to the Church. The only two to be deemed impenitent were absent: Francisco Rodríguez de Matos, the patriarch, who had died before the trial, and Baltasar, who had fled to Italy. Both were burned in effigy.

Francisca and Isabel were sentenced to four years penance in separate convents and were ordered to wear penitential garbs for the rest of their lives. Maríana and Catalina were sentenced to two years imprisonment in a convent, and Leonor was sentenced to one year because she was the youngest. But within four years, Leonor's husband, Jorge de Almeida, managed to convince the chief inquisitor in Madrid to reduce these sentences in exchange for a sizeable fee.[22] The Inquisition was unaware of the fact that Almeida too was a practicing Jew who had hosted many of the family's religious gatherings.

Thanks to Almeida, the women were released from the separate convents to which they had been assigned and moved together into a private house. Luis was transferred to a monastery nearby where he taught the natives Latin. A friar, Pedro de Oroz, was tasked by the Inquisition with watching over the family. To all appearances, the Carvajals attended mass daily, took communion and confessed regularly, prayed fervently, and kept Christian images in their house. Behind the scenes, however, they continued their Jewish practices: they commemorated feasts and fasts with other crypto-Jews, they kept the Sabbath, and they prayed daily toward Jerusalem.[23] Unbeknownst to them, the preparations for a second wave of trials were already underway.

## The Failure of Exploratory Torture

Neither Francisca nor Isabel's torture was purely exploratory. They had spent six and eight months in prison, respectively, before they were put to torture, a period the Inquisition exploited for gathering information about their family. Yet this was the Inquisition's first effort at infiltrating this particular community. A year's worth of interrogations, coerced and uncoerced, failed to reveal the extent of the family's Judaizing and their connections with a very large network of crypto-Jews in and around Mexico City.

Francisca and Isabel knew multiple conversos whose names they managed to withhold in the torture chamber. For example, the Inquisition later learned that the entire Carvajal family had celebrated Passover in the home of Leonor's husband, Jorge de Almeida, with Clara Henríquez, an aunt of Manuel de Lucena's. This took place in 1588, merely one year prior to their torture.[24] In 1589, on the eve of their arrest, all the Carvajal siblings and Francisca celebrated Passover with Clara Henríquez, Leonor Díaz, and two cousins of Manuel de Lucena (Constança Rodríguez and Pedro Rodríguez). Isabel had admitted under torture that she celebrated this Passover and mentioned her siblings, but she had omitted the names of others present. In the interrogations of 1595, all of these individuals would be exposed as Judaizers and all would be condemned at autos-da-fé. In 1589, however, the Inquisition failed to discover their heresies or their connections to the Carvajals.

It is likely that Francisca and Isabel knew many others prior to their torture. Soon after the end of their imprisonment, the Carvajal family observed holy days with multiple members of the converso community, including a Yom Kippur with eight others in 1591, and a Passover with nineteen others in 1592. If they knew some of these crypto-Jews in 1589, they did not reveal their names under torture. Manuel de Lucena and his wife, Catalina Henríquez, were present at all of these events and hosted the Carvajals at Yom Kippur in 1593. If Francisca and Isabel knew Manuel and Catalina in 1589, they managed to keep their identities secret. Because their torture was relatively exploratory, they Inquisition lacked the parallel information needed to make those connections. Indeed, Manuel de Lucena and Cristóbal Gómez, both close family friends and important Judaizers who would be condemned to death in subsequent trials, appeared as witnesses in these trials in 1589 but failed to attract the court's suspicions.

Other exploratory torture sessions that year revealed even less information. Manuel de Lucena's mother-in-law, Beatriz Henríquez (nicknamed "La Payba"), revealed nothing at all during her torture. Yet her house was a center for Jewish gatherings at which dozens of prominent crypto-Jews had celebrated Yom Kippur, Passover, and Purim in 1582, 1583, 1586, 1587, and 1589.[25] In the next round of trials, Luis de Carvajal, Manuel de Lucena, and many others witnesses would expose her central function in the community and she would be burned to death at the auto-da-fé of 1596.[26] But in this early period of investigations, she was deemed innocent because her interrogation in the torture chamber yielded no incriminating information.

Gonzalo Pérez Ferro, husband to Francisca's cousin Catalina, also suffered torture in 1589.[27] His torture revealed nothing, not even the extent of his own Judaizing. Unbeknownst to the Inquisition, he and his family had prayed and celebrated with the Carvajals. He had attended the weddings of both Leonor and Catalina, and he was at Luis's side when his father died and received Jewish burial rights. Ferro had discussed Jewish law with Luis de Carvajal and with Antonio Díaz de Cáceres, and he regularly observed the Sabbath with Tomás de Fonseca. He was a frequent guest in the home of Antonio Machado, whose home functioned as an informal synagogue for the Lucenas and Carvajals.[28] Because the Inquisition discovered none of this in 1589, not even by torturing him, he received the lightest sentence at the auto of 1590 and abjured *de levi*. The Inquisition realized its error in later years, when Luis and Lucena exposed Ferro's role in the community. His wife was executed in 1596 and he was condemned to permanent imprisonment in 1601.

Among the last to be tortured during this first round of trials was Tomás de Fonseca Castellanos, a cousin of Jorge de Almeida, who lived in Taxco. He was tried in 1590, was found innocent, but was arrested again that same year and tortured.[29] Fonseca Castellanos named no fellow Jews during this torture despite the fact that he had regularly celebrated Shabbat with Luis de Carvajal and Manuel de Lucena and had hosted a large gathering in his home on Yom Kippur the prior year.[30] Fonseca's son and uncle were practicing Jews and he knew Lucena's wife Catalina, Lucena's aunt Clara, Leonor Díaz, and many other members of this community to be crypto-Jews.

The Inquisition would spend the next four years collecting more information on this community. Fonseca Castellanos was arrested for a third time in 1595. This time the court had gathered testimony against him from twenty-one witnesses, including Lucena, Francisca de Carvajal, Luis, and three of his sisters. These witnesses described the holidays he celebrated with them, how he kept kosher, his opinions on Jewish law and prayer, his scorn for the Church. The difference between 1590 and 1595 is telling. If in 1590 his exploratory torture failed to yield even one name, five years later the mere threat of torture, combined with the evidence amassed against him, prompted Fonseca Castellanos to disclose everything he knew about the Carvajal and Lucena families and their Judaism. He continued to provide useful information to the Inquisition until March 1601, when he was garroted and burned.[31]

In 1589, the Inquisition had arrested a dozen suspects and conducted exploratory torture after weeks and months of interrogation. These interrogations failed to unmask the sizeable Jewish community of New Spain. In 1594, the Inquisition would arrest hundreds of suspects. It would hold these suspects in underground cells for years, not months. And it would conduct corroborative torture, not exploratory torture, which would aid in eliminating that community altogether.

# CORROBORATIVE TORTURE
## Mexico City (1594–1601)

The exploratory tortures committed in Mexico City in 1590 yielded poor information. The Inquisition had arrested key members of the crypto-Jewish community. It tortured five persons, all of whom had extensive contacts with the rest of the converso network; but they provided no names other than those of people deceased or absent. A year into its investigations, the Inquisition had no means of ascertaining whether suspects knew more than they were divulging. Influential figures, such as Manuel de Lucena, Beatriz Henríquez, or Tomás de Fonseca escaped that first wave without so much as a warning. The Inquisition accepted the remorse of the Carvajal family at face value and reconciled its members to the Church with lenient penalties that were soon forgiven. As a result, the Jewish life of the underground community in Mexico City continued undisturbed.

As additional witnesses continued to provide information about heretical practices, the Inquisition began to prepare a second round of trials. The interrogations that followed took place not after a year or two of investigation, as in 1590, but after five years of inquiry. The eleven tortures committed in this second wave were of an entirely different sort than the preceding tortures. They were corroborative, not exploratory. They occurred at the end of the proceedings, on the eve of the auto-da-fé of 1596, and targeted suspects who had spent multiple years in the prisons of the Inquisition. By relying on a combination of intelligence sources—material evidence, collaborators, intercepted messages, uncoerced testimony, and coerced testimony—this second round of investigations succeeded in decimating the crypto-Jewish community of Mexico City.

**TABLE 6.1** A sample of accusers, accused and torture (in bold) in Mexico, 1594–1601

| | ACCUSERS | | | | | | | | | | | |
|---|---|---|---|---|---|---|---|---|---|---|---|---|
| ACCUSED | Antonio Henríquez | Manuel de Lucena | Beatrize Henríquez | Pedro Henríquez | Catalina Henríquez | Constança Rodríguez | Justa Méndez | Leonor Díaz | Leonor de Carvajal | **Violante Rodríguez** | **Luis de Carvajal** | **Pedro Rodríguez Saz** |
| 11.18.1594: Antonio Henríquez | | | X | | X | X | X | X | | X | | |
| 12.12.1594: Manuel de Lucena | | | X | X | X | X | X | X | X | X | X | X |
| 12.29.1594: Beatrize Henríquez | | | | | | | | | | | | |
| 1.10.1594: Pedro Henríquez | | X | X | | X | X | X | | | | | |
| 1.12.1595: Catalina Henríquez | | X | X | X | | X | X | | | X | X | |
| 2.7.1595: Constança Rodríguez | | X | X | | X | | X | X | | | | X |
| 2.8.1595: Justa Méndez | | X | X | | X | X | X | | | | | |
| 3.30.1595: Leonor Díaz | | X | | | X | X | X | | | | | |
| 5.29.1595: Leonor de Carvajal | X | X | | X | | X | X | X | | | X | X |
| **1.27.1595: Violante Rodríguez** | | X | X | | X | | | | | | | |
| **2.8.1596: Luis de Carvajal** | | X | X | X | X | X | X | X | X | X | X | X |
| **5.16.1596: Pedro Rodríguez Saz** | | X | X | | X | X | X | X | | | X | |

Table 6.1 provides a snapshot of some of the mutual accusations that occurred over the course of this second wave of trials. These are a mere sample, randomly selected, from the scores of testimonies and trials held in Mexico City in this period, sorted chronologically. Evidence extracted by means of torture appears in bold.

Three patterns become immediately apparent. The first is that torture occurred toward the tail end of this wave of trials: Violante Rodríguez, Luis de Carvajal, and Pedro Rodríguez Saz suffered months of imprisonment after most of the other trials had concluded and most of the witnesses had cooperated willingly, as did the other conversos who were tortured (but are not included in this table). Second, those tortured had already been identified as Judaizers by multiple others prior to their torture. The Inquisition had little doubt about their culpability. Third, torture provided no new names. It confirmed names that had been offered by other witnesses in the absence of torture.

These patterns also go a long way toward explaining who was tortured and who was not. Because their torture occurred so late in the proceedings, the Inquisition had the opportunity to assemble significant information about each suspect. It tortured those who maintained their silence, despite mounting evidence of their Judaizing practices. As in the Old World, torture was not reserved for the most culpable or the most significant suspects.

For example, Violante Rodríguez was a marginal figure in the community, an aunt of Manuel de Lucena.[1] Arrested in April 1595, she refused to name other conversos in her community. Yet, as table 6.1 illustrates, the court had heard about her Judaizing from Antonio Henríquez, Manuel de Lucena, and Catalina Henríquez even before her arrest. Further witnesses testified against her during the first nine months of her imprisonment. Only then, in January 1596, after she met several reprimands with silence, was she tortured with three turns of the rope. I quoted from her torture at length in chapter 1. She incriminated five fellow Jews, including her own daughter, Isabel.

Violante Rodríguez was reconciled to the Church and condemned to life imprisonment, confirming yet another pattern observed in Iberian trials: torture did not correlate with the court's ultimate verdict. While Rodríguez escaped death at the stake, Manuel de Lucena, who was not tortured, burned to death.

# Manuel de Lucena

The second wave of trials against the crypto-Jews of Mexico began on October 15, 1594, when Domingo Gómez Navarro came before the court to volunteer his testimony. He related a troubling incident that occurred in 1589, prior to the first wave of trials. His brother, a merchant by the name of Manuel Gómez

Navarro, had fallen ill. Lucena and his wife were nursing Manuel back to health in their home. Luis de Carvajal was present when Manuel Gómez Navarro's brother, Domingo, came to pay a visit. The three men used this opportunity to try to convert Domingo, the only one among them who had not yet embraced his Jewish origins. Manuel told his brother to ignore the laws of the Christians and to accept the Law of Moses as the true faith. Domingo, outraged, threatened to report Carvajal, Lucena, and his own brother to the Inquisition.[2]

Domingo had already testified to these events in the first wave of trials at a time when the Inquisition lacked sufficient evidence to confirm or reject his testimony. Now it moved quickly to arrest Manuel Gómez Navarro and Lucena. It held off on arresting Carvajal in order to collect more evidence against him. Carvajal's case was of greater significance: he had slipped through their fingers once, and they had no intention of repeating that mistake again. Now that he had abjured *de vehementi*, a successful conviction against him would mean death at the stake.

Four days after Domingo's testimony, the court arrested his brother Manuel, who confirmed what his brother had related and joined in accusing Lucena and Carvajal.[3] In this and in three subsequent audiences, Manuel Gómez Navarro shared that it was Lucena who had taught him the Law of Moses and that he knew Lucena still to be awaiting the first coming of the Jewish Messiah. Lucena was arrested ten days later. He was formally accused of heresy and admonished, on three occasions, to speak the truth. He said nothing.[4]

The accusations of the Gómez Navarro brothers take up the first thirty-four pages of testimony in Lucena's trial manuscript. There now followed a procession of witnesses against Lucena in quick succession. Two days after Lucena's arrest, Manuel Gómez de Castelo Blanco testified against him and against ten other conversos.[5] A month later, Manuel González testified that he had witnessed Lucena castigating Manuel Gómez Navarro for eating "filthy" pork. González also linked Lucena to the Carvajal family, "who are known to be Jews."[6] A week later, a business partner of Lucena's named Gómez Pertiera offered testimony against Lucena.[7] Juan de la Serna, a clerk in one of Lucena's stores, testified on that same day that Lucena refused to eat pork or even eat from dishes on which pork had been served, and that he blew the *shofar*, the ram's horn, on the Jewish New Year.[8] Three days later, Fernando de Acuña claimed that he saw Lucena eat during Lent, that Lucena had not said mass over his dead father, and did not send his daughter to confession.[9]

The most damning testimony of all followed on December 13, 1594. In the intervening month and a half since his arrest, Lucena had refused to speak to the court. But he had been far from silent: he had poured out his heart to his cell mate, Luis Díaz. Unbeknownst to Lucena, Díaz was an informant for the Inquisition, placed in Lucena's cell to extract information. Díaz now shared with the court forty-six pages of incriminating evidence against Lucena: their theological conversations ("Christianity is as false as Islam"), Lucena's attempts to convert Díaz, the Jewish practices that Lucena had performed in the cell and had tried to teach to Díaz and, worst of all, the names of other Jews whom Lucena had mentioned.[10]

Prime among the names that Lucena confided to Díaz were those of Luis de Carvajal and his sisters. "You believe that the Jews who the Inquisition reconciled [in 1590] are converted but that's not true," he told Díaz, fatefully: "Luis de Carvajal is as Jewish as he was before."[11] Lucena had urged Díaz to look up Carvajal upon his release to learn more about Judaism, perhaps even learn how to perform his own circumcision. Lucena had also handed Díaz a letter, intended for Lucena's wife and for Carvajal, which included the *Amidah* prayer in Lucena's own handwriting: "My lips he will open and my mouth shall pronounce your praise." That letter was now an official court document and has survived, inserted into the trial manuscript.[12]

To ensure that the case against Lucena was airtight, the court had arranged for three court officials to witness secretly the conversations between Lucena and Díaz from outside their cell. The notary, the secretary, and the warden testified in order, corroborating Díaz's report and repeating the names of Judaizers

**FIGURE 6.1.**   Letter from Manuel de Lucena to Luis de Carvajal, inserted among the pages of Lucena's trial document. Bancroft MSS 96/95m, vol. 2. Image courtesy of University of California, Berkeley, Bancroft Library.

mentioned by Lucena, prime among them Carvajal, and Lucena's mother-in-law, Beatriz Henríquez, also known as La Payba.[13]

Ironically, the damning testimonies by Díaz and the three court clerks saved Lucena from torture. He must have learned of Díaz's betrayal for, a day later, he asked to speak to the court for the first time. Knowledge of what Díaz must have told the court freed Lucena to repeat the same names himself. Starting on December 20 and ending on December 22, he provided the names of eight fellow Jews, including Carvajal, whom he identified as an expert in Jewish law and practice.[14] Lucena was not entirely forthcoming: he denied that the Carvajal sisters were involved in Luis's Judaizing, despite warnings from the inquisitors that there was "information regarding the conversations between him and Luis Díaz that contradict what he just said."[15] But he did admit to practicing Judaism himself for the past seven years.

Two days later, the Inquisition raided Lucena's home and confiscated his property, including his books and his letters.[16] They now knew what he read and wrote. Next to undergo arrest was La Payba, Lucena's mother-in-law. Her son testified against her, against Lucena, and against six others in early January.[17] Then followed the most comprehensive testimony of all: Lucena's wife, Catalina Henríquez, testified against her husband and members of their community starting in January 1595. She was pregnant at the time and had suffered extreme labor pains in prison. Only after she had promised to make a full confession, and after an abbreviated reconciliation ceremony was held in her cell, did the Inquisition provide her with a midwife.[18] Henríquez's first testimony extends over sixteen pages.[19] She revealed more on August 22, on November 8, on August 16 of the next year, then provided daily testimony for five days between October 9 and October 14, 1596.[20] In all, Lucena's wife provided seventy-two pages of testimony in which she accused her husband and seventeen other Judaizers. She died in prison in 1601.

Evidence from all these sources allowed the court to press Lucena harder than before to explain discrepancies between the information it had assembled and the names Lucena had provided. At ever increasing pace, the judges provided Lucena with snippets of anonymized testimony about his Judaizing, signaling that they knew how much information he was withholding. On January 30, Lucena revealed that it was not only Luis de Carvajal who practiced Judaism but the entire Carvajal family.[21] Two days after that, on February 1, the Inquisition arrested Luis de Carvajal. It did not torture Carvajal or press him for names, not in February 1595 nor in the ensuing twelve months. Eager to avoid the mistake they had made in 1590, the inquisitors would assemble a full dossier against Carvajal and his community before interrogating him in February 1596. They invested the intervening months in arresting and interrogating accomplices named by Lucena and using their testimonies to provoke Lucena into providing further names.

Lucena provided information regarding seven new Judaizers on January 11, including his servant, Francisco Váez, his aunt, Violante Rodríguez, his cousin, Isabel Rodríguez, and her husband, Manuel Díaz (see table 6.1).[22]

Lucena provided ten more names on January 30, including that of his own brother, Hernán Váez.[23] The Inquisition arrested four of Lucena's relatives in the first half of February, all of whom testified against him and against one another.[24] On February 16, Lucena identified ten more members of the Jewish community, including his wife, Catalina Henríquez, and her cousin, Pedro Rodríguez Saz (discussed below).[25] He offered eighty-four pages of testimony against his wife. Six more conversos were arrested in the next four months, including the same Pedro Rodríguez Saz, Leonor de Carvajal, and Isabel de Carvajal.[26] Their testimonies confirmed prior witnesses and provoked further arrests.

Lucena would spend a total of twenty-six months in the prisons of the Inquisition before being taken out to be burned at the stake. In that period, he appeared before the tribunal time and again to affirm prior accusations and add new names to a growing list of suspects. The Inquisition had finally managed to crack open the tightly knit network of crypto-Jews that had eluded its grasp five years earlier.

Carvajal had once confided to a fellow Jew: "Lucena and I are one and the same, we understand each other, and together, the music of our souls is like a symphony." Another witness had told the court: "Whenever [Lucena] came to Mexico [City], he wouldn't stay anywhere but Luis de Carvajal's house in Santiago. For him, seeing Luis was glory."[27] Yet, on November 8, 1595, a full year after his arrest, Lucena offered the complete and explicit denunciation of Carvajal that the Inquisition had been waiting for.[28] The scribe concluded the transcript of this testimony with a list of the Carvajal family members whom Lucena had incriminated. To affirm his testimony, Lucena had to sign his name under the list (see figure 6.3).

At one of his last audiences, Lucena was asked to recite the Shema prayer, one of the most important prayers in Judaism. Lucena would have recited the prayer while standing, with his eyes closed, as was his custom, scrutinized by the tribunal.[29] The scribe recorded Lucena's words phonetically (see figure 6.4):

> Sema Ysrael
> aDonay Judio
> A Donay ha ha
> Barauh ¿? en que vot
> Mal Luto A lamba it

Lucena's prayer is a corruption of the Hebrew original.[30] His ancestors were forced to practice their Judaism in secret, without rabbis or teachers, for a full century. The expulsions from Spain and Portugal had meant an end to synagogues and rabbis, to houses of Jewish learning and to Jewish scholarship. It is unlikely that Lucena and his contemporaries spoke or understood Hebrew.[31]

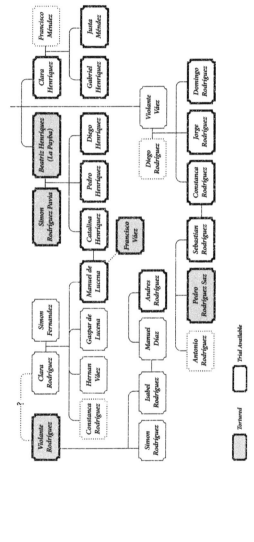

**FIGURE 6.2.** Manuel de Lucena and related community members.

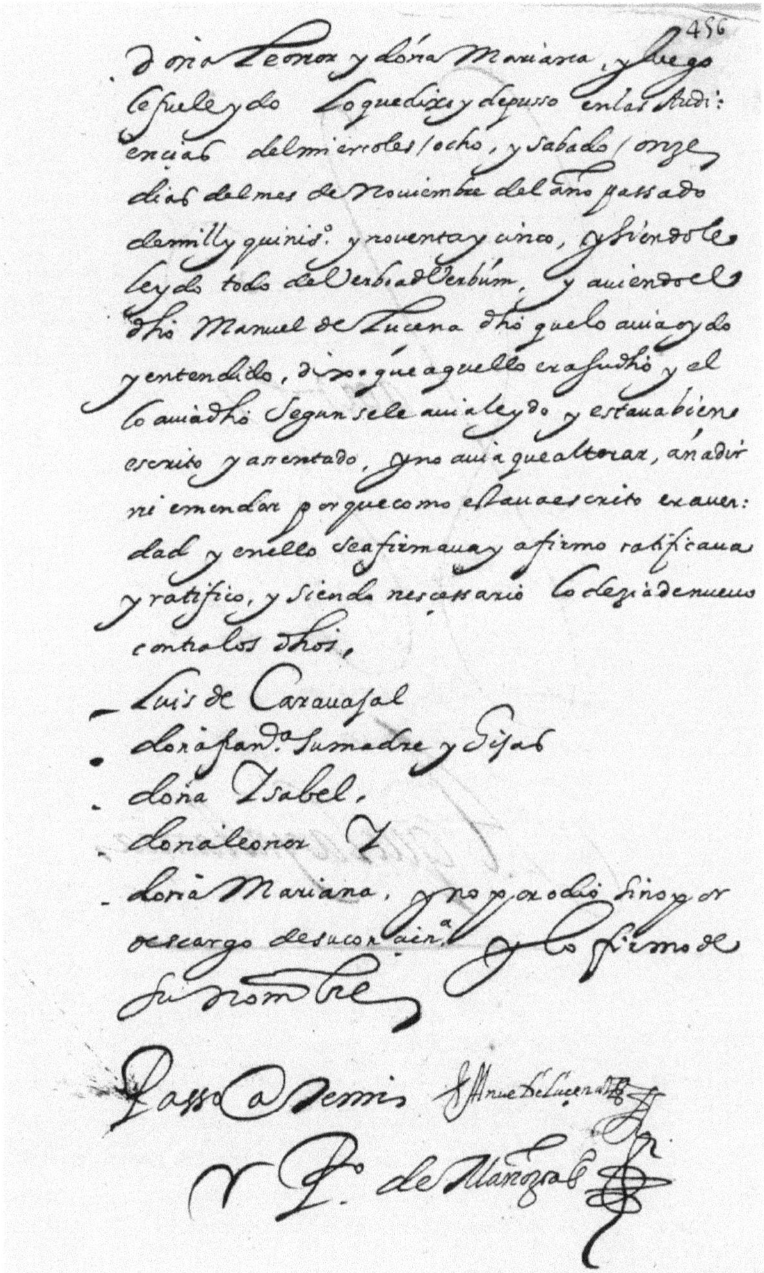

**FIGURE 6.3.** Lucena's affirmation of his accusation against the Carvajal family. Listed in order are the names of Luis de Carvajal, Doña Francisca his mother, Doña Isabel, Doña Leonor, and Doña Maríana. Beneath appear the signatures of Manuel de Lucena and the secretary, Pedro de Mañozca. Lucena Ms., 456r. Bancroft MSS 96/95m. Image courtesy of University of California, Berkeley, Bancroft Library.

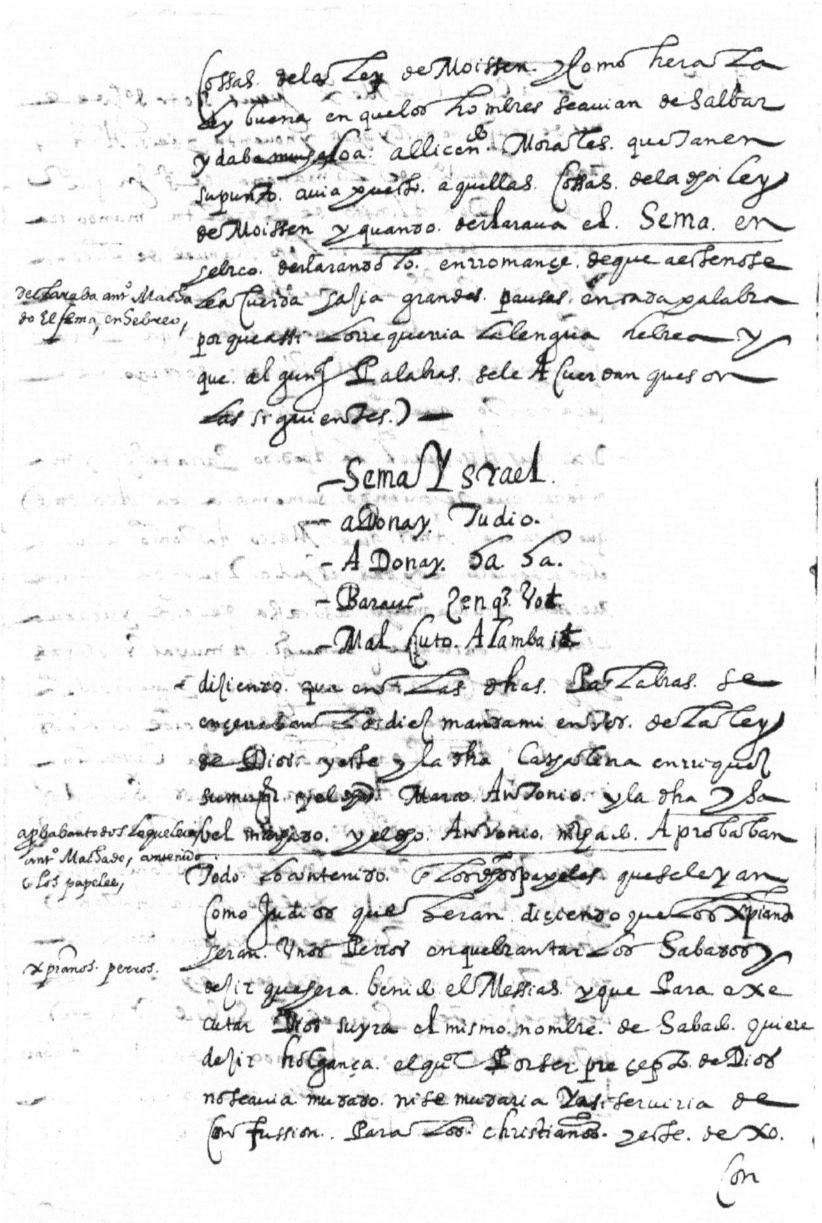

FIGURE 6.4.   Lucena recites the Shema prayer. Lucena manuscript, 646v. Bancroft MSS 96/95m. Image courtesy of University of California, Berkeley, Bancroft Library.

He had learned the prayer, he said, from Antonio Machado, an elderly invalid who had been a tailor in Spain. Perhaps the words had been corrupted over time as it passed from mouth to ear. Perhaps the court clerk, who certainly did not speak Hebrew, misrecorded what Lucena had said.[32] Regardless of its accuracy, I would like to believe that Lucena uttered the prayer with conviction, intention, and—given the terrible setting—great trepidation. One month later, Lucena was burned at the stake.

Why was Lucena willing to identify more than one hundred fellow Jews to the Inquisition? Certainly, the prolonged imprisonment took its toll on him: this was torture in all but name. No less significant was the fact that Lucena had some notion of what the Inquisition already knew, given his betrayal by Luis Díaz. The Inquisition had assembled overwhelming evidence against him. By the time Lucena offered his first testimony, the court had already gathered eighty pages of testimony from the first six witnesses who testified against him, had read all the books and papers confiscated from his home, and had intercepted the letter he had attempted to smuggle to Carvajal. Lucena avoided torture because his testimony was exhaustive to the extreme and because it matched information that the Inquisition had already obtained by other means. But was Lucena's testimony reliable? How might the court have evaluated his uncoerced testimony compared to that extracted by means of torture?

## The Torture of Pedro Rodríguez Saz

Because we have access to many of the same documents that the Inquisition used in its deliberations, we can reconstruct what the court knew from alternative sources prior to torture. Correlating this information requires organizing various testimonies in chronological order and searching for corresponding, or contradictory, names, events, or claims. That is, presumably, the process that the Inquisition used, relying on the indexes of names provided by scribes in the opening "summary" pages of trial manuscripts as well as on the highlight notes written into the margins of the text to emphasize crucial moments in trials.

Consider the torture of Pedro Rodríguez Saz, a distant relative of Lucena (the brother-in-law of Constança Rodríguez who was a cousin of Lucena's wife, see figure 6.2). Rodríguez Saz was one of the last conversos arrested in this wave of trials. He was imprisoned on April 28, 1595, and tortured more than a year later, on May 16, 1596:

> Once he was naked, and his arms were tied, he was admonished to tell the truth. He said that he had already told it and that witnesses who

testified against him had testified falsely. His arms were ordered to be tied tightly, and he was admonished to tell the truth and the minister ordered the first turn of the cord.

He complained loudly. He said: "Help me Lord, Jesus Christ, help me, I am here because of false witnesses." Another turn of the cord was ordered and he said: "Oh Christians! I will tell the truth! I beg for mercy! I will tell the truth!" The official who administered the torture was ordered to leave. He said: "It is true that, starting six to seven years ago, Luis de Carvajal started keeping the Laws of Moses."

He was told to confess the truth clearly and openly, to satisfy this Holy Office, for the salvation of his soul. He said: "About seven years ago, when Diego Henríquez, brother-in-law of Manuel de Lucena, and son of Beatriz Henríquez, La Payba, was arrested by the Holy Office, Manuel de Lucena taught me the Law of Moses, telling me that the Lord had promised to send a great prophet who will save the people. And that Jesus Christ was not the true God, but only God, who was in the highest heaven, will save the world. This God has a great day that the Jews call their Great Feast, on which they celebrate and fast.

On this Great Day of the Lord, I was there with Manuel de Lucena, his wife Catalina Henríquez, Clara Henríquez, her daughter Justa Méndez, Leonor Díaz, and a man called Juan Rodríguez. I don't remember whether Constança Rodríguez was there. We fasted and celebrated in Mexico City at the house of Manuel de Lucena, near the workplace of Juan Álvarez, in observance of the Law of Moses. I and the rest of the people I have listed, we danced and we celebrated, we wore festive clothing. We did not eat all day long until night, when I went to eat at my house, which is the house of Phelipe Núñez, where I stayed, and I ate in the company of Phelipe Núñez and his wife Phelipa López. We ate fish, garbanzos, eggs, and fruit. That's all that happened on the Great Day of the Lord."[33]

We can date precisely the "Great Day" of fasting and feasting that Pedro Rodríguez Saz is describing. It was Yom Kippur, September 19, 1589. It is possible to pinpoint the date exactly because, the following day, Manuel Gómez de Castelo Blanco approached the Inquisition to volunteer information on what he had seen: "Yesterday, at Lucena's home, Lucena and his wife, Catalina Henríquez, and Clara Henríquez, Constança Rodríguez, Beatriz Henríquez, the wife and daughter of Diego López Regalón [Anna López and Leonor Díaz], and Jorge Álvarez were there, assembled and well dressed."

Manuel Gómez was not a member of this Jewish community, so his unexpected appearance at the house of Lucena must have caused a great deal of concern to the Jews assembled there. We read about this same event again from a witness in a later trial, on February 9, 1595. Justa Méndez recounts how, upon arriving from Castile in 1589, she celebrated her first Yom Kippur at Manuel de Lucena's home. Present were Lucena, his wife Catalina Henríquez, Anna López, her daughters Leonor Díaz and Phelipa López, Beatriz Henríquez, and Catalina's aunt [Clara Henríquez]. "Then entered Manuel González, known at the time as Manuel Gómez, and Manuel Jorge, whose house he was staying in, and my first cousin Constança Rodríguez. This was at 10 or 11 in the morning and I stayed until noon and then left with Constança."[34]

The same event is recounted in the testimony of Leonor Díaz, given on March 2, 1595: "More or less five years ago, in the home of Manuel de Lucena, with his wife Catalina Henríquez, her mother Beatriz Henríquez, her sister Clara Henríquez, her daughter Justa Méndez, Constança Rodríguez, Juan Rodríguez de Silva, and Domingo Rodríguez. All fasted, observed the day, then all broke the fast at night with a meal."[35]

The same names reappear in testimonies by other attendees: Clara Henríquez (testimony of February 15, 1595), Anna López (testimony of July 18, 1595), Constança Rodríguez (testimony of August 29, 1595), among others.[36] Constança confirmed that Pedro Rodríguez Saz was there that day, as was her husband, Sebastian Rodríguez, who "wore clean clothes, washed his legs, and cut his nails" for the occasion. Sebastian Rodríguez, in turn, names the others and his wife as having participated in the celebration in his testimony of February 10, 1595.[37] Most important, the hosts, Manuel de Lucena, in his testimony of April 10, 1595, and his wife Catalina Henríquez, in her testimony of January 12, 1595, confirmed the list of attendees.[38] None of these testimonies involved torture.

In sum, we know Pedro Rodríguez Saz did not lie under torture for the same reason the Inquisition would have known that he did not lie under torture. They had been aware of the event he was describing for five years and had gathered testimony from all those present, confirming one another's testimonies, and attesting that Rodríguez Saz had been present as well. Rodríguez Saz could not have known about these testimonies: he had sat in the dungeons of the Inquisition since April 1595, a year prior to his torture. Indeed, that seems to be why he was tortured: despite ample evidence about his participation in this and other religious events, Rodríguez Saz refused to cooperate. His torture revealed nothing the Inquisition did not already know. Its purpose was to ensure he had stated everything he knew and his testimony matched that of other witnesses present.

This simple exercise of correlating evidence across cases can be performed for any of the many claims made by witnesses in the torture chamber. It is indistinguishable from the process the Inquisition used to corroborate uncoerced testimony, such as the comprehensive information that Lucena provided.

# The Torture of Luis de Carvajal

Such was also the case with the most extensive testimony under torture, the testimony of Luis de Carvajal. Carvajal was tortured in February 1596, a full year after his second arrest and seven years into the Inquisition's efforts to uproot the Jewish community in Mexico. By the time of his arrest, all key members of that community were already imprisoned and awaiting their trials, including his mother and sisters. By the time of his torture, at least twenty-one conversos had testified against Carvajal and named other community members, though there was no way for Carvajal to know who had testified and what they had said.

In Carvajal's case, as with Lucena, the Inquisition did not rely on its interrogations, let alone on torture, as its only source of evidence. The same informant, Luis Díaz, was placed in the cells of Manuel Gómez Navarro and Pedro Enríquez before he was placed in Carvajal's cell, whereupon Carvajal attempted to convert him to Judaism.[39] The conversations between Carvajal and Díaz, including information about Carvajal's beliefs, prayers spoken, rituals conducted in the prison cell, his fasts and Sabbath observance, and the prayer book that Carvajal had hidden in his cap, were relayed to the Inquisition by Díaz and the three court officials who had listened in on Lucena. The court read and summarized Carvajal's biography and heard testimony from witness after witness, implicating Carvajal and his family.

When prison guards discovered Carvajal was sending messages to other family members by inscribing them on an avocado pit, hidden inside a melon, they pretended not to notice the ruse so they could continue to glean information from his correspondence. Carvajal had inscribed the pit with the words: "the patience of Job." In the following days, he sent additional avocado pits, inscribed with quotes from scripture, including one hidden inside a banana, its skin sewn up to hide the missing interior.[40] Eventually, the warden left pen and paper in his cell so that he could send letters to his family. Luis wrote twenty such letters, seeking to inspire and encourage his sisters, describing the martyr's paradise that awaited them. Suspecting, perhaps, that the letters would be intercepted, he divulged no names or evidence regarding other Judaizers. He only implicated those whom he knew to have already been arrested (Manuel de Lucena and Manuel Gómez Navarro), safe (his brother Baltasar in Italy), or deceased (Antonio Machado).

Carvajal's refusal to divulge additional names to the Inquisition contrasts with his friend Lucena's detailed and uncoerced testimony. That is why Carvajal was tortured, after a year in a prison cell and three additional weeks of isolation in a dark dungeon. His torture began at eight-thirty in the morning on February 8, 1596:

Having been admonished to tell the truth, he said that he had nothing more to say. [In the margin: *Turns of the cord.*] The official was called into the chamber. Having been admonished to tell the truth, he was given one turn of the cord and said: "Ah! Oh, Lord, please forgive me Lord. Lord, please forgive me for my abominations. Have mercy on me." And that he would have told the truth if he knew of any other person.

Having been admonished again to tell the truth, he was given a second turn of the cord. He shouted, "Ah! Ah! Ah!" And said that his sister, Anica, kept the Law of Moses. And he added, crying, that he had told the truth and not to take vengeance upon him.

Having [again] been admonished to tell the truth, he was given a third turn of the cord. He shouted, "Lord, God of Israel, I have to tell a lie." And that, in the name of the one true God, he be shown mercy. "Oh, what sadness, I have to tell a lie." And he said that he had already told the truth. And he complained a great deal.

Having [again] been admonished to tell the truth, he was given a fourth turn of the cord. He complained very much and shouted, "Ah! Ah! Ah! Ah! I will tell the truth. I will tell the truth, Señor Inquisitor. I will tell the truth." He promised to tell the truth if the official left the room. And once the official left, he said that Anica kept the Law of Moses, however she did so as a child, meaning that she did not have the capacity to understand what was beneficial for her. She did not keep it with the same devotion as he did, or his mother, Doña Francisca, or his sisters, Doña Isabel, Doña Catalina, Doña Maríana, and Doña Leonor. . . .

He was told to tell the truth about everything else he knew because his answers were not satisfactory and was warned that torture would continue. He said that he had told the truth and that he would rather die during torture than tell a lie. Having [again] been admonished to tell the truth, the official was called in and he was given a fifth turn of the cord. He pled that the turns stop and said he would tell the truth frankly. And because he begged so much, and made such a commotion, the turns were stopped.

He said that he wants to tell the truth, which he had stopped telling so as not to wrong anyone and because he knew that it was a sin to reveal the names of others who he knew kept the Law of Moses. That if he had known it was not a sin from the beginning, he would have told the truth very frankly. And that the following people keep the Law of Moses.[41]

In the minutes that followed, Carvajal named as Judaizers Tomás de Fonseca, Héctor de Fonseca, Miguel Hernández, Manuel Álvarez, Jorge Álvarez, Antonio Díaz Márquez, Diego Enríquez, Pedro Enríquez, Pedro Rodríguez Saz, Ana López and her daughter Leonor Díaz, Manuel Rodríguez, Leonor Rodríguez, Ana Váez, Clara Enríquez, Gabriel Enríquez, Antonio López, Andres Rodríguez, Manuel Díaz, Catalina Enríquez, Beatriz Enríquez, Sebastian Rodríguez, Constança Rodríguez, Francisco Rodríguez, and Isabel Rodríguez.

The inquisitors responded dispassionately to this initial deluge of names: "He was asked whether he knew of others that follow the Law of Moses." Carvajal offered more names. At 2:00 p.m. the interrogation ceased so that the inquisitors could retire for lunch. Luis remained alone in the torture chamber. The questioning resumed that afternoon from three until seven. On the following two days, Carvajal was questioned from 8:30 a.m. to 5:00 p.m. The purpose of those interrogations was to draw out details regarding the names he had provided by asking open-ended questions: How did he know that this person was following the Law of Moses? When and where did he observe this behavior? How often did it happen? Who else was present? Who else knows that this person is a Judaizer? What else did they talk about on that day? Why did he not reveal this information earlier?

Carvajal was not interrogated during that weekend. On Monday, February 12, at 9:00 a.m., he was placed fully clothed on the rack. When he claimed that he had nothing more to say, he was stripped of his clothes once again. The inquisitor, Dr. Bartolomé Lobo Guerrero, demanded two turns of the rope but his associates, Don Alonso de Peralta and Dr. Juan de Cervantes insisted on six turns. Luis was tortured again and revealed even more names. At the end of the day, he was sent to his cell with paper, to provide a written summary of all the Judaizers in his community. Carvajal provided that list on February 14. It contained 119 names.

On February 15, Carvajal was asked to affirm what he had claimed under torture. He recanted it all: "Everything I have said from the time torture began has been a lie."[42] Upon leaving the audience chamber, Carvajal attempted suicide: He escaped his guards and flung himself out of a window into the courtyard, one floor below. He survived this suicide attempt.

Ten months later, Luis de Carvajal was burned at the stake alongside his mother, his sisters, and his friend, Manuel de Lucena. In the procession to the auto, Luis was placed in position of prominence, at the very rear of the line of convicted criminals. He had to be gagged to prevent him from shouting further encouragement to his mother and sisters, urging them to remain steadfast in their Judaism.[43] Because the Carvajal women had shown signs of contrition on the way to the execution, they were spared the torment of being burned alive. Instead, they were garroted before they were burned. Only Maríana was spared execution that day. She continued to provide useful information to the Inquisition and was held in its prisons until 1601. Then she, too, was garroted and burned (see figure 6.5).[44] Half a century later, the last of Carvajal's siblings, Ana de Carvajal, fell victim to the pyre. She was executed for Judaizing at the auto of April 11, 1649. "Little Anica" was eighty years old at the time.[45]

**FIGURE 6.5.**  *The Execution of Maríana de Carvajal*, as imagined by Primitivo Miranda, in Vicente Palacio, *El Libro Rojo* (1870), 61.

## Evaluating the Evidence

How did the Inquisition treat the information that Carvajal provided under torture compared to the copious information that Lucena provided without torture? Figure 6.6 illustrates the fortunes of the 119 individuals named by Carvajal and the 116 individuals named by Lucena. Because each trial manuscript includes information on the court's verdict, and because the records of the Inquisition

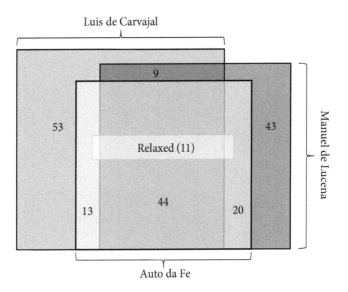

Luis de Carvajal

9

53    43

Relaxed (11)

Manuel de Lucena

44

13    20

Auto da Fe

**FIGURE 6.6.**   Individuals accused by Carvajal and Lucena and their fate.

include *relaciones de autos-da-fé*, information about participants at the auto-da-fé, it is possible to correlate who, among those named by Carvajal and Lucena, was publicly condemned by the Inquisition and who was not.[46]

In all, Carvajal and Lucena accused 182 alleged crypto-Jews. There is a significant overlap between their lists: both named the same 53 individuals, a nearly 50 percent match in their accusations. Of those 53, 44 appeared at the autos-da-fé of 1596 and 1601. In addition, 20 individuals named by Lucena but not Carvajal appeared at the autos, and 13 individuals named by Carvajal but not Lucena appeared.

In other words, the factor that doomed individuals was neither evidence from torture nor uncoerced testimony but a correspondence between both types of evidence. All of the individuals who were condemned at the auto were also named by other witnesses, in addition to Carvajal and Lucena. On average, three separate witnesses had to identify a suspect as a Judaizer prior to their appearance at an auto. Four separate witnesses had to agree in their testimonies, on average, before a sentence of death was proclaimed.

Put differently, the Inquisition relied on Carvajal's testimony under torture as one source among many in deciding whom to condemn at the auto and whom to execute. It certainly did not accord torture testimony a position of privilege. If anything, Carvajal's torture testimony carried slightly less weight than the voluntary disclosures of his friend Lucena: 48 percent of those Carvajal identified were condemned compared to 55 percent of Lucena's. Not once did the Inquisition condemn an individual based exclusively on Carvajal's testimony under torture. Indeed, sixty-two of those named by Carvajal (and fifty-two named by Lucena) do not seem to have been condemned at all, presumably because an insufficient number of independent witnesses could be found to corroborate their accusations.

## The Limits of Corroborative Torture

Antonio Díaz de Cáceres, brother-in-law to Luis de Carvajal, was one of the last Mexican conversos arrested and tortured in this second wave of trials.[47] He had succeeded in avoiding the Inquisition until December 1596. He had always been guarded in his Judaism, perhaps even ambivalent. Careful to maintain a Christian façade, he avoided most religious gatherings, conducted business on the Sabbath, and ate pork in public. But he also celebrated the Sabbath with the Carvajals, commemorated Passover with Jorge Almeida in 1583, discussed the Law of Moses with Gonzalo Pérez Ferro, and observed Yom Kippur with Clara Enríquez in 1593.[48]

Once arrested, Díaz named defense witnesses who, he hoped, would undermine the claims against him. Primarily, he wanted to prove that accusations made by his wife's family members, the Carvajals, were without merit and stemmed from their enmity toward him. The court interrogated ten of these witnesses in March 1597 but found their testimonies to be contradictory and unreliable.

He was left in his cell for nearly three years and was not interrogated again until December 2, 1600. In the intervening years, his daughter, his cell mates, and prisoners in nearby cells who had listened in on his conversations gave damning evidence against him. Luis de Carvajal testified against him under torture. His sister-in-law, Isabel de Carvajal, condemned him in July 1596. Yet he persisted in his denials. He claimed never to have heard of Yom Kippur. He thought that his sister-in-law's Jewish hymns were merely the ravings of a lunatic mind. Confronted with evidence that he had eaten kosher food, he responded, "I am not a cook. I ate what I was given."[49]

On March 2, 1601, Díaz suffered the most extreme torture recorded in this sequence of trials. He was hoisted to the ceiling by ropes tied to his contorted arms, then dropped rapidly, causing excruciating pain to his joints. This torture was repeated twelve times. The torturer then twisted ropes around his calves, thighs, and shins and turned these. This torture was also repeated twelve times. Water torture followed: He ingested seven jars of water. He screamed that they were killing him, but he revealed nothing. The Inquisition took this as proof of his innocence and reconciled him to the Church.[50]

Thus even corroborative torture had its limits. It could affirm accusations that exploratory torture had failed to reveal. But victims could still lie under torture, or provide evidence and later recant. In some cases, as with Díaz de Cáceres, strong-willed individuals who possessed a great deal of valuable information proved capable of overcoming the most extreme torture without providing their tormentors with a shred of useful information. Tragically, unbeknownst to Díaz, most of the friends and family members that he tried to protect throughout his extraordinary ordeal had long since died at the hands of the Inquisition.

# LESSONS FROM THE SPANISH INQUISITION

The preceding chapters offer several five-hundred-year-old lessons about the nature of interrogational torture. Drawing on archival sources, I have shown that the Inquisition succeeded at times in extracting useful information from torture victims. Suspects who refused to provide information during nonviolent interrogations, despite repeated opportunities to do so, sometimes revealed information later in the torture chamber. For example, in sixteenth-century Toledo, 29 percent of suspects who refused to collaborate and were tortured eventually provided information under duress that the Inquisition considered satisfactory. Moreover, that information was often accurate. Evidence provided in the torture chamber—names, places, events—was corroborated by witnesses outside the torture chamber and by material evidence collected by the court.

At the same time, these manuscripts reveal that the Inquisition treated interrogational torture with skepticism. It learned that (what I term) exploratory torture, conducted soon after an arrest and in the early stages of an investigation, provided little information that the court found useful or reliable. In the absence of independent means to corroborate that information, exploratory torture often targeted individuals who had no information to reveal, failed to identify those withholding significant information, and could not easily distinguish false or incomplete information from truthful claims.

As a consequence, the Inquisition learned to adopt a corroborative form of torture: torture that occurred toward the end of a prolonged investigation. This torture targeted suspects after months and years of confinement in the prisons of the Inquisition. The goal of this torture was not to uncover novel evidence but to corroborate information gathered by means other than torture and to extract as much information as possible from all potential witnesses. Even then, accusations made under torture were ignored unless they could be confirmed by other means. Not once, in the files I examined, did the court condemn a victim at an auto-da-fé based on evidence from torture alone.

Throughout, inquisitors displayed caution in drawing a line between interrogational torture, designed to unmask heretics and expose their communities, and alternative forms of torture that would not have served this purpose, such as penal or confessional torture. There was no relationship between the decision to employ torture during a trial and the outcome of that trial. The Inquisition had many forms of penal violence at its disposal, including death at the stake. It employed these punishments independently of its use of torture. The manuscripts I analyzed also display the court's awareness of the dangers inherent in conflating interrogational torture with confessional torture. Inquisitors did not seek proclamations of guilt or piety. They sought falsifiable information. They took care to avoid leading questions and instead urged suspects to "confess all they knew" without providing hints about the court's suspicions, specific intentions, the identity of other witnesses, or the testimony provided by those witnesses. This made it difficult for torture victims to offer false testimony to appease their tormentors or to reveal just enough information for torture to cease without disclosing too much.

The massive torture campaign that the Inquisition engaged in during the course of three centuries exacted a heavy price. For Jews and Muslims in the Spanish dominions, the Inquisition signaled the end of an era of cultural flourishing and the onset of expulsions, torment, and death. As these communities fled from the south of Spain, where the first courts were established, to the north, and from there to Portugal, or across the Atlantic to New Spain, the Inquisition followed. In 1482, the Inquisition established its first four permanent tribunals in Castile (Seville, Cordova) and Aragon (Valencia, Saragossa). By 1500, it boasted ten such tribunals across Spain. By 1520, four more had opened, including tribunals in the Canary Islands, Sicily, and Sardinia. Subsequently, it established five more tribunals, in such far-flung locations as Lima, Mexico City, and present-day Colombia.

The use of torture spread not only horizontally, across geographic regions, but also vertically. As the number of heretics diminished, and it became harder to collect evidence from voluntary witnesses, the frequency of torture went up. This, even though the Supreme Council of the Inquisition in Madrid placed significant constraints on local courts, drawing on increasingly elaborate sets of rules and restrictions regarding torture. The secrecy surrounding the Inquisition's procedures and rumors about the horrors of its torture chambers also played into the hands of Spain's rivals, primarily in Protestant England. They inflated the cruelty of the Inquisition's practices as a propaganda tool against the Spanish monarchy.[1]

Where prior analyses of torture had to rely on a patchwork of meager evidence and educated guesses, the archives of the Inquisition provide a vast universe of qualitative and quantitative data that can be analyzed carefully and objectively. Yet applying lessons from this historical experience to current concerns regarding torture as a counterterrorism tool demands extreme caution. The historical context in which the Inquisition tortured differed drastically from the circumstances in which torture is taking place today. It is true that inquisitors used many of the same methods that contemporary torturers employ. Indeed, American interrogators may have inherited variants of the torture methods that the Inquisition employed.[2] But that is where the similarities end and key differences between the cases become apparent. Inquisitors tortured for different reasons, with different goals, based on different assumptions, and in a social, political, and religious setting entirely alien to that of modern interrogators. The Inquisition functioned in an extraordinary environment. Its target population was confined within the realms of an authoritarian state in which the Inquisition wielded absolute authority. It tortured to uncover heresies already committed, not to prevent acts of terror yet to be executed. And it did so unconstrained by time, funding, or authority. No democracy can justify paying that social, political, or moral price for torture that yields modest, slow, and corroborative results.

Nonetheless, as I hope to show in this chapter, what little we know about contemporary torture confirms some of the patterns that emerge from my analysis of the Spanish Inquisition. As I suggested at the outset of this volume, information about contemporary torture is sparse and untrustworthy. In this chapter, I draw on two types of sources for information about contemporary torture. I cite from the testimonies of junior interrogators, who took an active part in torture, to establish current torture practices. These low-level officials are well positioned to evaluate how well rules regulating interrogation are implemented, and they can report abuses, including their own failure to follow protocols. However, because of their constrained vantage point, they are ill suited to evaluate how the information they have collected contributes to the broader intelligence picture because they are unaware of the nature of information gathered by other agencies and have little insight into the processing that occurs at higher levels in the intelligence analysis chain.

High-ranking intelligence officials are in a better position to assess the utility of intelligence extracted by means of torture, but their assessment is often colored by political or organizational bias, distorting evidence to support either an anti-torture or a pro-torture agenda. The tell-all memoires of CIA and FBI officials often serve to defend their own agency's position on torture and discredit the other agency's position. This bias is the very reason why historical analysis, such as the preceding study of the Spanish Inquisition, is necessary.

I draw on this second source whenever the testimonies of officials are in broad agreement with one another or where their statements about torture run counter to, or are neutral with respect to, their organizational preference. Where appropriate, I cite contradictory claims by officials from both sides of the debate to permit readers to reach their own conclusions. This is not a foolproof method for controlling against the bias inherent in these reports given some informal collaboration between these organizations, reliance on common sources, and even the shared use of ghostwriters across memoires. Nonetheless, I see no alternative to including these voices in this chapter. If I were to omit all accounts of torture by policymakers, we would be left with no direct evidence from the very organizations implicated in torture. I encourage readers to evaluate these reports critically and with a healthy dose of skepticism toward claims made both by advocates and by critics of US torture policy.

I conclude this chapter with a note of caution. There is a lot more about contemporary torture that we do not know than we do know. In the absence of a comprehensive archive, like that of the Spanish Inquisition, most assertions about contemporary torture rest on a feeble foundation of speculation, political bias, and wishful thinking. Primary among those is the unsubstantiated claim that torture is more or less effective than alternative interrogation methods. In the next and final chapter of this book, I shall argue that such utilitarian claims are also an unhelpful distraction from the moral problem of torture.

## Torture Can Provide Modest Intelligence

Even the Inquisition, in an extraordinary setting in which it was able to perfect a vast torture machinery, was able, at best, to extract nuggets of corroborative information from torture victims. Often, that information was false, misleading, or incomplete. This experience is echoed in contemporary torture accounts. Even the most confident proponents of contemporary interrogational torture concede that torture cannot provide full and decisive information about specific perpetrators or plots. In this sense, the intelligence derived from torture is no different than the intelligence derived from other sources: it can provide scraps of information that need to be corroborated, analyzed, and processed. This weakness is not unique to intelligence extracted from torture nor is it insurmountable. But it is a significant impediment and the resulting intelligence is often modest. This flies in the face of a public perception of torture as a loathsome yet effective "silver bullet" in the fight against global terrorism.[3]

For example, according to CIA accounts, disputed by the FBI, the torture of Abu Zubaydah (AZ) via 126 hours of sleep deprivation led to the identification and arrest of Jose Padilla. The confusion and distress induced by his lack of sleep, combined with the proposal (put to him by FBI agents) that his dream fragments might be divine guidance, led AZ to admit that he had sent two agents to Khalid Sheikh Muhammad (KSM) in order to initiate a dirty bomb attack in the United States. He called them Abu Ameriki and Abu Jamaki, but he did not know their real names. This description sufficed to alert a CIA officer in Pakistan, who remembered the names of two suspicious travelers leaving Pakistan ten days earlier. By the CIA's own account, neither the torture nor the suspicious traveler report would have sufficed to arrest Jose Padilla upon his arrival at Chicago's O'Hare airport.[4] The CIA further claims that once AZ became a cooperative witness as a result of torture, his uncoerced testimony was used to corroborate the names that another detainee, Abd al-Rahim al-Nashiri, provided during waterboarding.[5] It is noteworthy that, in both of these cases, the CIA engaged in exploratory and not corroborative torture.

The intelligence effort to locate Osama bin Laden offers an even more dramatic example of the piecemeal process in which multiple sources, including torture, are assembled to form a coherent intelligence assessment. In 2002, two detainees not in US custody identified Abu Ahmad al-Kuwaiti as an associate of bin Laden who traveled frequently to see him.[6] The interrogation of AZ in 2002 led to the capture of Ramzi bin al-Shibh, a key organizer of the 9/11 attacks. Al-Shibh's interrogation, combined with information extracted from AZ, led in turn to the capture of KSM in 2003.[7] Al-Kuwaiti's name appeared in materials seized during the capture of both AZ and KSM, but the former denied recognizing the name while the latter downplayed al-Kuwaiti's connection to bin Laden. Three additional detainees who suffered torture at the hand of the CIA, Khallad bin Attash, Ammar al-Baluchi, and Abu Faraj al-Libi, denied that he was bin Laden's courier. However, an al-Qaida operative by the name of Hassan Ghul, who claimed to have been unsure of al-Kuwaiti's connection to bin Laden prior to torture, may have confirmed that connection after torture and provided detailed information about al-Kuwaiti's last know whereabouts. If this account is to be believed, the torture of Ghul was used for corroborative purposes.[8]

Confronted with Ghul's claims, KSM and al-Libi's visceral responses persuaded CIA interrogators that al-Kuwaiti's identity was crucial, despite their statements to the contrary.[9] Moreover, interrogators discovered KSM's covert efforts to signal from his cell to other detainees not to discuss al-Kuwaiti. Using old intelligence records, CIA analysts then uncovered al-Kuwaiti's full name, a finding they allegedly confirmed using torture.[10] According to James Mitchell, who developed the CIA's enhanced interrogation program, yet another detainee,

Abu Yassir al-Jaza'iri, allegedly revealed information under torture about al-Kuwaiti's speech patterns that allowed the CIA to track his movements to Abbottabad.[11] By tracing calls made by bin Laden's bodyguard, US analysts were able to identify bin Laden's compound in Pakistan.[12] In all, the CIA claims that twenty-five detainees provided various clues about al-Kuwaiti's link to bin Laden. Of these, thirteen underwent some form of torture prior to disclosing the relevant information.[13] Clearly, some of these interrogations provided minor clues while others yielded false and even intentionally misleading information. Some of that information was new (exploratory) and some of it confirmed or undermined prior information (corroborative), but no single detainee revealed the location of Osama bin Laden under torture.

Like other sources of intelligence, contemporary torture often elicits false information that is difficult to distinguish from accurate information.[14] Guilty detainees have every incentive to fabricate claims in order to mislead interrogators. Innocent detainees have no information to offer and are thus forced to invent lies. As the US Army Field Manual notes: "The subject may not possess the information sought, but he will fabricate information to please the interrogator and bring an end to the force being applied."[15] Douglas A. Johnson, former executive director of the Center for the Victims of Torture, reported that nearly all victims of torture encountered by his center "gave up extraneous information, or supplied names of innocent friends or colleagues to their torturers ... such extraneous information distracts, rather than supports, valid investigation."[16] According to one CIA source, waterboarded detainees "get so desperate that they begin telling you what they think you want to hear."[17] Unchecked, the faulty intelligence resulting from torture can flood the system with false leads and may "bury" interrogators in useless information.

This reality forces investigator to engage in cross-checking to distinguish the more reliable and relevant intelligence (the "signal") from the less reliable and relevant intelligence ("the noise").[18] The same is true of material obtained from all other intelligence sources, be it signal intelligence (SIGINT), electronic intelligence (ELINT), or visual intelligence (VISINT). Information obtained from human sources (HUMINT) poses an additional challenge because the target may be aware of intelligence-gathering efforts and can falsify information intentionally.[19] But this challenge, too, is not unique to the interrogation of detainees. Enemies can "double" agents to provide misinformation, doctor radio messages, employ decoys to mislead image analysis, or forge documents.[20] Indeed, detainees provide misleading information when they are not tortured, as happens during noncoercive police interrogations.[21] In each case, the challenge faced by the intelligence analyst is to identify the intelligence that is relevant and then verify its authenticity by cross-referencing it with established knowledge.

Since this challenge is not unique to intelligence obtained from torture, interrogational torturers use the same tools that other interrogators use to distinguish truth from fiction.[22] They can draw on institutional knowledge about successful interrogation practices that their organization has accumulated over time as well as their own experience from multiple interrogations. Proficient interrogators use a wide repertoire of techniques to deceive detainees into revealing information. They will ask questions to which they already know the answers, either to corroborate that the detainee is being truthful or to demonstrate the futility of lying.[23] By misleading the detainee about what they know and what they wish to learn, experienced interrogators create uncertainty about what a detainee should and should not lie about. This also avoids the "confession trap," discussed below: detainees cannot parrot "what interrogators want to hear" if they are left in the dark about the interrogator's intentions.

All methods at the disposal of noncoercive interrogators are at the disposal of interrogators using torture. In addition, interrogators can respond to exposed lies by escalating torture. Some interrogators orchestrate "good cop/bad cop routines," while others release detainees from torture sessions into cells with seemingly friendly prisoners who act as informants.[24] Interrogators can also conduct parallel interrogations and then leverage snippets of information gleaned from one subject to verify information provided by another. They can reveal glimpses of that information in order to mislead subjects into thinking that the interrogators know more than they do.[25] For example, KSM became more susceptible to manipulation over the course of his imprisonment because interrogators were able to use information from concluded al-Qaeda attacks to mislead him into believing that these attacks had been foiled, that associates had betrayed the cause, or that plans he believed to be vital were no longer relevant.[26]

The most crucial step in distinguishing accurate from inaccurate information occurs outside the interrogation facility and after, or between, interrogation sessions, when the detainee's claims are cross-referenced against intelligence obtained from other sources. Since detainees are likely to lie, expecting that they are unlikely to be second-guessed, this cross-referencing is crucial to intelligence analysis.[27] The CIA's Jose Rodriguez claims that this was a time-consuming process:

> Often [interrogators] knew the answers to questions before they were asked. Always they double checked the information six ways from Sunday before accepting it as credible. As we got more and more al-Qa'ida leaders in custody, we were able to play one off against the other. We would ask a question, get a response, and then say, "Oh really? That's

not what KSM said, he said X." We would ask factual questions, such as "Where did you travel to in 1999?" When the detainee said, "Nowhere," we would say, "No, actually you went to Tanganyika and stayed at the Hill Top Hotel." They quickly learned not to mislead us. Still, we never assumed that what a detainee was telling us was true.[28]

According to Mitchell, CIA analysts were so suspicious of KSM's claims to having personally executed Daniel Pearl that they insisted on a reenactment of the beheading so that they could match the veins on KSM's forearms and hands to those of the executioner in the beheading video.[29] Whereas Rodriguez asserts that torturing KSM was crucial in identifying al-Kuwaiti, torture critic James Pfiffner claims that KSM offered no more than "a reinforcement of that discovery . . . merely another clue about al Kuwaiti's importance."[30] This is precisely the form of corroboration that underpins intelligence analysis.

The modest nature of much of the intelligence obtained by means of torture—some of it slight, some of it wrong—raises important questions about the moral costs that decision makers might be willing to pay for that intelligence. Torture advocates would argue that expecting any single source of intelligence to provide a "crucial" insight sets an unreasonable bar. If, as some torture critics argue, torture can only be justified when it provides crucial information that is unobtainable by other means, then torture is automatically disqualified as a policy option.[31]

## Torture Is Slow

Analyzing the intelligence obtained from torture and interlacing it with intelligence from parallel sources is a time-consuming process. But even the initial stage of extracting information from torture victims requires a great deal of time.[32] The rare instances for which torture timelines are available reveal that torture victims collaborated after weeks if not months.[33] Nguyen Van Tai, the highest-ranking North Vietnamese officer captured during the Vietnam War, endured four years of torment before he provided intelligence.[34] Abdul Hakim Murad admitted, after thirty-six days of torture by Philippine authorities, to plotting an attack during the pope's visit to Manila, by which time the pope's visit was long over.[35] AZ was in US custody for two months before he submitted to his interrogators.[36] KSM endured a month of gradually escalating torture, culminating in waterboarding, before sleep deprivation ultimately coerced his cooperation.[37] Muhammad al-Qahtani endured forty days of sleep deprivation, fifty-four days of torture, and sixty-four days of isolated imprisonment.[38] Omar al-Faruq, a confidant of bin Laden, was tortured by the CIA for three months before he began to cooperate.[39] Jamal Beghal, an al-Qaeda operative who could have led interrogators to Mohammad Atta's cell in Hamburg, was arrested on July 28, 2001, and was tortured but did not cooperate until September 23.[40] If the CIA is to be believed, torture yielded intelligence in all these cases. For example, KSM was "singing like a bird," leading interrogators to capture several other terrorists, and Beghal "talked and out poured a wealth of information . . . it was a real intelligence break."[41] But the process of obtaining intelligence through torture was slow, often so slow that the information obtained was no longer useful.

The fact that torture takes time is a crucial concern because torture policy is often discussed in reference to "ticking time bomb" scenarios. In these settings, information that is crucial to preventing an imminent mass terror attack has to be obtained rapidly before the attack can occur.[42] The ticking time bomb scenario is fanciful for a variety of reasons, not the least of which is the fact that the historical record does not provide a single incident in which a terrorist plot was foiled in this manner.[43] Nonetheless, the ticking time bomb scenario has made the successful transition from hypothetical thought experiment to policy guideline.[44] Intelligence officials have referenced the ticking bomb scenario to justify torture at Senate hearings, in internal government memoranda, and in their memoirs.[45] However, if successful torture is a protracted process, the bottom falls out of the ticking bomb argument.

Yet another reason why interrogational torture takes time is that it is not merely pain that elicits cooperation but the psychological effects that accompany pain, specifically prolonged isolation and fear of future torture, what I have called "the shadow of torture." As Milovan Djilas recollects in his memoir: "One does not become a traitor *under* torture, but *before* torture."[46] Henri Alleg, recounting his torture in Algeria, writes: "Rather than being kept in suspense, it was better to face the worst right away."[47] Threats are more effective than actual pain, the KUBARK interrogation manual explains, because detainees become conditioned to pain: "The threat of coercion usually weakens or destroys resistance more effectively than coercion itself."[48] Army interrogator Tony Lagouranis confirms: "Torture victims don't break on the pain they're experiencing, they break on the fear of more and worse pain to come."[49] These fears unfold over time.

As a result, interrogators do not expect to collect intelligence while torture occurs. "It wasn't pour water, demand a confession, pour water, ask a leading question," claims Mitchell.[50] Instead, interrogators introduce long pauses between torture sessions in order to foster the apprehension and dread that will elicit future cooperation outside the torture chamber.[51] Much torture consists of the psychological anguish of awaiting the initiation or resumption of pain. Interrogators threaten coercion, perhaps by exposing the detainee to the instruments of torture, as inquisitors did, by revealing the sounds of others being tortured, or by threatening the repetition of prior torture.[52] Alleg recollects his first encounter with a "magneto," an electroshock device, in a manner that calls to mind the Inquisition's practice of exposing victims to the instruments of torture: "He raised it to the level of my eyes, turning for my inspection the machine which had already been described to me a hundred times by its victims. 'You know what this is, don't you? You've often heard it spoken about? You've even written articles about it?'"[53]

According to Mitchell, torturing and debriefing are distinct responsibilities that occur at separate moments in an interrogation. The debriefer, who is a subject matter expert, interviews the cooperative detainee and authors the intelligence report after torture has ended and the interrogator is no longer in the room.[54] That was also the practice of the Inquisition. Such procedures would undermine the common criticism (discussed below) that victims will "say anything" under torture.[55] They would also weaken a series of torture critiques, leveled by neuroscientists and psychiatrists, arguing that pain undermines memory and recollection.[56] If these procedures were followed, neither the recollecting nor the saying would occur during a torture session but after, or between, torture sessions. But these routines do necessitate prolonged detention, gradual escalation, and recurring pauses as a key component of torture.

Of these, lengthy isolation is the most common technique to be coupled with torture. Soviet interrogators in the 1930s practiced "the long interrogation," questioning prisoners for four or five months, on average, prior to extracting false statements. Some intellectuals were interrogated for two and a half years, accompanied by inadequate sleep, freezing cells, and insufficient food, prompting physical and psychological disorders.[57] CIA behavior control experiments in the 1950s found that prolonged solitary confinement provoked an intense urge for human interaction among detainees.[58] Sustained imprisonment leads to disorientation, feelings of hopelessness, and the impression that the detainee has lost control over his own fate. The interrogator hopes that, with the passage of time, the detainee will realize the futility of withholding information and will wish to alleviate his own suffering.[59] Contemporary US interrogators found that isolated prisoners looked forward to interrogations, even harsh ones, as an opportunity to escape their oppressive cells and speak to a fellow human.[60] Even without these time-consuming measures, the escalation and repetition inherent in torture, the long pauses between torture sessions that elicit communication, and the time required for processing the intelligence obtained from torture all mean that torture is anything but quick.

## Interrogational Torture Fails When It Degenerates into Confessional Torture

When interrogators failed to maintain the distinction between interrogational and confessional torture, by insisting that detainees verify particular claims, for example, or when torture is used for purposes other than eliciting information, their efforts yielded unreliable results. I refer to this danger as "the confession trap." In confessional torture, pain is administered in order to attribute responsibility to a detainee, usually for the purpose of prosecution or public disclosure. This is the form of torture frequently employed by Communist interrogators in China, Korea, Vietnam, or the USSR, and it continues to be employed in several authoritarian regimes. Under confessional torture, detainees are likely to offer false admissions in order to escape their predicament, regardless of their innocence or guilt. The Roman jurist Ulpian argued in the second century CE that some people are so susceptible to pain that "they will tell any lie rather than suffer it."[61] The fifteenth century's *Malleus Maleficarum*, a handbook for interrogating those suspected of witchcraft, notes that "some are so soft-hearted and feeble-minded that at the least torture they will confess anything, whether it be true or not."[62]

Modern interrogators, including the Soviets under Stalin, the Japanese during World War II, and the Indonesians in their East Timor campaigns, were aware of the confession trap.[63] The CIA's 1963 KUBARK manual warns that "intense pain is quite likely to produce false confessions, concocted as a means of escaping from distress."[64] More recent historical evidence backs this claim. In Algeria under French occupation, many detainees talked under torture but offered deceptive responses.[65] In Vietnam, "if you were really hurting someone, they would tell you anything to stop it."[66] A Canadian citizen tortured in Syria, falsely accused of terror connections, nonetheless confessed to all accusations. He recalled: "You just give up . . . you become like an animal."[67]

Analytically speaking, interrogational torture is a distinct enterprise, even if interrogational and confessional torture often blend in practice. The purpose of interrogational torture is not affirmation but information. Interrogators conducting interrogational torture are not interested in a detainee's guilt or innocence but in operational details.[68] As Hayden and Mukasey put it, "Confessions aren't the point. Intelligence is."[69] The challenge for interrogators who employ torture is to distinguish one form from the other, thus avoiding the confession trap.

This difference between confessional and interrogational torture offers one reason why the FBI so vehemently opposes the interrogation practices of the CIA. The FBI considers "enhanced interrogation" to be illegal as well as counter to its law enforcement mission. When conducting counterterrorism, its goal is to elicit testimonies that link terror suspects to terror attacks for the purposes of prosecution. This is why FBI agents begin their interrogations, even those conducted outside the United States against non-US citizens, by reading detainees their Miranda Rights.[70] Once a detainee admits his responsibility to an FBI investigator, the investigator's primary task is accomplished. This is by no means an easy task since, as torture critics are loath to admit, there is no evidence to show that torture produces more false confessions than other forms of interrogation. Nonetheless, torture further undermines criminal investigations because the resulting evidence is inadmissible in US courts. Indeed, the FBI has been known to bar from its investigations any interrogators who were briefed on information obtained by torture, lest they inadvertently "taint" the investigation with that illegally obtained knowledge.[71]

The CIA, on the other hand, is not interested in the confessions of its detainees and is not concerned with securing legal evidence.[72] The goal of its counterterrorism interrogations is to uncover and foil ongoing and future plots. Its interrogators seek to uncover actionable intelligence, the more detailed the better. At Abu Ghraib, Army interrogators asked detainees seven specific questions, including: "Who and where are the mid-level Baathists?" "Which organizations and groups . . . will conduct high payoff attacks?" "What organizations are Baathist surrogates?"[73]

Interrogational torture fails when it degenerates into confessional torture.[74] Interrogators fall into the confession trap when they ask leading questions that reveal what answers they wish to hear or, as the KUBARK manual put it, "questions that suggest their own answer."[75] Experienced interrogators strive to avoid this trap. Mitchell asserts about his interrogation of AZ: "We weren't looking for a false confession and had to avoid asking him leading questions because we did not want him making up what he thought we wanted to hear."[76] Inept interrogators fail to take these precautions. For example, interrogators at Guantánamo harangued a detainee into admitting that he had appeared in a video with Osama bin Laden. After six weeks of torture, Sahfiq Rasul offered a false confession: "I was desperate for it to end and therefore eventually I just gave in and admitted to being in the video."[77] The interrogators who questioned Hanbali, seem to have been similarly careless with their leading questions: "Through statements read to him and constant repetition of questions, he was made aware of what type of answers his questioners wanted . . . he merely gave answers that were similar to what was being asked and what he inferred the interrogator or debriefer wanted, and when the pressure subsided or he was told that the information he gave was okay, he knew that he had provided the answer that was being sought."[78] KSM alleged, "During the harshest period of my interrogation, I gave a lot of false information in order to satisfy what I believed the interrogators wished to hear in order to make the ill-treatment stop."[79]

Mark Fallon provides a startling example of the failure to distinguish between interrogation and confession during the questioning of Mohamedou Ould Slahi by an unnamed interrogator:

> "We know you came to Canada to bomb the U.S.," said [name omitted].
> "And what was my evil plan?"
> "Maybe not exactly to harm the U.S. but to attack the CN Tower in Toronto?" he said. . . .
> "You realize if I admit to such a thing, I have to involve other people? What if it turns out I was lying?"
> [Name omitted] very much told me a precise crime I could admit that would comply with the Intel theory.[80]

The most prominent example of the confession trap involved Ibn al-Shaykh al-Libi, an al-Qaeda operative who provided helpful intelligence on camps and personnel in Afghanistan to US interrogators. When the CIA transferred him to Egypt under "extraordinary rendition," he was coerced under torture into affirming that Saddam Hussein had supplied al-Qaeda with weapons of mass destruction, a topic he knew nothing about. His claims were cited as a justification for the US decision to invade Iraq.[81]

## Torture Is Contagious

In the absence of a Supreme Council of the Inquisition and explicit rules delimiting torture, contemporary torture has proven difficult to contain. It is unwieldy and spreads easily, as interrogators exceed authorized limits and disobey orders.[82] Torture tends to spread beyond the appropriate boundaries in two ways. Vertically, interrogators will apply torture, or new forms of torture, to detainees who should not have been subjects to these new methods, or to any torture at all. Horizontally, torture or new forms of torture will "migrate" across organizational units.[83] This spread in the practice is particularly acute at times of perceived crisis, when interrogators are driven by both fear and self-empowerment.[84]

Scholars have identified several mechanisms to explain the unwieldy nature of torture. The first is psychological. Detainees become accustomed to pain. The more they resist interrogators, the more likely their frustrated interrogators are to escalate the use of force beyond authorized bounds. If interrogators believe that violence is an effective means of extracting information, they may also believe that more violence will lead to more information.[85] Threats are an integral component of these interrogations. Whenever interrogators follow through on threats, an escalation occurs. Since violence supplies no natural stopping point, these practices may lead to "force drift" and uncontrolled abuse.[86] "Once I got started, it seemed pointless to stop," Lagouranis claims, "and each escalation appeared seamless, natural, and justified."[87]

A second mechanism is legal. The laws regulating interrogation are vague and contestable. Lawmakers build interpretative latitude into these laws that allows them to be manipulated.[88] In Iraq and Afghanistan, US commanders kept changing and shifting the rules, making it difficult for interrogators to keep up. The interrogation rules of engagement varied from one prison environment to the next. According to Lagouranis, the rules constraining torture were "broad, self-contradictory, and malleable."[89]

The third mechanism is organizational. Different agencies learn from one another and emulate on another's torture practices.[90] But as they compete to extract information from detainees, they also seek to outdo one another in developing and implementing harsher techniques.[91] These new techniques do not die out: they spread.[92]

The testimonies of US interrogators suggest that even after Secretary of Defense Donald Rumsfeld approved harsher torture methods, interrogators exceeded approved techniques, trying as many different torture methods as they could.[93] In December 2002, Rumsfeld replaced officers at Guantánamo who felt bound by the Geneva Conventions with those willing to use harsher methods. Rumsfeld's impatience with the intelligence obtained from detainees subsequently led him to approve a broader list of interrogation techniques including "hooding," "stress positions," and "sleep adjustment." Yet guards at Guantánamo went far beyond these methods, allegedly beating detainees with broom handles, sexually abusing detainees, and depriving them of food and water.[94] Initial interrogation policy in Iraq permitted stress positions, sleep deprivation, loud music, and bright lights. In September 2004, according to Fallon, interrogators added dietary manipulation and environmental manipulation. In late October, controlled fear, isolation, and removal of comfort items were added to the list. In late November, military working dogs arrived at Abu Ghraib and were used against detainees.[95] Lagouranis maintains that, eventually, torture methods at Abu Ghraib came to include beatings, ice water, extreme temperatures, and rectal probing.[96]

This is the vertical escalation of torture. Seeing potential "ticking bombs" everywhere, aware that any one detainee might provide information that could save American lives, interrogators in Iraq applied harsh methods, intended for high-value detainees, to petty criminals.[97] Lagouranis avers, "As the stress positions, sleep deprivation, and isolation spread to the other prisoners, I hardly noticed. The bleed-over was unremarkable."[98] He observed that interrogators shifted from gathering specific information from detainees to collecting as much information as they could, prioritizing quantity over quality, and escalated their use of torture. Techniques that were initially prohibited were later permitted under exceptional circumstances. Eventually, they became the norm and were formalized and authorized. Lagouranis also suggests that officials ignored interrogators who reported abuse against prisoners.[99]

In parallel, torture spread horizontally. Techniques practiced at Fort Bragg were approved for use in Guantánamo, then spread to the detention facility at Bagram Air Force Base in Afghanistan, and from there to Abu Ghraib in Iraq.[100] Major General Geoffrey Miller (commander of the unified Task Force Guantánamo) used the April 16, 2004, secretary of defense guidelines for Guantánamo as a model to "Gitmo-ize" Abu Ghraib. Once Miller assumed control of all US Army prisons in Iraq in 2004, he instituted sweeping policy changes, including the decision to involve prison guards in interrogations despite their lack of training.[101] He also sent six personnel from Guantánamo to Abu Ghraib to assist in implementing his recommendations.[102]

Is this organizational contagion inevitable? It is hard to tell, because US Army interrogators, who provide the bulk of the evidence on how torture has been implemented by the army so far, were so poorly trained and supervised. Their testimonies speak volumes about how badly the army controlled torture, but they tell us little about whether a more disciplined organization could have done better. American agencies had neither studied nor sought to improve their interrogation practices since the Second World War. The first concerted effort to do so was only initiated in 2010.[103]

Army interrogators report that they received little to no training on how to torture, indeed, little to no training on how to interrogate. They claim that formal interrogation training included no mention of torture and a warning neither to threaten nor imply violence.[104] Neither the SERE (Survival, Evasion, Resistance, Escape) instructors who taught torture techniques nor their student interrogators had any interrogation experience.[105] At Guantánamo, the military had so few trained interrogators that it was forced to employ inexperienced and untrained civilian contractors. The officer in charge of interrogations at Abu Ghraib had no interrogation experience himself and no skilled interrogators working underneath him.[106] Members of Israel's security service were astounded at the high turnover among US interrogators, their reliance on untrained staff, and their willingness to outsource interrogation to "unprofessional" contractors.[107]

As a result, much of the violence that took place in these detention facilities was improvised. Lagouranis declares, "We had no idea what we were doing. We were just a bunch of frustrated enlisted men picking approved techniques off a menu. We weren't grounded in the history or theory; we were just trying shit out to see if it worked, venting our frustration, and acting like badasses when, in the dark art of torture, we were really just a bunch of rank amateurs."[108] Worse, for some army interrogators, torture became a macabre form of entertainment. As a sergeant of the Eighty-Second Airborne Division stated, "We would just get bored . . . we did that for amusement. . . . In a way it was sport."[109]

These are damning statements about US Army torture practices, but intelligence agencies can differ widely in their decision and ability to control torture. The more coherent and well integrated an organization is, the more professional its interrogators, and the greater its ability to verify the intelligence obtained from suspects, the more successful it will be at containing torture.[110]

Even torture critics concede that, in contrast to Army interrogators, torture by CIA interrogators was "relatively well monitored and limited in use," especially after an initial learning period.[111] CIA staff claim that the agency authorized only six specific torture techniques, all previously employed in SERE training, and that only fourteen operatives, equipped with psychological training, learned those techniques.[112] The training was meticulously detailed, "careful and precise," including instructions on how interrogators should position their hands and where they should place their fingers during torture. They further claim that these interrogators had to receive written permission from the deputy director for operations before escalating from any one technique to the next. Rodriguez writes, "Despite the popular misconception, we didn't freelance or just make things up as we went along. The parameters of significant actions are clearly laid out and the Agency is told what it can and cannot do, when and where it can do it, and what tools are at its disposal." According to Rodriguez and others at the CIA, the agency monitored the implementation of these procedures carefully. As a consequence, they claim that torture was rare, applied to only a dozen high-value al-Qaeda detainees, all of whom collaborated and none of whom died during interrogation.[113] According to the CIA, this program worked well and provided a good picture of the Iraq insurgency before poorly trained military-police prison guards were brought into the program, ultimately yielding the infamous Abu Ghraib abuses.[114]

Critics dispute these claims, arguing that the agency granted many more approvals to torture and that these approvals led to at least five deaths among detainees.[115] Even CIA officials admit to cases of excess in which interrogators used unapproved torture methods on detainees or continued torturing even after the detainee began cooperating.[116] That these interrogators were disciplined, removed from the program, and that policy was amended to try to prevent a recurrence of these incidents attests to the CIA's attempts at maintaining a control over the application of torture. But it also illustrates how difficult it is to establish that control.

## Torture Provokes Blowback

Torture is costly in the medium to long term. While it might provide some tactical advantage by providing information that can win battles, its strategic costs may lose the war. Torture campaigns create costs at four levels. At the most fundamental level, torture plays into the hands of one's opponents by emboldening detainees and their close associates. They may fight harder, for fear of being captured and tortured, and they may feel free to retaliate with torture of their own.[117] In the language of the KUBARK interrogation manual: physical brutality fosters resentment, hostility, and further defiance.[118] Analyzing terrorism data for the period 1976–2006, Daxecker and Hess have documented the backlash effect that repression produces in democracies, lengthening the life cycle of terrorist organizations and lowering the probability of counterterrorism outcomes favorable to the government.[119] According to Sullivan, torture has a similar effect in counterinsurgencies. It increases the incentives for insurgents to commit violence without reducing their capacity to do so.[120]

More broadly, torture undermines popular support for the government and radicalizes the target population, though the direction of the causal arrow is not always easy to establish.[121] Bell, Cingranelli, Murdie, and Caglayan show that political violence tends to rise when governments violate the physical integrity rights of their citizens by imprisoning, torturing, or "disappearing" individuals.[122] Torture can drive moderate civilians into the arms of radicals, turning marginal movements into organizations with mass appeal.[123] When British forces tortured Irish Republican Army members, a former MI5 operative reports, "It did nothing but exacerbate the situation. Most of those interned went back to terrorism. You'll end up radicalizing the entire population."[124] French torture against the Front de la Liberation Nationale helped grow the movement into a revolutionary party, enjoying mass support, by attracting the sympathy of Algeria's population and by sidelining moderates, such as the Algerian National Movement.[125] Robert Pape found references to the motivating effects of the Abu Ghraib tortures in twenty-six martyrdom videos recorded by suicide bombers.[126] Torture also deters informants from collaborating with authorities for fear that they, or those they inform on, will be tortured as well.[127] As an Iraqi detainee, who refused to provide information on a suspect to his American interrogators, stated: "If I give you his name, your soldiers will arrest him in his home and bring him here, and they will do to him what they did to me."[128]

At the broadest level of analysis, torture undermines the political capital of the country conducting torture by damaging its international reputation, as demonstrated by the damage to US moral leadership in the aftermath of the Abu Ghraib scandal.[129] These negative reputational effects act on the international level to discourage cooperation just as they do at the domestic level. Governments that might otherwise share intelligence because they perceive of their interests as aligned with the state conducting torture, now distance themselves from that state.[130] Even former CIA director Michael Hayden, who has testified to the efficacy of torture, has stated: "Look, even though we say it is effective, the consequences of doing it vis-à-vis our allies could outweigh any benefit we might gain."[131] President Obama's former national director of intelligence, Admiral Dennis Blair, who acknowledged that torture yielded "high value information," also affirmed that "the bottom line is these techniques have hurt our image around the world, the damage they have done to our interests far outweighed whatever benefit they gave us and they are not essential to our national security."[132]

A final blowback caused by torture occurs within the organization exercising torture and the society that supports it. Torture has a pernicious effect on the torturers, both moral and psychological, that can undermine their ability to serve those institutions effectively.[133] It can transform their loyalty and devotion to the state into a sense of betrayal and distrust.[134] Studies examining the effects of torture on the torturers found that the psychological damage to torturers can manifest itself in symptoms that are very similar to those of victims, including anxiety, intrusive traumatic memories, and impaired cognitive and social functioning.[135] Several US guards who participated in torture reported suffering from PTSD, nightmares, panic attacks, flashbacks, and depression.[136] Jennifer Bryson, a former Guantánamo interrogator, notes: "Engaging in torture damages the torturer. The starting point for torture is the dehumanization of a detainee. Those who dehumanize others corrupt themselves in the process."[137] Indeed, torture may exert a corrupting effect on civil society if it fosters increased acceptance of brutality in law enforcement. Torture, as Camus put it, degrades a nation "in its own eyes and the world's."[138]

# What We Do Not Know about Torture

The evidence regarding the nature of interrogational torture by US agents, spotty and inconsistent as it may be, permits some preliminary conclusions. Torture can provide intelligence, but that intelligence is partial, at best. The process of obtaining information from torture is slow, and it fails entirely when interrogators lapse into confessional torture. As an organizational practice, torture is difficult to contain, and it provokes blowback in the medium to long term. This much can be cautiously surmised from declassified information.

Does contemporary torture provide better information than alternative methods? Even the Spanish Inquisition, after centuries of experience backed by carefully collected data, made no such claim. It envisioned torture as a complement to alternative sources of information, not as a substitute and certainly not as a superior alternative. Inquisitors understood that torture was rarely necessary, that it yielded information in some cases but not in others, and that it often provided incomplete or altogether false information.

In the absence of precise and reliable data on contemporary torture, the relative utility of modern torture cannot be assessed, to the dismay of torture proponents and critics alike. Torture critics have argued that noncoercive interrogation methods, including psychological tricks, threats, clues gleaned from alternative information sources, information provided by volunteers, or the creation of friendly rapport between interrogators and detainees, have provided intelligence as good, if not better, than intelligence obtained by means of torture.[139] Social science experiments seem to demonstrate that false testimonies and resistance to interrogation increase in direct proportion to the coerciveness of interrogation while the detainee's ability to recollect precise information, and the interrogator's ability to tell truth from lie, decrease during harsh interrogations.[140] Rejali asks and answers: "Is torture more effective than these other ways of gathering information? Torture is definitely inferior."[141] A Pentagon adviser confirms: "It's not torture but acts of kindness that lead to concessions."[142] In a survey of experienced military and intelligence interrogators, all forty-two experts voiced the belief that noncoercive methods are superior to coercive approaches.[143]

There are four problems with this claim, the primary of which is that it is untestable, given appropriate social science norms and procedures. It offers a counterfactual that has not and will never be demonstrated. Short of discovering a natural experiment in which detainees were randomly assigned to be tortured or interrogated noncoercively and then rigorously comparing the results, the claim that noncoercive interrogation works better than torture is as speculative as the opposite claim that torture works better than noncoercive interrogation.[144] No intelligence agency or social science laboratory has ever attempted an odious experiment of this sort.

Research on the relative efficacy of torture relies on experiments in which psychologists and neuroscientists explore more and less confrontational scenarios in a laboratory setting.[145] This literature has provided fascinating insight into certain aspects of coercion and interrogation. Indeed, these findings align with some of the results of my analysis of the Spanish Inquisition, such as the inherent difficulty that interrogators face in identifying false statements, or the effects of stress and sleep deprivation on the degradation of memory and the production of false memory.

But these experiments involve no torture, since even experimental torture on primates is considered beyond the pale.[146] Instead, most torture studies tend to involve students in a laboratory setting undergoing some distant proxy for torture.[147] The "external validity" of these experiments (meaning, what they can teach us about the world outside a laboratory) is suspect. Even experiments that expose soldiers to high-stress interrogations are of limited external validity. They tend to be soldiers undergoing interrogation training who are well aware that they are not, in fact, in enemy hands and who know, with full certainty, that threats and rough treatment will fall short of torture.[148] These studies thus provide some parallels for how torture might work, but they provide limited insight into how torture actually works.

States do not experiment with torture at all. They either eschew torture altogether or mix coercive and noncoercive interrogation methods. Neither option permits scholars or critics to compare torture to noncoercive interrogation. In the first scenario, the complete absence of torture provides no clues about how well interrogators might have done had they used torture. For example, Rejali speculates that informants who aided British police in investigating the July 2005 bombings would not have come forward had they suspected that the British practiced torture.[149] Since torture was neither considered nor attempted in parallel, there is no basis for conjectures about how a policy of torture would have influenced informants. To wit, US authorities were able to capture KSM thanks to an informer, attracted by the promise of a financial reward and motivated by an ideological disagreement with al-Qaeda, despite the fact that the US practices torture.[150]

In the second scenario, prevailing in the United States, for example, agencies mix torture and noncoercive interrogation in a nonrandom manner, then pool information obtained from both sources. This makes it difficult to contrast the success of one method with the other because the results of one "contaminate" the results of the other.

This mixing of methods raises a second, related, problem that hampers the comparison between violent and nonviolent interrogation. Even during the friendliest interrogation, "the shadow of torture" looms large. Detainees undergoing noncoercive interrogation know that torture is a distinct possibility if they do not cooperate, particularly if torture has already occurred. For example, Nguyen refused to reveal useful information to his Vietnamese interrogators under torture. But once he was handed over to American interrogators, who claim not to have tortured him, he provided "useful (albeit limited) information."[151] Can this be credited to the skillful questions and psychological ploys used by American interrogators? Or should it be credited to a palpable fear of being handed back to the Vietnamese if he did not cooperate?

The shadow of torture looms over interrogators as well. If interrogators know that their counterparts might employ torture if noncoercive interrogation fails to deliver results, that threat is likely to surface, explicitly or implicitly, and influence their interrogation. How successful would noncoercive interrogation be if torture did not loom over it? Glenn Carle, a CIA officer who interrogated Afghan banker Pacha Wazir, claimed to have disavowed all torture: "I simply would not allow or have anything to do with any physical coercive measure. I would not do it."[152] Yet he warned Wazir that "others were not as nice, or as patient, as I was."[153] Was his interrogation successful because he eschewed torture or because he mentioned torture as a palpable alternative?[154]

The difficulty in extricating one form of interrogation from the other is apparent in the primary case cited by champions of noncoercive interrogation, the interrogation of Abu Zubaydah (AZ). Critics argue that AZ's friendly interrogation by the FBI yielded far more information than his subsequent torture by the CIA. A closer look at the evidence, even as it is presented by the FBI, unravels this claim.[155] AZ was not interrogated by the FBI and CIA in sequence. He was handed back and forth between the two agencies multiple times over the course of hours and days, transitioning rapidly from noncoercive interrogation to torture and back again. All FBI interrogations occurred under CIA auspices and with CIA interference.[156] After a successful FBI interrogation, CIA interrogators stripped AZ of his clothes, blasted cold air and loud music at him and deprived him of sleep. These efforts proved unsuccessful, so FBI agents resumed their interrogation, with more success. Were they successful because they used noncoercive interrogation or because their CIA counterparts were threatening to resume torture? Unbeknownst to the FBI interrogators, CIA agents were manipulating the temperatures in AZ's cell while he underwent noncoercive interrogation. Soon thereafter, the CIA took charge of the interrogation again, implementing sleep deprivation, loud music, and forced nudity. FBI representatives returned for one final round of interrogations before they left the compound in disgust, at which point the CIA began full-fledged torture. If the CIA is to be believed, this approach proved fruitful. Yet the FBI's Soufan concludes: "We gained information using a tried and tested scientific approach while what [the CIA] was doing was un-American and ineffective."[157] Even if the FBI's version of events is to be believed, skeptics ought to ask: How much information would the agency have gained with its "good cop" approach had it not been for intermittent CIA "bad cop" treatment? There is no way to tell.

A third difficulty in comparing torture with its alternatives is that many intelligence agencies do not treat torture and noncoercive methods as substitutes but as complements. Torture is never the sole source of intelligence. It is not obvious why other means should work less well when they are being supplemented by torture. By the FBI's own account, its rapport building with AZ worked well despite the fact that CIA torture occurred in parallel. Nor is it obvious that torture is unhelpful when it serves to corroborate information obtained by other means. For example, torture critics claim that AZ's divulging of KSM's alias under torture was redundant because two other sources, the Emir of Qatar and a CIA tipster, had provided the same name.[158] How helpful AZ's confirmation of this alias was depends, among other things, on how reliable these alternative two sources were and how many contradictory claims about KSM's alias analysts encountered. Corroboration may not be morally robust enough a goal to justify torture, but it certainly is a crucial component in any intelligence analysis.

This complementary role played by torture and alternative intelligence-gathering methods is apparent in a second case often cited by torture critics, the interrogation of Abdul Hakim Murad. His torture by Philippine police in 1995 revealed the name of his accomplice, Ramzi Ahmed Yousef, their plans to execute an attack during the pope's visit to Manila, their plans to bomb airliners, and their plan to fly planes into public buildings in Washington, DC.[159]

Torture critics assert that much of the information extracted by means of torture was available on the laptop found in his apartment.[160] This claim is problematic for several reasons. For one, the information on the laptop was encrypted and Philippine authorities were unable to read it. It was subsequently deciphered by US authorities.[161] Moreover, the flight numbers and airline itineraries found on the laptop "baffled investigators" since the laptop provided no information on the suspects' plans regarding these flights. Torture revealed that it was their intention to leave explosive with timing devices hidden on the airplanes, set to go off after the terrorists had deplaned at stopover airports. Nor did the laptop reveal the separate plots to fly airliners into the CIA headquarters, the White House, and the Pentagon, plans now recognized as early versions of the 9/11 plot.[162] The redundancy provided by these multiple sources was not an obstacle to intelligence analysis but a boon. Torture performed a corroborative role. Combined, Murad's interrogation, his laptop, and objects found in his apartment allowed investigators to piece together an outline of his plots.

A fourth and final challenge for scholars who allege that noncoercive interrogation is superior to torture is that purely "noncoercive" interrogation is rare in high-stakes situations. When dealing with detainees who are believed to hold crucial intelligence, interrogators often push noncoercive interrogation beyond its breaking point. They may humiliate detainees, issue death threats, or threaten the detainee's family members and loved ones.[163] Nguyen's American interrogators may claim that he was not tortured in US captivity, but he was kept in isolation for three full years, denied sleep and food, and subjected to extreme temperatures.[164] Rejali claims that skillful Communist interrogators avoided the use of torture.[165] In reality, NKVD and KGB interrogators held prisoners in isolated cells in uncomfortable temperatures, deprived them of sleep and food, and subjected them to eighteen to twenty-four hours of standing, producing excruciating pain and even death. They merely refused to categorize these techniques as "torture."[166]

The FBI's interrogation of AZ presents an equally egregious case. AZ had been severely wounded during his arrest, shot in the thigh, groin, and stomach. Nonetheless, and despite the severe pain he was in, FBI agents interrogated AZ immediately after his capture, at an undisclosed location outside the United States.[167] According to the FBI's own accounts, he was kept awake for nearly five days while CIA and FBI interrogators worked on him in "tag teams."[168] His condition became so critical that the interrogation had to be halted so that he could be rushed to a nearby emergency room. An agent had to improvise a tracheotomy in the vehicle on the way to the hospital that saved AZ's life. Because the hospital was not a secure location, AZ's FBI interrogators urged him "not to make a scene" at the hospital, warning: "If you play any games, you're only endangering yourself."[169] Was there no perception on AZ's part that his medical treatment would be discontinued if he did not cooperate?

By the FBI's own account, the agency interrogated AZ during this entire time, including long periods in which he was handcuffed to a hospital bed and recovering from emergency surgery, "as soon as he opened his eyes and it was clear he was lucid." The interrogation had to be conducted using an Arabic letter chart because AZ had a breathing tube in his mouth and could not speak.[170] He was denied pain killers.[171] He was subsequently questioned in the hospital "every moment [we] could" pausing only "when he had to sleep or when doctors treated him."[172] How is this not torture?

In conclusion, scholars cannot answer the vague question "does torture work?" The evidence available suffices to answer a simpler question: "Does torture sometimes provide actionable intelligence?" The evidence does not yet suffice to answer a more important question: "Does torture provide better intelligence than alternative forms of interrogation?" And the evidence will never suffice to answer the most important question of all: "Does the intelligence extracted by means of torture justify the moral cost of torture?"

## Looking Ahead

My goal in this book has been to contribute robust empirical evidence to the study of torture, a field that has so far rested many of its claims on anecdotal evidence. My work seeks to build on the findings of prior scholars, and it corroborates several of their insights. The files of the Spanish Inquisition confirm that extracting evidence by means of torture is a lengthy, complex, costly, and unwieldy process that often yields misleading results. They similarly confirm the dangers of asking leading questions (confessional torture) and the futility of expecting torture to provide quick and novel information (exploratory torture). As modern torture scholars have suspected, pain and sleep deprivation can degrade memory and recall, which is why the Inquisition aimed to collect and confirm evidence outside the torture chamber, between torture sessions. The evidence I explored also affirms the crucial role that prolonged incarceration, and the threat of future torture (the "shadow of torture") play in the interrogation process.

But my findings undermine other assumptions commonly held by torture scholars such as the claim that torture cannot provide reliable information or the definitive assertation that other forms of interrogation are more effective than torture. Corroborative torture has forced victims to reveal accurate information. That information tends not to be very surprising or very significant (and would not be trusted if it were surprising and significant) but corroboration performs a crucial function of its own in intelligence analysis. Scholars have amassed some experimental evidence to show that aggressive interrogations can be less effective than friendly interrogations, but they have not established this finding in the realm of physical torture.

The research program on torture is still in its infancy and my contributions in this volume are not merely modest but also tenuous. Brief forays into the archives of the Spanish Inquisition cannot possibly suffice to establish generalizable conclusions about torture throughout the sixteenth and seventeenth centuries or throughout the Spanish dominions as a whole, let alone uncover the causes and effects of torture in the present. The initial probe in these pages does, however, suggest two potential research trajectories, each fraught with its own challenges.

The most obvious next step in this research agenda is to explore whether my findings regarding Ciudad Real, Toledo, and Mexico City apply to the courts in these cities beyond the periods I have analyzed and whether they extend to other tribunals of the Inquisition in other locales. Sevilla, Córdoba, Granada, Valencia, Zaragoza, and other Spanish cities hosted significant tribunals for extended periods of time. As in Ciudad Real, their practices evolved over time as they experimented with different forms of interrogation, as rules became institutionalized, and as they learned from one another. Their use of torture was also affected by changing political, social, religious, legal, and financial circumstances, so tracking the tribunals over time will prove valuable. Further afield, the Inquisitions in Lima, the Canary Islands, and Sicily would make for fascinating comparisons as would the contemporaneous Inquisition in Portugal and Rome.

This archival work will be bedeviled by problems of access, interpretation, and selection. The written material is geographically dispersed across institutions. Much of it has not been catalogued and very little of it has been digitized. Libraries and archives may prevent scholars from accessing vulnerable manuscripts, or severely limit access in time or volume. The manuscripts are numerous, very numerous, and can be lengthy and detailed. Language barriers, antiquated script, and idiosyncratic conventions in notation or organization pose additional obstacles. Texts can be hard to locate and decipher, especially if one does not know precisely what to look for. Unless scholars are accompanied by small armies of translators and research assistants, they will have to be very selective about the collections they choose to focus on. But how can they know what collections to choose prior to accessing, deciphering, and analyzing the manuscripts in those collections?

Prior scholarship by historians can provide clues about potentially fertile venues of research, even if their histories are not dedicated to the topic of torture. In my research for this book, I leaned on work by Chaim Beinart, Henry Charles Lea, Martin A. Cohen, and others to identify which archival collections might yield the most fruitful manuscripts for analysis. Their hints were not always helpful (and at times outright misleading), but they proved far superior to jumping blindly into the bottomless pit of the Inquisition archives. At minimum, preexisting scholarship offered some information about of the parameters of particular archives: How much material was available, how accessible it would be, and what condition it was in. On occasion, my predecessors commented on references to torture that they had encountered in their research.

Much time can be saved, and uncertainty avoided, by analyzing sources that have already undergone some "processing" by archivists or scholars. I was able to curtail some of my research travels by obtaining scanned or transcribed copies of Spanish and Mexican files from libraries in Germany and the United States. I could read Beinart's transcriptions of the Ciudad Real proceedings in my university's library, could lean on Lea's meticulous handwritten notes regarding the Toledo tribunal, and I could rely on Cohen's narrative description of the setting in which the Mexico City trials took place.

Knowing where to look leaves open the question of methodology. Much is to be gained from collecting rudimentary information across a very large universe of cases, spanning time and space, revealing trends and exceptions to trends at thirty thousand feet. To provide robust results, the data need to be of consistent quality, sufficient quantity, and display interesting variation across variables of interest. The in-depth analysis of detailed cases across time offers alternative insight into the logic of torture that can be fine grained and reveal distinct motivations, mechanisms, and outcomes. Indeed, only by tracking down manuscripts that capture events prior to torture and subsequent to torture, for each and every case analyzed, can we hope to ascertain whether that torture victim possessed the information sought by the Inquisition and whether the information they revealed under torture was truthful or useful to the Inquisition. Those seeking to build on my analysis of torture under the Spanish Inquisition will have to decide which of these approaches to privilege or combine in their own work.

A second way to further the empirical research of torture is to focus on more recent torture campaigns. The analysis of modern torture poses new problems that mirror the challenges of studying inquisitorial torture. If the archives of the Inquisition are too voluminous, the data on modern torture are too thin. Most of the important evidence remains classified and is unlikely to see the light of day in our time. Modern sources on torture may be easier to read and interpret but they are far less reliable precisely because the painful events they describe are still fresh in our collective minds. These sources are drawn not from legal files compiled by indifferent scribes centuries ago but from the personal accounts of individual torturers and victims, some of whom still live among us. If analyzing the archives of the Inquisition requires difficult methodological choices, no such choices encumber the study of contemporary torture. The evidence is so sparse that quantitative analysis is out of the question. Even detailed and consistent narratives are difficult to piece together, as I sought to demonstrate when I described current US torture policy in chapter 1.

The French tortured tens of thousands in Algeria, the Nazis tortured hundreds of thousands, and authoritarian leaders in the postwar era have tortured millions. None of these torture campaigns have produced comprehensive archives that are currently available to scholars. The perpetrators avoided documenting their actions, hid the evidence, or destroyed the documents. This is true for democracies as well. Darius Rejali conducted the most ambitious survey of torture campaigns by democracies worldwide, but his meticulous analyses could not lean on any systematic database.[173] Courtenay Conrad, Jillienne Haglund, and Will Moore assembled a global dataset of statewide torture levels, and specific instances of torture, for every year between 1995 and 2005. Their data is based on allegations made by Amnesty International.[174] Christopher Einolf was able to piece together a history of the American torture effort in the Philippines in the late nineteenth century by combing for clues in disparate reports, histories, biographies, and single court cases.[175] He found more detailed evidence on torture in the archives of the Ba'ath regime in Iraq. Seventy testimonies by individuals tortured under Saddam Hussein, several of whom were members of the resistance against his regime, provided a first glimpse into the nature of interrogations in Iraq's torture chambers.[176]

Governments may yet surprise us by declassifying information on relatively recent torture operations, especially if they wish to disassociate themselves from the torture policies of their predecessors. In 1991, Germany established the Federal Commissioner for the Records of the State Security Service of the former German Democratic Republic, colloquially known as the Stasi Records Agency, to declassify the files of the former East German intelligence and secret police agency.[177] If laid out in a row one page after another, these archives, which also include 39 million index cards, 1.4 million photos, and 34,000 video and audio recordings, would extend for more than sixty-nine miles.[178] So far, more than seven million individuals and institutions have requested access to these files. Alas, only 2 percent of the files have been digitized.[179] Half of these documents can be found in the Stasi Record Agency's headquarters in Berlin, the other half is distributed across twelve regional offices in Germany. These files await analysis. It remains to be seen how many cases of torture they documented, how detailed or reliable the information is, and what it reveals about the causes and consequences of torture in the former GDR.

Because the study of torture is a new enterprise, it poses all the challenges entailed in launching a novel research program and more. Even in the context of security studies and terrorism studies, the theme of torture is uniquely controversial and disturbing. Furthermore, the visceral reality of the topic, the depictions of brutality and suffering embedded in each and every document, can pose a real harm to the scholar's emotional health. Students of torture will struggle to strike a balance between reflecting the grim reality of torture in their work and abstracting from that horror to arrive at dispassionate conclusions. The greatest challenge of all is to grapple with the ethical implications of this research and the moral implications of its findings, a topic to which I now turn.

# ETHICS AND THE STUDY OF TORTURE

On Monday, July 7, 1941, at ten o'clock in the morning, four SS men accompanied by two Romanian soldiers barged into the home of Rabbi Abraham Mark.[1] Mark was the chief rabbi of Czernowitz, at the time a city of 100,000 residents, of whom half were Jewish. The Germans demanded that the rabbi provide the names and addresses of wealthiest Jewish community members. Rabbi Mark refused to collaborate and was taken away. He was then tortured, physically and psychologically. The physical torture took place in the basement of the Hotel Zum Schwarzen Adler, the temporary headquarters of Einsatzkommando 10B. There, Rabbi Mark and other community leaders were incarcerated in the bottom of the elevator shaft where they were beaten and humiliated. The psychological torture occurred on the roof of the hotel. On July 8, Mark was taken to the roof, overlooking his nearby synagogue. As he watched, the synagogue was set ablaze with barrels of gasoline and the sacred Torah scrolls were thrown into the fire. His tormentors jeered: "Look, there is your synagogue, burning." It is not known whether this act of desecration led the rabbi to provide the names sought by the SS. The next day, Wednesday, July 9, he was executed at the banks of the Prut River together with more than six hundred other Jews. Thousands more were killed in the coming weeks before the Jewish community was forced into a ghetto, expelled, and annihilated.

Interrogational torture is not a five-hundred-year-old historical puzzle, captured in leather-bound manuscripts, tucked away in vast archives. Governments continue to engage in torture, and detractors and advocates continue to debate its nature, as scholars strive to learn more about its causes and effects and contribute to an ever-growing research program on torture.

My purpose in this epilogue is to consider the implications of my findings for the ethics of torture policy, criticism, and scholarship. First, I depart from those who claim that policy deliberations about torture have a simple answer because torture always, or never, yields results. Instead, I propose that torture poses a real policy dilemma for decision makers because it can yield tangible, if modest, results under extreme conditions. Second, I argue that torture critics should cease basing their denunciation of torture on speculative consequentialist grounds. They should direct the force of their criticisms away from the efficacy of torture and onto the much more credible moral challenge posed by torture. Finally, I discuss the difficult issue of ethical restraint in the scholarship of torture and offer several considerations for future debates on how ethics might inform the study of torture.

## Implications for Policymakers and Critics

As the prior pages in this book demonstrated, neither of the extreme positions on the efficacy of torture is tenable. Torture is not a quick and efficient way to uncover substantial information in "ticking bomb" scenarios. At the same time, torture does sometimes extract accurate information from unwilling informants. We do not know, and we never will know, whether it is inferior or superior to alternative interrogation methods. In terms of policy (but not ethics) this reality places decision makers in a difficult position. Like nuclear weapons, drones, and landmines, torture is a brutal means that exacts high costs. If decision makers deem this means to be effective for accomplishing particular goals, they will have to weigh those costs against the costs of foregoing those goals. Torture presents decision makers with a truly tragic choice.[2]

Pretending that this is an easy decision to make, either by imagining that torture is always effective or by claiming that it is never effective, eliminates an abstract moral dilemma but fails to resolve the underlying policy dilemma. Given the historical record on torture, it is unrealistic to expect that future leaders will not contemplate its use. How they will resolve such quandaries will depend on their own assessment of the efficacy of torture, their confidence in the belief that informants have valuable information, the value they place on obtaining that information, and their judgments regarding the cost of not uncovering that information.

This predicament is already visible in US attempts to justify torture by bending and stretching the "ticking bomb" metaphor. For example, James Mitchell justified the torture of Khalid Sheikh Muhammad by claiming that the situation "felt" like a ticking bomb: an attack "possibly involving a nuclear device, was in the works and could occur at any moment."[3] Note the qualifiers: "possibly," "in the works," "could." There was no nuclear bomb, there was no plan, there was no looming deadline, but the situation "felt" as if all of these parameters were alarming enough, in tandem, to justify torture. In the absence of actual ticking bomb scenarios, or the ability of torture to address such scenarios, leaders will have to ask themselves: How closely does a scenario need to resemble a ticking bomb before I should contemplate torture, if at all? How confident must my assessments be before I permit interrogators to use force? How will I justify this decision to my electorate and to myself?

Torture critics face a much easier task, if only because they do not have to contend with concrete policy dilemmas, nor with the dire consequences of action or inaction. They can, at best, hope to influence policy by means of persuasive arguments. Yet in espousing unrealistic views regarding the efficacy of torture, many torture critics have made the unfortunate decision to embrace a consequentialist stance on torture, at great loss of credibility. For example, John W. Schiemann writes:

> Interrogational torture does not work . . . for anyone who has ever had so much as a root canal, it sure seems like it *should* work. But it does not. Interrogational torture generates bad information. It results in false information by innocent detainees. It results in ambiguous information of unclear value. It results in no information at all.[4]

The evidence presented in this book undermines these statements. Certainly, torture, like all other intelligence sources, sometimes provides false, ambiguous, or no information. I have also documented in the prior chapter the many ways in which torture has proven pathological to the institutions that practice it and detrimental to their strategic goals. But all too often, torture has provided accurate and reliable information. Indeed, the preceding chapters documented scores of instances in which torture victims revealed information that was neither bad, nor false, nor ambiguous. It was clear, explicit, plentiful, and it doomed them and their communities.

Consequentialist arguments are much weaker than moral critiques for several reasons. The first fundamental problem with all consequentialist critiques of torture is that the costs of torture that critics emphasize can always be weighed against the benefits that torture proponents emphasize. This weighing of the pros and cons of torture often assumes the form of a "war of anecdotes": for every example of unnecessary, excessive, or fruitless torture that a critic offers, a defender of torture can counter with an example of crucial, efficient, and successful torture.[5]

In this war of anecdotes, information asymmetry favors the torture apologist. This is a second reason why consequentialist critiques of torture are dangerous. The decision makers who are responsible for determining whether torture should be employed know a great deal more about its efficacy than critics who lack access to classified information. Stumbling half-blind through the meager evidence available to them, critics risk making assumptions about torture that perpetrators know to be factually incorrect. When this happens, critics fail to persuade their audiences, at best, or discredit their legitimacy as expert advocates, at worst.

Third, torture "technology" is continuously advancing. Both the physical and the psychological tools available to interrogators are constantly shifting. Even if one could show that interrogational torture is not effective today, and there are insufficient grounds for any such assessment, torture may prove effective tomorrow. A single dramatic innovation in torture technology, be it improvements in the use of polygraph machines during torture or a hypothetical new "truth serum" used in conjunction with torture, could thus pull the rug out from under the critics' feet.[6]

But the most important reason to reconsider consequentialist critiques of torture is not because they are based on wishful thinking, nor because they are easily undermined. The most important reason to abandon consequentialist critiques of torture is that they are irrelevant to the morality of torture. To a deontologist who believes that torture is evil because it is dehumanizing, it cannot matter whether torture works sometimes, often, or always. The only scenario in which the efficacy of torture could possibly have a bearing on its morality would be a universe in which torture is never ever effective. Only in such a universe would it be impossible to justify torture on consequentialist grounds. That is not the universe we inhabit.

How then should torture opponents phrase their dissent? They should rest their opposition to torture on absolutist (deontological) grounds.[7] They can object to torture because it dehumanizes its victims.[8] Torture treats individuals as instruments rather than as beings of value, of rational, aesthetic, or spiritual capacities. As Ronald Dworkin has argued, torture is inconsistent with viewing others as full members of the human community.[9] Torture instrumentalizes pain and undermines the victim's capacity for self-government and agency. This, as David Sussman points out, is more than mere cruelty. It forces victims to collude against themselves through their own affects and emotions, to be simultaneously powerless and yet actively complicit in their own violation.[10] During torture, the body betrays the self, and humans are reduced to base flesh, denied of rationality.[11] Unlike killing in war, in which those attacked can defend themselves, torture is an attack on the defenseless, who cannot shield themselves, evade, or retaliate, and who cannot know when or whether the attack will ever end.[12] It strips its victims of all human dignity, tyrannizes, and dominates them.[13]

Torture opponents should reject torture *despite* the fact that it may at times work, and despite the costs that a refusal to torture might carry. The Israeli Supreme Court, in its decision to prohibit torture, presented a sober view of the sacrifices required to uphold moral principles: "A democratic society does not accept that investigators use any means for the purpose of uncovering truth. . . . At times, the price of truth is so high that a democratic society is not prepared to pay it."[14]

The international community does not oppose ethnic cleansing or chemical weapons on efficacy grounds. Its members know with certainty that nuclear weapons work yet oppose their use regardless. Critics should not judge the morality of torture on its efficacy either. If torture is evil, its efficacy is irrelevant.[15] Those who know it to be evil should reject torture outright, regardless of how efficacious it may or may not be.

Is this moral argument futile because it won't persuade potential torturers? Recent surveys suggest that American adults find moral arguments against torture to be far more persuasive than inefficacy arguments about torture.[16] Perhaps decision makers care more about results than they care about morality. That question, in and of itself, stacks the deck in favor of consequentialism: if you believe that only results matter then, yes, you should set aside sound moral arguments that fail to persuade. The problem with this meta-consequentialist attitude is that torture critics possess no good alternative to the moral (absolutist) argument. I have presented some evidence to show that torture yields modest and slow results, at great costs and under unique circumstances. Nonetheless, the evidence necessary to confidently state that "torture does not work" does not exist. Intelligence officials are likely to expose any claim to the contrary as misinformed, speculative, or biased. After all, they know all too well how often torture has or has not proven of utility to them. The absolutist argument is powerful, regardless of whether all government officials find it compelling, not only because it is more fundamental than the consequentialist argument but also because it is more sound.

Weak consequentialist arguments do not suddenly become good arguments because they succeed in convincing someone. We should not reject absolutist claims merely because they are unpersuasive, and we should not adopt dubious consequentialist claims merely because we are desperate to persuade. If we do, we shall fail both on consequentialist grounds (because the facts will undermine our claims) and on absolutist grounds. Torture critics should make arguments that are true regardless of whether they convince, not arguments that are convincing regardless of whether they are true.

# Implications for Scholars

While torture opponents anchor their objections in ethical foundations, scholars should continue to amass the empirical information necessary to rigorously assess the costs and consequences of interrogational torture. This scholarly enterprise is crucial because government-sanctioned torture is an ongoing reality: it continues, unabated, driven in large part by misconceptions about the requirements, nature, and effects of torture.

Studying torture is a separate enterprise from criticizing or endorsing torture. It is both possible and necessary to study torture in a dispassionate manner. But this enterprise poses ethical dilemmas of its own. How ought scholars to balance their professional ethics against the moral problem of torture? These questions have not troubled scholar-activists who employ their research as an anti-torture cudgel. Like misguided interrogators, they have been asking leading questions and have only accepted the answers they wanted to hear. As a result, much of the early scholarship on torture has upheld convenient fictions, such as the illusion that torture yields quick and crucial results or, conversely, the wrongheaded notion that all interrogators are incompetent bunglers, blissfully unaware of the dangers of confessional torture, or the unpersuasive claim that torture victims cannot recall important information.

The scholarship of torture is gradually progressing beyond that early, politicized stage. Scholars who wish to publish findings regarding torture that are grounded in evidence will have to contend with the fact that their findings may run counter to their intuition and may contradict their personal policy preferences. If they are professional in their scholarship, they will not know with certainty at the outset of their research what findings their analysis may yield. Scholarly ethics suggests that they not distort the findings of that analysis, no matter how distasteful they find them. Should scholars publish everything they discover? How can they possibly foresee the effects of their research on government policy in the distant or very distant future? If those are the implications of conducting professional scholarship on torture, can we justify this academic endeavor?

These are not questions with which scholars of torture need to grapple alone. Scientists in fields as diverse as nuclear physics, robotics, or genetics have asked themselves parallel questions precisely because the answers are neither easy nor obvious. Now that the scholarship on torture has started to professionalize, this debate has started to surface in this field as well. For example, M. Gregg Bloche, who has written at length about medical ethics, has proposed three ethical guidelines for scholars in the behavioral sciences who advise interrogators.[17] First, their consultation should be based on hard science, not hunches or intuitions. Second, behavioral science professionals should refrain from advising any interrogation program that breaches human rights law or the law of armed conflict. Third, they should define more clearly what the permissible boundaries of manipulation and experimentation are within their field.

Social scientists whose work draws on archives, surveys, and interviews rather than experiments will have to devise ethical guidelines of their own. All scholars ought to identify their own moral compass and make explicit, at least to themselves, how they envision the ethical constraints on their research. In writing this book, I have fallen back time and again on a very old system of ethics, identified in the thirteenth century by Thomas Aquinas.[18] Aquinas's Doctrine of Double Effect is an ethical tool that seeks to assess any action that may have both morally good and morally bad consequences.[19] It can provide insight into some of the moral deliberations surrounding scholarship even though (like all moral guidelines) it does not provide definitive rules. Indeed, its fourth condition raises more questions than it answers.

Aquinas's first condition, as I paraphrase it, is that the problematic act under consideration (in this case, scholarship) must itself be morally good or at least morally indifferent. Second, the agent may not intend the act's bad effect. If they could attain the good effect without the bad effect, they would do so. Third, the good effect must not be a consequence of the bad effect but must flow directly from the action. Fourth, the good effect must outweigh the bad affect.

How might these four rules shed light on the morality of studying torture? Scholars can and should engage in vigorous debate about what the good and bad effects of studying torture might be. It seems to me that scholarship has two primary good effects: an increase in knowledge, and the impacts of this knowledge on policy that one might consider morally laudable. The morally bad effects of scholarship seem to me to be entirely in the realm of policy: foreseeable and unforeseeable consequences on practice that are morally contemptible.

I thus understand Aquinas as making four demands on scholars of torture of which the first three, to my mind, are straightforward. First, that the scholarship they engage in is itself a moral good or value neutral. Second, that the student of torture not intend (or magnify or promote) the malicious effects that their scholarship might trigger. They ought to intend only its good effects. Third, that these good effects, say, greater insight into the history of torture, or a greater level of restraint in US torture policy, should not be a consequence of any bad effects, say the adoption of some new torture method, but rather be a direct consequence of the scholarship. Fourth, and most challenging of all, that the moral benefits of scholarship outweigh the moral costs.

This final criterion is very difficult to meet or even assess, for a variety of reasons. Unless they happen to collaborate directly with institutions that engage in torture, students of torture will have a difficult time evaluating what their impact on policy might be. One cannot identify the weaknesses in a tactic, strategy, doctrine, or weapon without empowering both those who wish to employ it and those who wish to oppose it. Any analysis of torture, regardless of its findings, can play into the hands of those who seek to minimize torture and those who seek to exploit it further. The only means of avoiding this trap is to claim, disingenuously and unpersuasively, that a policy has only immutable weaknesses or only unassailable strengths.

This challenge is apparent in the debates within the High-Value Detainee Interrogation Group. This group, initiated by President Barak Obama's executive order to review interrogation practices, is open about the political goals of its research: to "fix the problem of the use of abusive interrogation methods by US government personnel."[20] Yet its participants deliberated at length about whether to classify their findings for fear of inadvertently aiding and abetting future torture programs.[21] Similarly, the decision by the American Psychological Association to distance itself from US government interrogation practices prompted controversy. Some members felt that it was the absence of large cadres of trained psychologists, not the presence of two poorly trained psychologists, that accounted for a great deal of the ignorance in government circles about the psychological effects of torture.[22]

Should one decide that one's findings might too easily be abused by the powers that be, how does one eliminate the evidence and suppress the findings? Historical documents are available for all to analyze. Experiments are open to all to replicate. Survey data are available to all to collect. Not unlike investigations into nuclear fission, once launched, the scholarship on torture is a wheel that cannot easily be uninvented. These are difficult ethical questions. Those who claim otherwise (in the pretense that torture almost always, or almost never, works) are of little help in addressing these questions.

I do not think that the appropriate conclusion is that one ought to pursue honest scholarship at all costs, and may the world perish, nor do I think that scholars should abstain from studying topics that might yield controversial results. Arguably, those are precisely the areas of research that scholars should not surrender to politicians or activists. The editor of one prestigious political science journal refused to review my first research paper on torture on the grounds that "one needs to ask about the ends to which such research would be put."[23] These were strange grounds for rejection from a journal that had published recent articles on US counterinsurgency doctrine, foreign-imposed regime change, counterterrorism, and nuclear deterrence. One can only hope that, as the scholarship on torture moves farther away from praise or critique and toward rigor and scholarly accountability, members of this growing field of research will grapple with these ethical questions with intelligence and care.

When I present my research, I am often asked, directly or indirectly, to declare my personal stance on torture. "Is he contributing to torture prevention or is he not?" asked one reviewer.[24] Such ad hominem questions strike me as unconstructive. At best, they shame the scholar and their scholarship. They suggest that audiences need to correct for biases in scholarship based on the agenda of the author. At worst, they demean the audience. They imply that readers are only receptive to the ideas of scholars who share their agenda.

Such purity tests are yet another testament to how young the research program on torture is and how much more it needs to mature before it can be considered a professionalized field of inquiry. The obligation of the scholar is not to set their audience's minds at ease. Rather, their obligation is to put checks in place to ensure that the scholarly enterprise is ethical while, at the same time, guarding personal preferences from distorting their analysis and findings.

I will not declare my personal stance on torture. It has no bearing on my findings. I will say only this: Rabbi Mark was my great-grandfather. The victims of the Inquisition in Ciudad Real, Toledo, and Mexico City are my ancestors. I will leave it at that.

# Acknowledgments

I have never relied as heavily or as gladly on the kindness, patience, and diligence of peers, students, friends, and strangers as I have in completing this project. Social science research is always a team effort and the research for this book pushed me well beyond my training in the study of religion and international conflict into two new fields, early modern Spanish history and intelligence analysis. I was welcomed into both fields by colleagues who supported my efforts with constructive criticism and with gifts of time, labor, and insight.

In the earliest stages of the project, I benefited from feedback at numerous academic venues. Colleagues at Berkeley's MIRTH seminar, at Yale's MacMillan International Relations Seminar Series, at the Political Science Seminar of the University of Tokyo, and at George Washington University's Security Policy Workshop offered invaluable feedback on early drafts as did audience members at the annual conferences of the American Political Science Association and the International Studies Association. I received helpful comments from Nicholas Anderson, Allan Dafoe, Alexander Debbs, Doyle Hodges, Nuno Monteiro, Darius Rejali, and Bruce Russett.

Some early elements of this manuscript appeared in "What Do We Know about Interrogational Torture?" *International Journal of Intelligence and Counterintelligence* 33, no. 1 (2019); and in "The Cost of Torture: Evidence from the Spanish Inquisition," *Security Studies* 29, no. 3 (June–July 2020). I thank the editors of those journals and the anonymous reviewers they recruited for investing in those early versions of my research and for helping me think through some of the more complicated challenges that the analyses posed.

In collecting, transcribing, translating, and analyzing the data for this book, I depended on the aid of a team of research assistants more than in any prior project. Alejandro Mendoza, Courtney Tran, Rudrani Ghosh, and Emanuelle Le Chat combed through scores of sources, often in vain, to discover fragments of the puzzle that I was trying to assemble. Their patience in hunting down, translating, and summarizing documents was remarkable. Two young scholars went above and beyond any call of duty to support my work. Omar Rivera Barrientos translated numerous passages for chapter 3. He also transcribed Lea's handwritten notes and organized much of the data for my analysis in chapter 4, displaying curiosity, initiative, and a knack for creative problem solving. Andrea Miranda-González translated mountains of material related to the trials in Mexico City for chapters 5 and 6, interspersing her notes with her own intuitions and suggestions. She did so tirelessly and without demurring, despite my continued (and transparently false) promises that there would soon be an end to her efforts. My work to decode these manuscripts would have amounted to nothing had it not been for Omar and Andrea's professionalism and devotion.

The guardians of these manuscripts proved equally crucial. At the Center for Jewish History in New York, Ilya Slavutskiy furnished me with transcriptions of manuscripts from the Archivo General de la Nación (Mexico). Gunnar Knutsen in Norway and Jean-Pierre Dedieu in France shared some of their analyses on the Toledo tribunal. Markus Wagner at the Historische Sammlungen, Martin-Luther-Universität Halle-Wittenberg, found and scanned the manuscripts from Toledo that Lea had read in Halle in 1902. John H. Pollack, the curator in the Kislak Center for Special Collections, Rare Books and Manuscripts at the University of Pennsylvania Libraries, helped me track down Charles Henry Lea's handwritten notes on the Halle manuscript and toured me around Lea's old library. In Spain, Antonio Blázquez at the Archivo Histórico Nacional helped in accessing the original Ciudad Real manuscripts.

Back home, at the University of California at Berkeley's Bancroft Library, José Adrián Barragán-Álvarez, curator of Latin Americana, guided me through the manuscripts acquired by Berkeley and helped me find my way through the holdings of the Archivo General de la Nación in Mexico. He and I leafed through the leather-bound Lucena and Carvajal manuscripts in the Bancroft Library together, transcribing and translating one page at a time. Eventually, we fell under their spell and spent hours and days pouring over key passages, deciphering allusions and idioms. Those sessions were a highlight of my research for this book and I am grateful to José Adrián for the joy he took in sharing his craft with me. Charles Faulhaber, who was responsible for acquiring these manuscripts for Berkeley, offered a thoughtful reading of the relevant draft chapters for this book. Jerry Craddock, his colleague in Berkeley's Department of Spanish and Portuguese, provided crucial corrections and suggestions.

Roger Haydon and Mahinder Kingra shepherded this manuscript through the Cornell University Press review and production process offering encouragement and important suggestions along the way. Several reviewers, in-house and external, submitted valuable input about my manuscript to the press that influenced my thinking and rewriting. Among these anonymous reports, one exceeded all expectation or precedent, extending over sixty single-spaced pages of criticism, praise, sources, corrections, frameworks, gentle nudges, and blunt denunciations. This ranks as one of the most remarkable acts of scholarly charity that I have had the good fortune of experiencing. I incorporated as much of that feedback as I could. This book is the better thanks to this reviewer's remarkable investment in my manuscript. I am also deeply indebted to James Pfiffner and to Tracy Lightcap for their careful comments on earlier drafts. Jane Hambleton designed the beautiful family trees scattered throughout this volume.

I later learned that another anonymous reviewer, who had provided valuable feedback on the historical chapters of this book, was David M. Gitlitz, eminent scholar of Sephardic Judaism and Crypto-Judaism. His recent book *Living in Silverado*, on the secret lives of Jews in colonial Mexico, had proved a great source of information and inspiration for chapters 5 and 6 of this volume. I would have liked to meet him and thank him for his help, but I learned of his identity two weeks too late. On December 30, 2020, David Gitlitz passed away from Covid-19 in his home in Oaxaca, Mexico. May his memory be a blessing.

# Notes

## 1. HOW LITTLE WE KNOW ABOUT TORTURE

1. The full text of the convention, formally titled The Convention against Torture and Other Cruel, Inhuman or Degrading Treatment or Punishment, available at https://treaties. un.org/doc/Treaties/1987/06/19870626%2002-38%20AM/Ch_IV_9p.pdf.

2. See, for example, Jay Bybee memorandum to Alberto Gonzales, "Standards for Conduct for Interrogation under 18 U.S.C. 2340–2340A," US Department of Justice, Office of Legal Counsel, August 1, 2002, available at http://www.gwu.edu/~nsarchiv/NSAEBB/ NSAEBB127/02.08.01.pdf.

3. Alfred W. McCoy, *A Question of Torture: CIA Interrogation from the Cold War to the War on Terror* (New York: Metropolitan Books, 2006), 19, 83.

4. Philippe Sands, "The Green Light," *Vanity Fair*, April 2, 2008.

5. "Inquiry into the Treatment of Detainees in U.S. Custody," US Senate, Committee on Armed Services, November 20, 2008, 62 and note 447, my emphasis.

6. Brian Ross and Richard Esposito, "CIA's Harsh Interrogation Techniques Described," *ABC News*, November 18, 2005. Rejali is justified in pondering why it is that cellophane would lead to gagging, as opposed to asphyxiation. Darius Rejali, *Torture and Democracy* (Princeton: Princeton University Press, 2007), 285.

7. Jay Bybee, "Standards for Conduct." This description is in line with a declassified report from the CIA's Office of Medical Staff which mentions a saturated cloth placed over the mouth and nose and in which water fills the nasal cavity but not the lungs. "OMS Guidelines on Medical and Psychological Support to Detainee Rendition, Interrogation, and Detention," Central Intelligence Agency, December 1, 2004, available at https://www. cia.gov/library/readingroom/docs/0006541536.pdf.

8. Jose Rodriguez, *Hard Measures: How Aggressive CIA Actions after 9/11 Saved American Lives* (New York: Threshold Editions, 2012), 236–37. Italics in the original. See also James E. Mitchell, *Enhanced Interrogation: Inside the Minds and Motives of the Islamic Terrorists Trying to Destroy America* (New York: Crown, 2016), 53.

9. Mark Fallon, *Unjustifiable Means: The Inside Story of How the CIA, Pentagon, and US Government Conspired to Torture* (New York: Regan Arts, 2017), 84. My italics.

10. Rejali, *Torture and Democracy*, 284, citing Michael Slackman, "What's Wrong With Torturing a Qaeda Higher-Up?" *New York Times*, May 16, 2004, sec.4, 4; and Jane Mayer, "Outsourcing Torture: The Secret History of America's 'Extraordinary Rendition' Program," *New Yorker*, February 14, 2005.

11. Mark Benjamin, "Waterboarding for Dummies," *Salon.com*, March 9, 2010. Yet the same review states that "water may enter—and accumulate in—the detainee's mouth and nasal cavity," with no mention of the detainee's lungs, 'and expresses concern that "the detainee might aspire some of the water and the resulting water in the lungs might lead to pneumonia," language that implies that this exceptional outcome is to be avoided.

12. Jane Mayer, *The Dark Side: The Inside Story of How the War on Terror Turned into a War on American Ideals* (New York: Anchor Books, 2009), 173.

13. McCoy, *A Question of Torture*, 122; 19, 59, 83, and 127.

14. Rejali, *Torture and Democracy*, 284.

15. Ali H. Soufan, *The Black Banners: Inside the Story of 9/11 and the War Against al-Qaeda* (New York: W. W. Norton, 2011), 368; and Rodriguez, *Hard Measures*, 177, 236; Mitchell, *Enhanced Interrogation*, 70; and Mayer *The Dark Side*, 172–73.

16. James Pfiffner, "The Efficacy of Coercive Interrogation," in *Examining Torture: Empirical Studies of States Repression*, eds. Tracy Lightcap and James P. Pfiffner (New York: Palgrave, 2014), 127–58; Rodriguez, *Hard Measures*, 236; Soufan, *The Black Banners*, 515 and 536; and Mitchell, *Enhanced Interrogation*, 252.

17. See, for example, Rejali, *Torture and Democracy*; McCoy, *A Question of Torture*; Tracy Lightcap and James P. Pfiffner, eds., *Examining Torture: Empirical Studies of States Repression* (New York: Palgrave, 2014); Sanford Levison, ed., *Torture: A Collection* (Oxford: Oxford University Press, 2004); Fritz Allhoff, *Terrorism, Ticking Time Bombs, and Torture* (Chicago: University of Chicago Press, 2012); John W. Schiemann, *Does Torture Work?* (Oxford: Oxford University Press, 2016); Shane O'Mara, *Why Torture Doesn't Work* (Cambridge, MA: Harvard University Press, 2015); James Pfiffner, *Torture as Public Policy* (Boulder, CO: Paradigm, 2011); and Tracy Lightcap, *The Politics of Torture* (New York: Palgrave Macmillan, 2011).

18. Mark Bowden, "The Dark Art of Interrogation," *The Atlantic*, October 2003; and Louis Michael Seidman, "Torture's Truth," *University of Chicago Law Review* 72, no. 3 (2005): 881–83.

19. Pfiffner, "Efficacy of Coercive Interrogation," 127, 147.

20. For examples, see Mary Ellen O'Connell, "Affirming the Ban on Harsh Interrogation," *Ohio State Law Journal* 66 (2005): 1261n130.

21. See Rodriguez, *Hard Measures*; and Soufan, *The Black Banners*.

22. Rodriguez, *Hard Measures*, xiii, 103–4, 242.

23. Mitchell, *Enhanced Interrogation*, 197.

24. Michael Hayden and Michael B. Mukasey, "The President Ties His Own Hands on Terror," *Wall Street Journal*, April 17, 2009; George J. Tenet, Porter J. Goss, Michael V. Hayden, John E. McLaughlin, Albert M. Calland, and Stephen R. Kappes, "Ex-CIA Directors: Interrogations Saved Lives," *Wall Street Journal*, December 10, 2014; and Rodriguez, *Hard Measures*, 112.

25. Rodriguez, *Hard Measures*, 241.

26. Rodriguez, *Hard Measures*, 250.

27. Greg Miller, "John Brennan CIA Hearing Exposes Skepticism about U.S. Antiterrorism Efforts," *Washington Post*, February 7, 2013, https://www.washingtonpost.com/world/national-security/brennan-defends-drone-strike-policies/2013/02/07/.

28. Spencer Ackerman, "Some Will Call Me a Torturer: CIA Man Reveals Secret Jail," wired.com, July 1, 2011.

29. Ross and Esposito, "CIA's Harsh Interrogation Techniques Described."

30. Steven G. Bradbury, "Memorandum for John A. Rizzo, Senior Deputy General Counsel, Central Intelligence Agency, 'Re: Application of United States Obligations Under Book 16 of the Convention Against Torture to Certain Techniques that May Be Used in the Interrogation of High Value al Qaeda Detainees,'" May 30, 2005, 10.

31. Rejali, *Torture and Democracy*, 503.

32. Rejali, *Torture and Democracy*, 508–10.

33. McCoy, *A Question of Torture*, 120–21 and 141; and Tony Lagouranis, *Fear Up Harsh: An Army Interrogator's Dark Journey Through Iraq* (New York: New American Library, 2007): 181.

34. Senate Select Committee on Intelligence, "Committee Study of the Central Intelligence Agency's Detention and Interrogation Program (Report)," US Senate, December 3, 2014.

35. Director, Central Intelligence Agency, *CIA Comments on the Senate Select Committee on Intelligence Report on the Rendition, Detention, and Interrogation Program*

(Washington: DC, Government Printing Office, June 27, 2013); and Tenet et al., "Ex-CIA Directors: Interrogations Saved Lives," 3–4, 91–92, and 280–81.

36. Siobhan Gorman, Devlin Barrett, Felicia Schwartz, and Dion Nissenbaum, "Senate Report Calls CIA Interrogation Tactics Ineffective," *Wall Street Journal*, December 9, 2014. For additional criticisms of the SCCI report see David Cole, "Did the Torture Report Give the CIA a Bum Rap?" *New York Times*, February 20, 2015, available at https://www. nytimes.com/2015/02/22/opinion/sunday/did-the-torture-report-give-the-cia-a-bum-rap.html; and Robert Jervis, "The Torture Blame Game: The Botched Senate Report on the CIA's Misdeeds," *Foreign Affairs*, May–June 2015, https://www.foreignaffairs.com/ reviews/2015-04-20/torture-blame-game.

37. Rodriguez, *Hard Measures*, 110; Soufan, *The Black Banners*, 515 and 536; Pfiffner, "The Efficacy of Coercive Interrogation," 147; and Mitchell, *Enhanced Interrogation*, 164–65.

38. Mayer, *The Dark Side*, 269, 276.

39. Mitchell, *Enhanced Interrogation*, 149, 164–65.

40. Pfiffner, "The Efficacy of Coercive Interrogation," 147.

41. Rodriguez, *Hard Measures*, 58, 71, 80 and 85; Mitchell, *Enhanced Interrogation*, 71–74, 96.

42. Soufan, *The Black Banners*, 408.

43. Rodriguez, *Hard Measures*, 60–61; and Soufan, *The Black Banners*, 398, 400, 406, 413, 423.

44. Rodriguez, *Hard Measures*, 176, 242.

45. Mitchell, *Enhanced Interrogation*, 28–43.

46. Sanford Levinson, "Contemplating Torture," in *Torture: A Collection*, ed. Sanford Levinson (Oxford: Oxford University Press, 2004), 33.

47. Philip N. S. Rumney, "Is Coercive Interrogation of Terrorist Suspects Effective? A Response to Bagaric and Clarke," *University of San Francisco Law Review* 40 (winter 2006): 485n26, citing Marcy Strauss, "Torture," *New York Law School Review* 48, no. 201 (2004): 263.

48. Louis Michael Seidman, "Torture's Truth," *University of Chicago Law Review* 72, no. 3 (2005): 882.

49. Lisa Silverman, *Tortured Subjects: Pain, Truth, and the Body in Early Modern France* (Chicago: University of Chicago Press, 2001), 89–90, 192.

50. See for example Robert Lifton, *Thought Reform and the Psychology of Totalism* (New York: Norton 1961); Nathan Leites and Elsa Bernaut, *Ritual of Liquidation: The Case of the Moscow Trials* (Glencoe, IL: Free Press, 1954); and Rejali, *Torture and Democracy*, 476.

51. Rejali, *Torture and Democracy*, 494–99.

52. Darius Rejali, "The Field of Torture Today: Ten Years On from Torture and Democracy," in Steven J. Barela, Mark Fallon, Gloria Gaggioli, and Jens David Ohlin, *Interrogation and Torture: Integrating Efficacy with Law and Morality* (Oxford: Oxford University Press, 2020), 93.

53. Rejali, *Torture and Democracy*, 462, citing Ian Cobain, "The Secrets of the London Cage," *Guardian*, November 12, 2005, 8.

54. Cobain, "The Secrets of the London Cage," 8.

55. Albert D. Biderman, *March to Calumny: The Story of American POW's in the Korean War*; and Albert D. Biderman, "Communist Techniques of Coercive Interrogation," Air Force Personnel and Training Research Center: Office for Social Science Programs, December 1956.

56. Fallon, *Unjustifiable Means*, 17, 117. The manual is the *CIA Document of Human Manipulation: KUBARK Counterintelligence Manual* (New York: BN Publishing, 2012), 94. Though the KUBARK Manual is the most recent declassified CIA interrogation manual, it is fifty years old and dedicates only two ambiguous paragraphs to torture.

57. Rejali, *Torture and Democracy*, 482–23, citing John McGuffin, *The Guineapigs* (Harmondsworth: Penguin, 1974), 135.

58. Rejali, *Torture and Democracy*, 493.

59. Rejali, *Torture and Democracy*, 491–92; and McCoy, *A Question of Torture*, 19.

60. Martin Edwin Andersen, "Is Torture an Option in the War on Terror?" *Insight on the News*, June 17, 2002.

61. Rejali, *Torture and Democracy*, 491–92.

62. Rejali, *Torture and Democracy*, 513–35; Mark Moyar, *Phoenix and the Birds of Prey* (Annapolis, MD: Naval Institute Press, 1997), 60, 102–3; and Anderson, "Is Torture an Option in War on Terror?"

63. McCoy, *A Question of Torture*, 102.

64. McCoy, *A Question of Torture*, 180.

65. William Ranney Levi, "Interrogation's Law," *Yale Law Review* 118, no. 1434 (2009): 1477.

66. Bowden, "The Dark Art of Interrogation."

67. Alan M. Dershowitz, *Why Terrorism Works: Understanding the Threat, Responding to the Challenge* (New Haven: Yale University Press, 2002), 150.

68. Ron Hassner, "The Myth of the Ticking Bomb," *Washington Quarterly* 41, no. 1 (March 2018).

69. Lu Ann Homza, ed. and trans., *The Spanish Inquisition: 1478–1614, An Anthology of Sources* (Indianapolis: Hackett, 2006): 45–46.

70. See for example Jean-Pierre Dedieu, *L'administration de la Foi: L'Inquisition de Tolède (XVIe–XVIIIe Siècle)* (Madrid: Bibliothèque de la Casa de Velázquez, 1992); Ricardo García-Cárcel, *Orígenes de la Inquisición Española: El Tribunal de Valencia, 1478–1530* (Barcelona: Ediciones Península, 1976); and Gustav Henningsen, "The Database of the Spanish Inquisition: The Relaciones de Causas Project Revisited," in Heinz Mohnhaupt and Dieter Simon, eds., *Vorträge zur Justizforschung* (Frankfurt: Vittorio Klostermann, 1993), 43–85.

71. Michael I. Handel, "Intelligence and the Problem of Strategic Surprise," *Journal of Strategic Studies* 7, no. 3 (1984): 229–81; Roberta Wohlstetter, "Cuba and Pearl Harbor: Hindsight and Foresight," *Foreign Affairs* 43 (1965): 691–707; Janice Stein, "The 1973 Intelligence Failure: A Reconsideration," *Jerusalem Quarterly* 24 (summer 1982): 41–50; Michael Herman, *Intelligence Power in Peace and War* (Cambridge: Cambridge University Press, 1996).

## 2. THREE MYTHS ABOUT THE SPANISH INQUISITION

1. Edward Peters, *Inquisition* (Berkeley: University of California Press, 1989), 65.

2. Toby Green, *Inquisition: The Reign of Fear* (New York: Thomas Dunne, 2007), 72, citing Jiménez Monteserin, *Introducción a la Inquisición Española* (Madrid: Editora Nacional, 1980), 426–27.

3. Green, *Inquisition*, 68–69, drawing on comparisons with criminal courts in Castile, Cataluña, Granada, Portugal, and Brazil; and Peters, *Inquisition*, 92, drawing on inquisitorial literature. For dissenting opinions on the brutality of the Inquisition see Green, *Inquisition*, 69–70.

4. Henry Kamen, *The Spanish Inquisition: A Historical Revision* (New Haven: Yale, 2014), 238.

5. Henry Charles Lea, *A History of the Inquisition of Spain* (New York: Macmillan, 1907), 3:8.

6. Jane S. Gerber, *The Jews of Spain: A History of the Sephardic Experience* (New York: Free Press, 1992), 120–43.

7. Peters, *Inquisition*, 65.

8. Haliczer, *Inquisition and Society in the Kingdom of Valencia* (Berkeley, CA: California University Press, 1990), 67–68, 79; Lea, *A History of the Inquisition of Spain*, 3:5.

9. Peters, *Inquisition*, 92; Lea, *A History of the Inquisition of Spain*, 3:2.

10. Kamen, *The Spanish Inquisition*, 247.

11. Haliczer, *Inquisition and Society*, 74–75, 79, 374n87; E. William Monter, *Frontiers of Heresy* (Cambridge, MA: Cambridge University Press, 1990), 74–75; Kamen, *The Spanish Inquisition*, 239, citing Ricardo García-Cárcel: *Herejia y Sociedad en el Siglo XVI: La Inquisición en Valencia 1530–1609* (Barcelona: Ediciones Península, 1980); Bartolomé Bennassar, ed., *L'Inquisition Espagnole XVe-XIXe Siècle* (Paris: Hachette, 1979), 115–16; and Bartolomé Benassar, *Inquisición Española: Poder Político y Control Social* (Barcelona: Grijalbo, 1981), 15–39. For a critique of these statistics, see Kamen, *The Spanish Inquisition*, 248.

12. Green, *Inquisition*, 69.

13. Lea, *A History of the Inquisition of Spain*, 3:33.

14. Haliczer, *Inquisition and Society*, 67–68; Lea, *A History of the Inquisition of Spain*, 3:2.

15. Peters, *Inquisition*, 16.

16. Lisa Silverman, *Tortured Subjects: Pain, Truth, and the Body in Early Modern France* (Chicago: University of Chicago Press, 2001); and Lea, *A History of the Inquisition of Spain*, 3:3.

17. Green, *Inquisition*, 72.

18. Lea, *A History of the Inquisition of Spain*, 3:7.

19. Lea, *A History of the Inquisition of Spain*, 3:7.

20. Lea, *A History of the Inquisition of Spain*, 3:2 and 17–18.

21. Monter, *Frontiers of Heresy*, 75.

22. Lea, *A History of the Inquisition of Spain*, 3:3, 23, and 27–30.

23. Peters, *Inquisition*, 65, 79–80.

24. Kamen, *The Spanish Inquisition*, 239. Halizcer found that less than 1 percent of the torture sessions in his survey recurred. Haliczer, *Inquisition and Society*, 79–80.

25. Haim Beinart: *Conversos on Trial: The Inquisition in Ciudad Real* (Jerusalem: Magnes Press, 1981), 237; Lea, *A History of the Inquisition of Spain*, 3:232; and Monter, *Frontiers of Heresy*, 216.

26. Monter, *Frontiers of Heresy*, 216.

27. John W. Schiemann, *Does Torture Work?* (Oxford: Oxford University Press, 2016), 89; Edward Peters, *Torture* (Philadelphia: University of Pennsylvania Press, 1985), 68; Henry Charles Leah and Edward Peters, eds., *Torture* (Philadelphia: University of Pennsylvania Press, 1973), 111; and John H. Langbein, *Torture and the Law of Proof: Europe and England in the Ancien Regime* (Chicago: University of Chicago Press, 1978), 7.

28. James Pfiffner, "The Efficacy of Coercive Interrogation," in *Examining Torture: Empirical Studies of States Repression*, eds. Tracy Lightcap and James P. Pfiffner (New York: Palgrave, 2014), 142, 151–52; Darius Rejali, *Torture and Democracy* (Princeton: Princeton University Press, 2007, 462; Jane Mayer, "Outsourcing Torture: The Secret History of America's 'Extraordinary Rendition' Program," *New Yorker*, February 14, 2005; and Schiemann, *Does Torture Work*, 211.

29. Lea, *A History of the Inquisition of Spain*, 3:18.

30. "Manuel de Lucena, 1594, Mexico City," Bancroft MSS 96/95m, 2, Berkeley: U.C. Berkeley Bancroft Library, 283v–284r.

31. Kamen, *The Spanish Inquisition*, 231; and Halizcer, *Inquisition and* Society, 68.

32. Lea, *A History of the Inquisition of Spain*, 3:24–25, translating from the Archivo Histórico Nacional, Inquisición de Toledo, Leg. 138.

33. Lea, *A History of the Inquisition of Spain*, 3:26, and 234.

34. Monter, *Frontiers of Heresy*, 75.

35. Indeed, heresy (in contrast to witchcraft) was by definition a group act, so the Inquisition sought to save not only the soul of the individual involved but also their fellow heretics. Peters, *Torture*, 66.

36. Peters, *Torture*, 11.

37. Peters, *Inquisition*, 65 and 93.

38. Gerber, *The Jews of Spain*, 133.

39. Green, *Inquisition*, 69–70.

40. Green, *Inquisition*, 92.

41. Monter, *Frontiers of Heresy*, 152–54.

42. On imprisonment as a form of interrogation, see James Buchanan Given, *Inquisition and Medieval Society: Power, Discipline, and Resistance in Languedoc* (Ithaca: Cornell University Press, 2001). Robert Conquest, in his study of the Stalinist Terror, refers to this form of interrogation as "the Long Interrogation." Robert Conquest, *The Great Terror: A Reassessment* (Oxford, UK: Oxford University Press, 2008): 125.

43. Martin A. Cohen, *The Martyr: Luis de Carvajal, A Secret Jew in Sixteenth-Century Mexico* (Albuquerque: University of New Mexico Press, 1973): 151.

44. Nicolas Eymerich, *Directorium Inquisitorum*, composed around 1376. Roman edition of 1578, 341. Yale University, Division of Rare and Manuscript Collections, available at http://ebooks.library.cornell.edu/cgi/t/text/text-idx?c=witch;idno=wit045.


## 3. LEARNING TO TORTURE

1. Toby Green, *Inquisition: The Reign of Fear* (New York: Thomas Dunne, 2007), 78.

2. Henry Charles Lea, *A History of the Inquisition of Spain* (New York: Macmillan, 1907): 3:8, 72, 76, 82.

3. Henry Kamen, *The Spanish Inquisition A Historical Revision* (New Haven: Yale, 2014), 49.

4. Martin A. Cohen, *The Martyr: Luis de Carvajal, A Secret Jew in Sixteenth-Century Mexico* (Albuquerque: University of New Mexico Press, 1973), 149.

5. Haim Beinart, *Records of the Trials of the Spanish Inquisition in Ciudad Real* (Jerusalem: Israel National Academy of Sciences and Humanities, 1974), 1:xix–xx; Kamen, *The Spanish Inquisition*, 65.

6. Haim Beinart: *Conversos on Trial: The Inquisition in Ciudad Real* (Jerusalem: Magnes Press, 1981): 101, 120.

7. Beinart, *Conversos on Trial*, 72–78.

8. Beinart, *Records*, I:xiv.

9. Beinart, *Records*, I:xv–xviii.

10. Beinart, *Records*, I:trial 3, 70–90.

11. Beinart, *Conversos on Trial*, 62–72.

12. Beinart, *Records*, I:trial 14, 262.

13. Beinart, *Records*, I:trial 14, 262–71.

14. Beinart, *Records*, I:trial 80, 487–504.

15. Beinart, *Records*, I:trial 47.

16. Beinart, *Records*, I:xx; and Green, *Inquisition*, 38.

17. Beinart, *Records*, I:trial 6, 133–62.

18. "Familiars" were lay servants of the Inquisition who received a salary for assisting the prosecutor in his inquiries. They enjoyed exceptional civil privileges as well as an advantaged (and hereditary) position in society. Edward Peters, *Inquisition* (Berkeley: University of California Press, 1989), 91.

19. Beinart, *Records*, I:trial 9, 182–211.

20. Beinart, *Records*, I:trial 81, 505–28.

21. Beinart, *Records*, I:trial 4 and 84, 91 and 551–67.

22. Beinart, *Records*, IV:447.

23. Beinart, *Records*, II:trial 91.

24. Lu Ann Homza, ed. and trans., *The Spanish Inquisition, 1478–1614: An Anthology of Sources* (Indianapolis, IN: Hackett, 2006), 29.

25. Homza, *Spanish Inquisition*, 38.

26. Beinart, *Records*, I:trial 85, 568–79.

27. Beinart, *Records*, I:trial 30.

28. Beinart, *Records*, II:trial 98.

29. Beinart, *Records*, I:trial 19, 315–34.

30. Beinart, *Records*, II:trials 93, 101, and 107.

31. Beinart, *Records*, II:trials 108 and 109.

32. Beinart, *Records*, II:trial 108, my translation.

33. The Bribia, or Brivia or Briuia, was a translation of the Bible into Romance. Stephen Gilman, *Spain of Fernando de Rojas: The Intellectual and Social Landscape of La Celestina* (Princeton, NJ: Princeton University Press, 2015), 241n79.

34. Beinart, *Records*:II, trial 108, my translation.

35. This seems to confirm the claims, made by psychologists who study torture, about the deleterious effects of pain on memory and recall. For a review of those claims, see Shane O'Mara, *Why Torture Doesn't Work* (Cambridge, MA: Harvard University Press, 2015); and Darius Rejali, "The Field of Torture Today: Ten Years On from Torture and Democracy," in Steven J. Barela, Mark Fallon, Gloria Gaggioli, and Jens David Ohlin, *Interrogation and Torture: Integrating Efficacy with Law and Morality* (Oxford: Oxford University Press, 2020), 96–97.

36. Beinart, *Records*, II:trial 108, my translation.

37. Beinart, *Records*, II:trial 108.

38. Beinart, *Record*, II:trial 100.

39. Homza, *Spanish Inquisition*, 51.

40. Beinart, *Record*, II:trial 100, 297; Homza, *Spanish Inquisition*, 54–55.

41. Beinart, *Records*, II:trial 101.

42. Beinart, *Records*, II:trials 102, 103, 104. These trial documents have not survived.

43. Beinart, *Records*, II:trial 105.

44. Beinart, *Records*, II:trial 106.

45. Beinart, *Trials*, II:trial 100, my translation.

46. Beinart, *Trials*, II:trial 103.

47. Beinart, *Trials*, II:trials 101, 105, 107, 113, 114.

48. Beinart, *Trials*, II:106.

49. Beinart, *Trials*, II:115.

50. Beinart, *Trials*, II:108.

51. Beinart, *Trials*, II:116.

52. The prohibition on eating certain animal fats, called *chelev* (suet), is first mentioned in Leviticus, chapter 7.

53. Beinart, *Trials*, II:116, my translation.

54. Beinart, *Trials*, II:trial 112.

## 4. CORRELATES OF TORTURE

1. Spanische Inquisitions-Acten, MSS Yc 2° 20 (1), *Historische Sammlungen der Martin-Luther-Universität Halle-Wittenberg* (hereafter, Halle Ms.).

2. Henry Charles Lea papers, Ms. Coll. 111 Box 102, Folder 1732, Henry Charles Lea Research Collection on the Inquisition, University of Pennsylvania, Philadelphia, PA (hereafter, Lea Ms.).

3. Jaime Contreras and Gustav Henningsen, "Forty-Four Thousand Cases of the Spanish Inquisition (1540–1700): Analysis of a Historical Data Bank," in *The Inquisition*

*in Early Modern Europe*, ed. Gustav Henningsen and John Tedeschi (Dekalb, IL: Northern Illinois University Press, 1986): 100–129; and Robin Vose, "Introduction to Inquisition Trial Transcripts and Records," Hesburgh Libraries of Notre Dame, Department of Rare Books and Special Collections, University of Notre Dame, 2010.

4. George Ryley Scott, *The History of Torture Throughout the Ages* (New York: Columbia University Press), 172.

5. Lea Ms., 9, 36, 118, 11, 65.

6. Lea Ms., 27.

7. Lea Ms., 128, 140.

8. Lea Ms., 105, 64, 52, 70.

9. Lea Ms., 19, 67, 68, and 74, 78.

10. Lea Ms., 41, 54, 55, 71, 104, 124.

11. Lea Ms., 60.

12. Lea Ms., 76, 105, 126, 133.

13. Lea Ms., 54, 57, 61.

14. Lea Ms., 119, 135.

15. Lea Ms., 64.

16. Lea Ms., 144, 67, 77, 144.

17. Henry Charles Lea, *History of the Inquisition of Spain* (New York: Macmillan, 1907), 7.

18. Lea Ms., 121, 128, 64, 73, 137.

19. Lea Ms., 78, 118, 125, 126, 142.

20. Henry Kamen, *The Spanish Inquisition: A Historical Revision* (New Haven, CT: Yale University Press, 2014), 232, 247.


## 5. EXPLORATORY TORTURE

1. I have standardized the spelling of names in these chapters following Martin A. Cohen's work, which served as my primary reference point. For example, in the trial manuscripts the surname Carvajal appears in several variations, including Carbajal, Carabajal, and Caravajal. Similarly, I follow Cohen in preferring Constança over the more modern Constanza, Enríquez over Henríquez, Almeida rather than Almeyda, etc. Martin A. Cohen, *The Martyr: Luis de Carvajal, A Secret Jew in Sixteenth-Century Mexico* (Albuquerque: University of New Mexico Press, 2001).

2. Cohen, *The Martyr*, 245; Toby Green, *Inquisition: The Reign of Fear* (New York: Thomas Dunne, 2007), 84–87, 157–63; and Anna Lanyon, *Fire & Song: The Story of Luis de Carvajal and the Mexican Inquisition* (New York: Allen & Unwin, 2012).

3. I thank Charles Faulhaber for sharing this information with me. See also "Rare Documents Shed Light on Grisly Mexican Inquisition," *Jewish News of Northern California*, October 11, 1996. In Cohen's authoritative account of the Carvajal trials, the Lucena file is listed as "case missing." Cohen, *The Martyr*, 279.

4. David Gitlitz, *Living in Silverado: Secret Jews in the Silver Mining Towns of Colonial Mexico* (Albuquerque: University of New Mexico Press, 2019), appendix 2 and appendix 3, 310–27.

5. See Martin A. Cohen, trans., "The Autobiography of Luis de Carvajal, the Younger," *American Jewish Historical Quarterly* 55, no. 3 (March 1966): 277–318; and Seymour B. Liebman, *The Enlightened: The Writings of Luis de Carvajal, el Mozo*, trans. and ed. (Coral Gables, FL: University of Miami Press, 1967).

6. The history that follows draws on Arnold Wiznitzer, "Crypto-Jews in Mexico during the Sixteenth Century," *American Jewish Historical Quarterly* 51, no. 3 (March 1962): 168–97, 199–214; Stanley M. Hordes, *To the Ends of the Earth: A History of the Crypto-Jews of New Mexico* (New York: Columbia University Press, 2005), 72–103; Alfonso Toro,

*La Familia Carvajal* (Mexico City: Editorial Patria, 1944); Seymour B. Liebman, *The Jews in News Spain: Faith, Flame, and the Inquisition* (Coral Gables, FL: University of Miami Press, 1970); Richard E. Greenleaf, *The Mexican Inquisition of the Sixteenth Century* (Albuquerque: University of New Mexico Press, 1969); Samuel Temkin, *Luis de Carvajal: The Origins of Nuevo Reino de Leon* (Santa Fe: Sunstone Press, 2011); Cohen, *The Martyr*; Green, *Inquisition*; and Gitlitz, *Living in Silverado*.

7. On the Inquisition in Mexico, see Solange Alberro, *Inquisición y Sociedad en México, 1571–1700* (Mexico: Fondo de Cultura Económica, 1988); and John Chuchiak IV, ed., *The Inquisition in New Spain, 1536–1820: A Documentary History* (Baltimore: The Johns Hopkins University Press, 2012).

8. Wiznitzer, "Crypto-Jews in Mexico," 169, 175.

9. Gitlitz, *Living in Silverado*, 293.

10. Cohen, *The Martyr*, 83; and Wiznitzer, "Crypto-Jews in Mexico," 184.

11. Cohen, *The Martyr*, 85–90.

12. Cohen, *The Martyr*, 142, citing testimony of Felipe Núñez of March 7 and 8, 1589, trial of Isabel de Andrada.

13. A full English translation of this indictment appears in Cohen, *The Martyr*, 160–62.

14. "Trial of Doña Francisca de Caravajal, Spanish Transcript of Processo," series 1, box 2, folder 2, Mexican Inquisition Collection, American Jewish Historical Society, New York, 235. My translation.

15. See for example Vicente Riva Palacio, *El Libro Rojo: 1520–1857* (Mexico: Díaz de León y White, 1870).

16. "Trial of Doña Francisca," 238. My translation.

17. "Trial of Doña Francisca," 245.

18. "Trial of Doña Francisca," 259–86.

19. "Trial of Doña Francisca," 88.

20. "Trial of Doña Francisca," 92.

21. Temkin, *Luis de Carvajal*, 162–63; and Wiznitzer, "Crypto-Jews in Mexico," 186–87.

22. Wiznitzer, "Crypto-Jews in Mexico," 199.

23. Green, *Inquisition*, 161–62.

24. Gitlitz, *Living in Silverado*, appendix 2, 310–24.

25. Gitlitz, *Living in Silverado*, appendix 2, 310–24.

26. "Trial of Beatriz Enríquez La Payua, Spanish Transcript of Processo," Series I, Box 8, Folder 1, Mexican Inquisition Collection, American Jewish Historical Society, New York.

27. "Processo contra Gonzalo Pérez Ferro, 1589," Archivo General de la Nación, Mexico, 61, 126, 11.

28. Gitlitz *Living in Silverado*, 115 and 122; Cohen, *The Martyr*, 101.

29. "Processo contra Tomás de Fonseca, 1590," Archivo General de la Nación, Mexico, 61, 127, 1; and "Processo contra Tomás de Fonseca, 1595," Archivo General de la Nación, Mexico, 61, 156, 4.

30. Gitlitz, *Living in Silverado*, 213 and appendix 2, 310–24.

31. Gitlitz, *Living in Silverado*, 261–62.

## 6. CORROBORATIVE TORTURE

1. Her testimony is recounted in full in several trials, including "Trial of Beatriz Enríquez La Payua, Spanish Transcript of Processo," Series I, Box 8, Folder 1, Mexican Inquisition Collection, American Jewish Historical Society, New York, 157–58.

2. "Manuel de Lucena, 1594, Mexico City," Bancroft MSS 96/95m, 2 (Berkeley: University of California, Berkeley, Bancroft Library) (hereafter Lucena Ms.), 15–22.

3. Lucena Ms., 27–30.

4. Lucena Ms., 282–85 verso.

5. Lucena Ms., 23–26.

6. Lucena Ms., 32.

7. Lucena Ms., 37–40.

8. Lucena Ms., 41–43.

9. Lucena Ms., 44–45.

10. Lucena Ms., 46–69.

11. Lucena Ms., 74 verso.

12. Lucena Ms., 288.

13. Lucena Ms., 70–85.

14. Lucena Ms., 295–304.

15. Lucena Ms., 302.

16. Lucena Ms., 6.

17. Lucena Ms., 147–52.

18. David Gitlitz, *Living in Silverado: Secret Jews in the Silver Mining Towns of Colonial Mexico* (Albuquerque: University of New Mexico Press, 2019), 272.

19. Lucena Ms., 86–94.

20. Lucena Ms., 94–122.

21. Lucena Ms., 317–19 verso.

22. Lucena Ms., 305.

23. Lucena Ms., 317–19 verso.

24. Lucena Ms., 123–46, and 175–89.

25. Lucena Ms., 323–82.

26. Lucena Ms., 153–56, 157–74, 190–92.

27. Gitlitz, *Living in Silverado*, 215–16.

28. Lucena Ms., 450–53 verso.

29. Gitzliz, *Living in Silverado*, 213.

30. The standard version of this prayer, anglicized, is, "Sh'ma Yisra'eil Adonai Eloheinu Adonai echad; Barukh sheim k'vod malkhuto l'olam va'ed." Doña Leonor de Carvajal offered her own version of the prayer in her 1595 trial: "Shema Israel Adonay Eloin Paro es em que vos Malcuto Eloin Bael." Gitlitz, *Living in Silverado*, 202.

31. Cohen, *The Martyr*, 94–96.

32. Gitlitz, *Living in Silverado*, 202.

33. The trial of Pedro Rodríguez Saz is not available but his testimony is recounted in full in several trials, including "Juan Rodríguez de Silva: Spanish Transcript of Processo," Series I, Box 10, Folder 1, Mexican Inquisition Collection, American Jewish Historical Society, New York, 15–20. My translation.

34. Her testimony is recounted in full in several trials, including in "Trial of Constança Rodríguez, Spanish Transcript of Processo," Series I, Box 10, Folder 3, Mexican Inquisition Collection, American Jewish Historical Society, New York, 41. My translation.

35. "Trial of Constança Rodríguez," 58–59. My translation.

36. Trial of Constança Rodríguez," 66–68, 86–88, 135–37.

37. "Trial of Constança Rodríguez," 75.

38. Lucena Ms., 340 and 305.

39. The trial manuscripts for Luis de Carvajal were reprinted as Luis de Carvajal, *Procesos de Luis de Carvajal (el mozo)* (Mexico: Talleres Gráficos de la Nación, 1935). The events are recounted in Martin A. Cohen, *The Martyr: Luis de Carvajal, A Secret Jew in Sixteenth-Century Mexico* (Albuquerque: University of New Mexico Press, 1973), 226–75; and Toby Green, *Inquisition: The Reign of Fear* (New York: Thomas Dunne, 2007), 84–87, 157–63.

40. Green, *Inquisition*, 84–85.

41. Carvajal, *Procesos*, 307–9. My translation.

42. Cohen, *The Martyr*, 246n27, citing Carvajal, "Processo," 366.

43. Cohen, *The Martyr*, 255.

44. Green, *Inquisition*, 163; Cohen, *The Martyr*, 257.

45. Cohen, *The Martyr*, 267.

46. The Inquisition sentenced minor offenders in private sessions. These convictions are not included in my analysis here.

47. "Processo Contra Antonio Díaz de Cáceres, 1596," Archivo General de la Nación, Mexico, 61, 159, 1.

48. Gitlitz, *Living in Silverado*, 227, 254, and appendix 2, 312–13.

49. Cohen, *The Martyr*, 262–63, Gitlitz, *Living in Silverado*, 256–57.

50. Cohen, *The Martyr*, 263, Gitlitz, *Living in Silverado*, 257.

## 7. LESSONS FROM THE SPANISH INQUISITION

1. Scholars have referred to this anti-Spanish and anti-Catholic disinformation campaign, in which myths about the Inquisition came to play a central part, as the "Black Legend." See Edward Peters, *Inquisition* (Berkeley: University of California Press, 1989); and Henry Kamen, *The Spanish Inquisition: A Historical Revision* (New Haven: Yale University Press, 2014).

2. According to Christopher Einolf, American soldiers learned water torture from their Filipino allies, the Macabebe Scouts, who had practiced it for years, having learned it from the Tagalogs. The Tagalogs were an ethnic group that fought alongside the Spanish during the Philippine Revolution of 1896. They may thus have passed on a variation of the old inquisitorial practice. In this variant of waterboarding, sometimes referred to as "pumping," soldiers forced a prisoner's mouth open with a club or a gag or a gun barrel, poured water down the throat and nose until the stomach was filled with water, then hit the stomach with the butt of a gun. Christopher J. Einolf, *America in the Philippines, 1899–1902: The First Torture Scandal* (New York: Palgrave Macmillan, 2014), 51–58. See also Darius Rejali, "The Field of Torture Today: Ten Years On from Torture and Democracy," in Steven J. Barela, Mark Fallon, Gloria Gaggioli, and Jens David Ohlin, *Interrogation and Torture: Integrating Efficacy with Law and Morality* (Oxford: Oxford University Press, 2020), 82.

3. Kelly M. Greenhill, "'24' on the Brain," *Los Angeles Times*, May 28, 2007, available at http://articles.latimes.com/2007/may/28/opinion/oe-greenhill28.

4. James E. Mitchell, *Enhanced Interrogation: Inside the Minds and Motives of the Islamic Terrorists Trying to Destroy America* (New York: Crown, 2016), 31–34.

5. Mitchell, *Enhanced Interrogation*, 97–98.

6. US Senate, "Senate Intelligence Committee Study on CIA Detention and Interrogation Program," December 13, 2012, 384–88, available at http://www.feinstein.senate.gov/public/index.cfm/files/serve?File_id=7c85429a-ec38-4bb5-968f-289799bf6d0e&SK=D500C4EBC500E1D256BA519211895909.

7. Michael Hayden and Michael B. Mukasey, "The President Ties His Own Hands on Terror," *Wall Street Journal*, April 17, 2009; Mitchell, *Enhanced Interrogation*, 76, 132–34.

8. Rodriguez suggests that Ghul offered this information under torture but a report by the Senate Intelligence Committee claims that he did so prior to undergoing torture. Mitchell provides a detailed account of what Ghul divulged prior to torture as opposed to after torture. Jose Rodriguez, *Hard Measures: How Aggressive CIA Actions after 9/11 Saved American Lives* (New York: Threshold Editions, 2012), 108–9; Mitchell, *Enhanced Interrogation*, 193; and US Senate, "Senate Intelligence Committee Study," 387–88, note 2190.

9. Rodriguez, *Hard Measures*, 111.

10. Mitchell, *Enhanced Interrogation*, 191–92.

11. Mitchell, *Enhanced Interrogation*, 196.

12. Owais Tohid, "Bin Laden Bodyguard's Satellite Phone Calls Helped Lead US Forces to Hiding Place," *Christian Science Monitor*, May 2, 2011.

13. US Senate, "Senate Intelligence Committee Study," 390. The report places some of this information in doubt.

14. Darius Rejali, *Torture and Democracy* (Princeton: Princeton University Press, 2007), 463; and John W. Schiemann, *Does Torture Work?* (Oxford: Oxford University Press, 2016).

15. Rejali, *Torture and Democracy*, 463, citing US Army, *U.S. Army Field Manual 30–15 Intelligence Interrogations* (Washington, DC: Headquarters, Department of the Army, 1982).

16. Philip N. S. Rumney, "Is Coercive Interrogation of Terrorist Suspects Effective? A Response to Bagaric and Clarke," *University of San Francisco Law Review* 40 (winter 2006): 496.

17. Brian Ross and Richard Esposito, "CIA's Harsh Interrogation Techniques Described," *ABC News*, November 18, 2005.

18. Rejali, *Torture and Democracy*, 488, 500; Neil Boorman, "5 Arguments against Torture," July 28, 2011, online at amnesty.org.uk; and sources cited in Mark Costanzo and Ellen Gerrity, "The Effects and Effectiveness of Using Torture as an Interrogation Device: Using Research to Inform the Policy Debate," *Social Issues in Policy Review* 3, no.1 (2009): 183.

19. I thank Doyle Hodges for bringing this point to my attention.

20. Samantha Newbery, Bob Brecher, Philippe Sands, and Brian Stewart, "Interrogation, Intelligence, and the Issue of Human Rights," *Intelligence and National Security* 24, no.5 (October 2009): 642.

21. Aldert Vrij, *Detecting Lies and Deceit: The Psychology of Lying and the Implications for Professional Practice* (New York: John Wiley and Sons, 2000); and Ariel Neuman and Daniel Salinas-Serrano, "Custodial Interrogations: What We Know, What We Do, and What We Can Learn from Law Enforcement Experiences," in *Educing Information: Interrogation—Science and Art* (Washington, DC: National Defense Intelligence College, 2005).

22. Contrast, for example, Rodriguez's description of cross-checking during coercive interrogation, quoted below, with Soufan's nearly identical description of the same process during noncoercive interrogation. Rodriguez, *Hard Measure*, 233; and Ali H. Soufan, *The Black Banners: Inside the Story of 9/11 and the War Against al-Qaeda* (New York: W. W. Norton, 2011), 317.

23. Rodriguez, *Hard Measures*, 233; Mitchell, *Enhanced Interrogation*, 66; and Hayden and Mukasey, "The President Ties His Own Hands."

24. Mark Bowden, "The Dark Art of Interrogation," *The Atlantic*, October 2003.

25. Rodriguez, *Hard Measures*, 233.

26. Bowden, "The Dark Art of Interrogation."

27. Rejali, *Torture and Democracy*, 461.

28. Rodriguez, *Hard Measures*, 233.

29. Mitchell, *Enhanced Interrogation*, 166–68.

30. James Pfiffner, "The Efficacy of Coercive Interrogation," in *Examining Torture: Empirical Studies of States Repression*, eds. Tracy Lightcap and James P. Pfiffner (New York: Palgrave, 2014), 147. For similar claims regarding the torture of al-Qahtani, see Jane Mayer, *The Dark Side: The Inside Story of How the War on Terror Turned into a War on American Ideals* (New York: Anchor Books, 2009), 211.

31. Rumney, "Is Coercive Interrogation of Terrorist Suspects Effective?" 489–90, citing B'Tselem, "Legislation Allowing the Use of Physical Force and Mental Coercion in Interrogations by the General Security Services" (Jerusalem: The Israeli Information Center for Human Rights, 2000), 50.

32. Rejali, *Torture and Democracy*, 474; Soufan, *Black Banners*, 425; and Rodriguez, *Hard Measures*, 62. For a rare dissenting opinion see Fritz Allhoff, *Terrorism, Ticking Time Bombs, and Torture* (Chicago: University of Chicago Press, 2012), 146.

33. The timelines do not suffice to ascertain precisely how much of this time con-sisted of torture as opposed to nonviolent interrogation prior to torture or pauses between torture sessions. Mitchell proposes that thirty days usually suffice for torture to reveal whether a detainee "would be willing to cooperate" but he also notes that most detainees "started trying to cooperate" after seventy-two hours of torture. Since he does not define successful cooperation, and since the protocol he developed for the CIA assumes that noncoercive methods are attempted prior to torture, there may be no tension between his briefer timelines and the longer timelines proposed by others. Mitchell, *Enhanced Inter-rogation*, 43, 157, 201.

34. Alfred W. McCoy, *A Question of Torture: CIA Interrogation from the Cold War to the War on Terror* (New York: Metropolitan Books, 2006), 70.

35. Rejali, *Torture and Democracy*, 507–8; and Rumney, "Is Coercive Interrogation of Terrorist Suspects Effective?" 488.

36. Raymond Bonner, Don Van Natta Jr., and Amy Waldman, "Threats and Responses: Interrogations; Questioning Terror Suspects in a Dark and Surreal World," *New York Times*, March 9, 2003. Rodriguez proposes that AZ was tortured even longer—for five months—before he cooperated. Rodriguez, *Hard Measures*, 62, 80–81, 183–84.

37. Rodriguez, *Hard Measures*, 92, 104.

38. Philippe Sands, "The Green Light," *Vanity Fair*, April 2, 2008; and Pfiffner, "The Efficacy of Coercive Interrogation," 130.

39. Bonner, Van Natta Jr., and Waldman, "Threats and Responses."

40. Steven Erlanger and Chris Hedges, "A Nation Challenged: The Trail; Terror Cells Slip Through Europe's Grasp," *New York Times*, December 28, 2001.

41. Mayer, *The Dark Side*, 269; and Erlanger and Hedges, "A Nation Challenged."

42. See, for example, Martin Edwin Andersen, "Is Torture an Option in the War on Ter-ror?" *Insight on the News*, June 17, 2002; and Mirko Bagarig and Julie Clarke, "Not Enough Official Torture in the World? The Circumstances in Which Torture is Morally Justifiable," *University of San Francisco Law Review* 39 (spring 2005): 612.

43. Ron Hassner, "The Myth of the Ticking Bomb," *Washington Quarterly* 41, no. 1 (March 2018): 83–94.

44. Alan M. Dershowitz, *Why Terrorism Works: Understanding the Threat, Responding to the Challenge* (New Haven: Yale University Press, 2002), 140.

45. See for example Mark Mazzetti, "Panetta Open to Tougher Methods in Some CIA Interrogation," *New York Times*, February 5, 2009, available at http://www.nytimes.com/2009/02/06/us/politics/06cia.html; Adam Serwer, "Did General Petraeus Change His Position on Torture?" *Washington Post*, June 24, 2011, available at https://www.washingtonpost.com/blogs/plum-line/post/did-general-petraeus-change-his-position-on-torture/2011/03/04/AGxR04iH_blog.html?utm_term=.178e9811b622; Memorandum from Steven G. Bradbury to John A. Rizzo, "Regarding Application of 18 U.S.C. Sec-tions 2340–2340A to Certain Techniques that May Be Used in the Interrogation of a High Value al-Qaeda Detainee," May 2005, 41; Rodriguez, *Hard Measures*, 231, 253; and Tony Lagouranis, *Fear Up Harsh: An Army Interrogator's Dark Journey Through Iraq* (New York: New American Library, 2007), 60, 246.

46. Rejali, *Torture and Democracy*, 476, citing Milovan Djilas, *Of Prisons and Ideas* (San Diego: Harcourt Brace Jovanovich, 1986), 5.

47. Henri Alleg, *The Question*, John Calder trans. (Lincoln: University of Nebraska Press, 1958), 40.

48. *CIA Document of Human Manipulation: KUBARK Counterintelligence Manual* (New York: BN Publishing, 2012), 90. See also Alleg, *The Question*, 47, 62–63.

49. Lagouranis, *Fear Up Harsh*, 95.

50. Mitchell, *Enhanced Interrogation*, 159–61.

51. Mitchell, *Enhanced Interrogation*, 71.

52. Rodriguez, *Hard Measures*, 103; and Charles Fried and Gregory Fried, *Because It Is Wrong: Torture, Privacy, and Presidential Power in the Age of Terror* (New York: W. W. Norton, 2010), 69.

53. Alleg, *The Question*, 43.

54. Mitchell, *Enhanced Interrogation*, 159–61.

55. Pfiffner, "The Efficacy of Coercive Interrogation," 142, 151–52; Rejali, *Torture and Democracy*, 462; and Jane Mayer, "Outsourcing Torture: The Secret History of America's 'Extraordinary Rendition' Program," *New Yorker*, February 14, 2005.

56. For a review of those arguments, see Shane O'Mara, *Why Torture Doesn't Work* (Cambridge, MA: Harvard University Press, 2015).

57. Robert Conquest, *The Great Terror: A Reassessment* (Oxford: Oxford University Press, 2008), 125.

58. McCoy, *A Question of Torture*, 42.

59. Rodriguez, *Hard Measures*, 64, 115, 233; and McCoy, *A Question of Torture*, 10.

60. Lagouranis, *Fear Up Harsh*, 33.

61. Costanzo and Gerrity, "The Effects and Effectiveness of Using Torture," 182.

62. Rumney, "Is Coercive Interrogation of Terrorist Suspects Effective?" 491.

63. Rejali, *Torture and Democracy*, 462–63; Conquest, *The Great Terror*, 121–22.

64. *KUBARK*, 94.

65. Rejali, *Torture and Democracy*, 488.

66. Mark Moyar, *Phoenix and the Birds of Prey* (Annapolis, MD: Naval Institute Press, 1997), 102.

67. Mayer "Outsourcing Torture."

68. Mitchell, *Enhanced Interrogation*, 97.

69. Hayden and Mukasey, "The President Ties His Own Hands."

70. Soufan, *The Black Banners*, 293, 309, 312, 445.

71. Soufan, *The Black Banners*, 22.

72. Mitchell, *Enhanced Interrogation*, 27.

73. McCoy, *A Question of Torture*, 139.

74. Lagouranis, *Fear Up Harsh*, 112, 181 and 246; Pfiffner, "Efficacy of Coercive Interrogation," 139; Schiemann, *Does Torture Work* 89; O'Mara, *Why Torture Fails*, 252.

75. KUBARK, 110.

76. Mitchell, *Enhanced Interrogation*, 71.

77. Rumney, "Is Coercive Interrogation of Terrorist Suspects Effective?" 494.

78. Schieman, *Does Torture Work?*, 242, citing Senate Intelligence Committee, "Study on CIA Detention and Interrogation Program," 134, 282–83.

79. Soufan, *The Black Banners*, 423.

80. Mark Fallon, *Unjustifiable Means*,130, citing Mohamedou Ould Slahi, *Guantánamo Diary* (New York: Back Bay Books; 2015).

81. Rejali, *Torture and Democracy*, 504–5; Mayer, "Outsourcing Torture," 105–6, 135; and Rodriguez, *Hard Measures*, 52–53.

82. Rejali, *Torture and Democracy*, 454–55 and 486–87; Rumney, "Is Coercive Interrogation of Terrorist Suspects Effective?" 498; and Rejali, "The Field of Torture Today," 89–91.

83. Sands, "The Green Light."

84. McCoy, *A Question of Torture*, 209.

85. Sands, "The Green Light."

86. Lagouranis, *Fear Up Harsh*, 244–45; Matthew Alexander and John Bruning, *How to Break a Terrorist: The US Interrogators Who Used Brains, not Brutality, to Take Down the Deadliest Man in Iraq* (New York: Simon and Schuster, 2008), 75; Costanzo and Gerrity, "The Effects and Effectiveness of Using Torture," 196–98; David Luban, "Liberalism,

Torture, and the Ticking Bomb," in *Intervention, Terrorism, and Torture*, ed. S. P. Lee (Springer: Netherlands, 2007), 256–58; and McCoy, *A Question of Torture*, 128.

87. Lagouranis, *Fear Up Harsh*, 244–45.

88. William Ranney Levi, "Interrogation's Law," *Yale Law Revie*, 118, no. 1434 (2009)1434–83; and Mayer, "Outsourcing Torture," 248.

89. Lagouranis, *Fear Up Harsh*, 85. See also Tracy Lightcap, *The Politics of Torture* (New York: Palgrave Macmillan, 2011).

90. Pfiffner, "The Efficacy of Coercive Interrogation," 152.

91. Mayer, "Outsourcing Torture," 195.

92. Rejali, *Torture and Democracy*, 486–47. For evidence to the contrary, including the cessation of torture by France and Britain and the regulation of torture by Israeli courts, see Eric Posner and Adrian Vermeule, "Should Coercive Interrogation Be Legal?" *Public Law and Theory Working Papers* (University of Chicago Law School, 2005), 17; and Joseph Lelyveld, "Interrogating Ourselves," *New York Times Magazine*, June 12, 2005.

93. Rejali, *Torture and Democracy*, 454–55.

94. Pfiffner, "The Efficacy of Coercive Interrogation," 129–31.

95. Mark Fallon, *Unjustifiable Means: The Inside Story of How the CIA, Pentagon, and US Government Conspired to Torture* (New York: Regan Arts, 2017), 148.

96. Lagouranis, *Fear Up Harsh*, 80, 144.

97. Seymour Hersh, "The Grey Zone: How a Secret Pentagon Program Came to Abu Ghraib," *New Yorker*, May 24, 2004; James Pfiffner, *Torture as Public Policy* (Boulder, CO: Paradigm, 2011); Pfiffner, "The Efficacy of Coercive Interrogation," 139; Lagouranis, *Fear Up Harsh*, 246; and Fallon, *Unjustifiable Means*, 123.

98. Lagouranis, *Fear Up Harsh*, 92.

99. Lagouranis, *Fear Up Harsh*, 47, 160; and McCoy, *A Question of Torture*, 124.

100. Pfiffner, "The Efficacy of Coercive Interrogation," 129–31; Lagouranis, *Fear Up Harsh*, 35; Fallon, *Unjustifiable Means*, 108–9, 168. Mitchell contests this account and argues that the military became interested in "enhanced interrogation" in December 2001, long before the CIA did. Mitchell, *Enhanced Interrogation*, 258.

101. Mayer, *The Dark Side*, 189, 235, 241.

102. Fallon, *Unjustifiable Means*, 138–39, 144–48.

103. Mark Fallon and Susan E. Brandon, "The HIG Project: A Road to Scientific Research on Interrogation," in *Interrogation and Torture: Integrating Efficacy with Law and Morality*, eds. Steven J. Barela, Mark Fallon, Gloria Gaggioli, and Jens David Ohlin (Oxford: Oxford University Press, 2020), 126.

104. Lagouranis, *Fear Up Harsh*, 31.

105. Fallon, *Unjustifiable Means*, 58 and 117.

106. Stephen Budiansky, "Truth Extraction: A Classic Text on Interrogating Enemy Captives Offers a Counterintuitive Lesson on the Best Way to Get Information," *The Atlantic*, June 2005.

107. Lelyveld, "Interrogating Ourselves."

108. Lagouranis, *Fear Up Harsh*, 118–19; 30, 36, 50, 63.

109. Rumney, "Is Coercive Interrogation of Terrorist Suspects Effective?" 505, citing Human Rights Watch, "Leadership Failure: Firsthand Accounts of Torture of Iraqi Detainees by the US Army's 82nd Airborne Division 1–2," (2005), 12.

110. Rejali, *Torture and Democracy*, 478.

111. Ross and Esposito, "CIA's Harsh Interrogation Techniques Described"; and Schiemann, *Does Torture Work*, 48–58.

112. Ross and Esposito, "CIA's Harsh Interrogation Techniques Described"; and Mitchell, *Enhanced Interrogation*, 42.

113. Rodriguez, *Hard Measures*, 67, 80–83, 119.

114. Hersh, "The Grey Zone"; and Sands, "The Green Light."

115. Rejali, *Torture and Democracy*, 500; and Hina Shamsi, *Command's Responsibility: Detainee Deaths in U.S. Custody in Iraq and Afghanistan* (New York: Human Rights First, 2006).

116. Mitchell, *Enhanced Interrogation*, 111–22, 130–35; and Rodriguez, *Hard Measures*, 84.

117. Costanzo and Gerrity, "The Effects and Effectiveness of Using Torture," 202, citing John Conroy, *Unspeakable Acts, Ordinary People* (New York: Knopf, 2000); and Andersen, "Is Torture an Option in the War on Terror?"

118. Rumney, "Is Coercive Interrogation of Terrorist Suspects Effective?" 492–93.

119. Ursula E. Daxecker and Michael L. Hess, "Repression Hurts: Coercive Government Responses and the Demise of Terrorist Campaigns," *British Journal of Political Science* 43, no. 3 (2013): 559–77.

120. Christopher Michael Sullivan, "The (In)effectiveness of Torture for Combating Insurgency," *Journal of Peace Research* 51, no.3 (2014); and Lightcap, *Politics of Torture*.

121. Robert Pape, "Review by Robert Pape, University of Chicago," in *ISSF Forum on the Senate Select Committee on Intelligence (SSCI) Report and the United States' Post-9/11 Policy on Torture*, H-Diplo, ISSF Forum, no. 5 (2015), https://networks.h-net.org/node/28443/discussions/61352/issf-forum-senate-select-committee-intelligence-ssci-report-and#_Toc411763046; and Costanzo and Gerrity, "The Effects and Effectiveness of Using Torture," 202.

122. Amanda Murdie, "It Works on 24 but Not in Real Life: Peer-Reviewed Evidence that Torture Will Increase Terrorism," *Duck of Minerva*, January 25, 2017, available at http://duckofminerva.com/2017/01/peer-reviewed-evidence-that-torture-will-increase-terrorism.html.

123. Michael P. O'Connor and Celia M. Runmann, "Into the Fire: How to Avoid Getting Burned by the Same Mistakes Made Fighting Terrorism in Northern Ireland," *Cardozo Law Review* 24, no. 1657 (2002–3): 1750; and Rejali, *Torture and Democracy*, 493.

124. Mayer, "Outsourcing Torture."

125. Rumney, "Is Coercive Interrogation of Terrorist Suspects Effective?" 498.

126. Pape, "Review by Robert Pape."

127. Rejali, *Torture and Democracy*, 493, 503.

128. Lagouranis, *Fear Up Harsh*, 99.

129. For an overview of this argument, see Douglas A. Johnson, Alberto Mora, and Averell Schmidt, "The Strategic Costs of Torture: How 'Enhanced Interrogation' Hurt America," *Foreign Affairs*, September/October 2016, 121–32; Rejali, *Torture and Democracy*, 503; McCoy, *A Question of Torture*, 201–2; Posner and Vermeule, "Should Coercive Interrogation Be Legal?" 21; Boorman, "5 Arguments against Torture"; and Mayer, *The Dark Side*, 330–31.

130. James I. Walsh and James A. Piazza, "Why Respecting Physical Integrity Rights Reduces Terrorism," *Comparative Political Studies* 43, no. 5 (March 2010): 551–77; Mary Manjikian, "But My Hands Are Clean: The Ethics of Intelligence Sharing and the Problem of Complicity," *International Journal of Intelligence and Counterintelligence* 28, no. 4 (2015): 692–709; Jason Vest, "CIA Veterans Speak Out Against Torture," *Government Executive*, November 23, 2005; and Fallon, *Unjustifiable Means*, 191.

131. Asa Hutchinson and James R. Jones, *The Report of The Constitution Project's Task Force on Detainee Treatment* (Washington, DC: The Constitution Project, 2013), 279.

132. Hutchinson and Jones, *Report of the Constitution Project's Task Force*, 244, citing Peter Baker, "Banned Techniques Yielded 'High Value Information,' Memo Says," *New York Times*, April 21, 2009.

133. William R. Johnson, "Tricks of the Trade: Counterintelligence Interrogation," *International Journal of Intelligence and Counterintelligence* 1, no. 2 (1986): 103–13; Vest, "CIA Veterans Speak Out Against Torture"; and Costanzo and Gerrity, "The Effects and Effectiveness of Using Torture," 193–96.

134. Rejali, *Torture and Democracy*, 493, 502; and Mayer, *The Dark Side*, 119, 174.

135. Costanzo and Gerrity, "The Effects and Effectiveness of Using Torture," 154n54; O'Mara, *Why Torture Doesn't Work*, 205–6.

136. Hutchinson and Jones, *Report of the Constitution Project's Task Force*, 276–78; Carol Rosenberg, "Guantánamo Hearing: Ex-Interrogator Felt Sorry for Khadr," *Miami Herald* (May 5, 2010); Justine Sharrock, "Am I a Torturer?" *Mother Jones* (March 2008); James Randerson, "Guantánamo Guards Suffer Psychological Trauma," *Guardian* (UK), Feb. 25, 2008; and Lougranis, *Fear Up Harsh*, 236–37.

137. Jennifer S. Bryson, "My Guantánamo Experience: Support Interrogation, Reject Torture," Public Discourse, September 9, 2011, available at http://www.thepublicdiscourse.com/2011/09/3934, cited in Hutchinson and Jones, *Report of the Constitution Project's Task Force*, 276.

138. Vest, "CIA Veterans Speak Out Against Torture," citing Albert Camus, *Preface to the Algerian Reports*; and Bob Brecher, *Torture and the Ticking Bomb* (Malden, MA: Blackwell, 2007), 57.

139. Pfiffner, "The Efficacy of Coercive Interrogation," 138–40, 145; Alexander and Bruning, *How to Break a Terrorist*, 83; Stephen Budiansky, "Truth Extraction: A Classic Text on Interrogating Enemy Captives Offers a Counterintuitive Lesson on the Best Way to Get Information," *The Atlantic*, June 2005; Hutchinson and Jones, *Report of the Constitution Project's Task Force*, 263–66; Mark Fallon, *Unjustifiable Means*, 17.

140. Naturally, these experiments have not explored the effects of torture. See sources cited in Costanzo and Gerrity, "The Effects and Effectiveness of Using Torture," 183; Aldert Vrij, Christian Messiner, Ronald P. Fisher, Saul M. Kassin, Charles A. Morgan III, and Steven M. Kleinman, "Psychological Perspectives on Interrogation," *Perspectives on Psychological Science* 12, no. 6 (2017): 927–55; and Hutchinson and Jones, *Report of the Constitution Project's Task Force*, 259.

141. Rejali, *Torture and Democracy*, 458.

142. Rumney, "Is Coercive Interrogation of Terrorist Suspects Effective?" 497, citing Seymour Hersh, *Chain of Command: The Road from 9/11 to Abu Ghraib* (New York: Penguin Books, 2004).

143. Melissa B. Russano, Fadia M. Narchet, Steven M. Kleinman, and Christian A. Meissner, "Structured Interviews of Experienced HUMINT Interrogators," *Applied Cognitive Psychology* 28, no. 6 (2014): 847–59.

144. Misty C. Duke and Damien Van Puyvelde, "What Science Can Teach Us about 'Enhanced Interrogation,'" *International Journal of Intelligence and Counterintelligence* 30 (2017): 312.

145. Duke and Van Puyvelde, "What Science Can Teach Us," 312–14, 327; Costanzo and Gerrity, "The Effects and Effectiveness of Using Torture," 183; Simon Oleszkiewicz, Pär Anders Granhag, and Sebastian Cancino Montecinos, "The Scharff-Technique: Eliciting Intelligence from Human Sources," *Law and Human Behavior* 38, no. 5 (2014): 478–89; Laurence J. Alison, Emily Alison, Geraldine Noone, Stamatis Elntib, and Paul Christiansen, "Why Tough Tactics Fail and Rapport Gets Results: Observing Rapport-Based Interpersonal Techniques (ORBIT) to Generate Useful Information from Terrorists," *Psychology, Public Policy, and Law* 19, no. 4 (2013): 411–31; and Robert Fine, ed., *Educing Information: Interrogation: Science and Art: Foundation for the Future* (Washington, DC: National Defense Intelligence College, 2006).

146. O'Mara, *Why Torture Doesn't Work*, 121.

147. In one experiment, participants were asked to play a ball-toss game online to simulate the psychological effects of solitary confinement. In another experiment, the researchers investigated sleep deprivation as a form of torture by interviewing hard-working MBA students. Fallon and Brandon, "The HIG Project," 129, 227–30, citing Loran F. Nordgren, Mary-Hunter Morris McDonnell, and George Loewenstein, "What Constitutes Torture? Psychological Impediments to an Objective Evaluation of Enhanced Interrogation Tactics," *Psychological Science* 22, no. 5 (2011): 689–94. Rejali, "The Field of Torture Today," 96–97.

148. One such experiment involved twenty-three cadets from the Royal Norwegian Naval Academy who were undergoing interrogation training. They underwent a faux kidnapping, were placed in stress positions, and underwent eight hours of aggressive interrogation. Jon Christian Laberg, Jarle Eid, Bjørn Helge Johnsen, Bård S. Eriksen, and Kenneth K. Zachariassen, "Coping with Interrogations," in *The Human in Command* (Boston, MA: Springer, 2000), 333–44. Charles Morgan and his colleagues studied soldiers during SERE training who were exposed to high-stress conditions in a "mock POW camp," including physical confrontations, food deprivation, and sleep deprivation. Charles A. Morgan III, Steven Southwick, George Steffian, Gary A. Hazlett, and Elizabeth Loftus, "Misinformation Can Influence Memory for Recently Experienced, Highly Stressful Events," *International Journal of Law and Psychiatry*, 36, no. 1 (2013): 11–17; and Charles A Morgan III, Gary Hazlett, Madelon Baranoski, Anthony Doran, Steven Southwick, and Elizabeth Loftus, "Accuracy of Eyewitness Identification Is Significantly Associated with Performance on a Standardized Test of Face Recognition," *International Journal of Law and Psychiatry* 30, no. 3 (2007): 213–23. I thank an anonymous reviewer for pointing me to these sources.

149. Rejali, *Torture and Democracy*, 458–59, 476, 503.

150. Rodriguez, *Hard Measures*, 87.

151. Vest, "CIA Veterans Speak Out Against Torture."

152. Ackerman, "Some Will Call Me a Torturer."

153. Schiemann, *Does Torture Work*, 170, citing Glenn Carle, *The Interrogator: An Education* (New York: Nation Books, 2011), 74.

154. Schiemann, *Does Torture Work*, 171.

155. Soufan, *The Black Banners*, 375, 395–409, 414–23.

156. Mitchell goes further and argues that CIA and FBI agents sometimes interrogated AZ at the same time. Mitchell, *Enhanced Interrogation*, 25.

157. Soufan, *The Black Banners*, 430.

158. Rejali, *Torture and Democracy*, 505.

159. Doug Struck, Howard Schneider, Karl Vick, and Peter Baker, "Borderless Network of Terror," *Washington Post*, September 23, 2001.

160. Rejali, *Torture and Democracy*, 507–8; and McCoy, *A Question of Torture*, 112.

161. Fritz Allhoff, *Terrorism, Ticking Time Bombs, and Torture* (Chicago: University of Chicago Press, 2012), 166.

162. Matthew Brzezinski, "Bust and Boom," *Washington Post*, December 30, 2001.

163. Allhoff, *Terrorism, Ticking Time Bombs, and Torture*, 159–60, citing (and criticizing) Matthew Alexander and John R. Bruning, *How to Break a Terrorist* (New York: Free Press, 2008).

164. Frank Snepp, "Tortured by the Past," *LA Times*, April 27, 2009.

165. Rejali, *Torture and Democracy*, 452, citing Biderman, *March to Calumny: The Story of American POW's in the Korean War* (New York: Macmillan, 1963), 136.

166. McCoy, *A Question of Torture*, 46, citing Lawrence E. Hinkle and Harold G. Wolff, "Communist Interrogation and Indoctrination of 'Enemies of the State': Analysis of

Methods Used by the Communist State Police (a Special Report)," *Archives of Neurology and Psychiatry* 76 (1956): 115–74.

167. Soufan, *The Black Banners*, 374–76.

168. Mitchell, *Enhanced Interrogation*, 34.

169. Soufan, *The Black Banners*, 382–84.

170. Schiemann, *Does Torture Work?* 2.

171. Bonner, Van Natta Jr., and Waldman, "Threats and Responses."

172. Soufan, *The Black Banners*, 384, 390.

173. Rejali, *Torture and Democracy*. On torture reform in democracies, see Henry Frank Carey, *Reaping What You Sow: A Comparative Examination of Torture Reform in the United States, France, Argentina, and Israel* (ABC-CLIO, 2011); and Henry Frank Carey, "Torture Reform in Democracies: A Causal Interpretation," in *Examining Torture*, eds. Lightcap and Pfiffner, 185–211. On legal and institutional constraints on torture in democracies and dictatorships, see Courtenay Ryals Conrad and Will H. Moore, "What Stops the Torture?" *American Journal of Political Science* 54 (2010): 459–76; Courtenay R. Conrad, "Divergent Incentives for Dictators: Domestic Institutions and (International Promises Not to) Torture," *Journal of Conflict Resolution* 58, no.1 (2014): 34–67; and Courtenay R. Conrad, Daniel W. Hill Jr, and Will H. Moore, "Torture and the Limits of Democratic Institutions," *Journal of Peace Research* 55, no.1 (2018): 3–17.

174. Courtenay R. Conrad, Jillienne Haglund, and Will H. Moore, "Disaggregating Torture Allegations: Introducing the Ill-Treatment and Torture (ITT) Country-Year Data," *International Studies Perspectives* 14, no. 2 (2013): 199–220.

175. Einolf, *America in the Philippines*.

176. Christopher Einolf, "Does Torture Work? An Empirical Test Using Archival Data," paper presented at the September 2018 conference of the Association of Human Rights Institutes in Edinburgh, Scotland.

177. Bundesbeauftragter für die Unterlagen des Staatssicherheitsdienstes der ehemaligen Deutschen Demokratischen Republik, at https://www.bstu.de/ueber-uns/bstu-in-zahlen/.

178. Helen Pidd, "Stasi Files Row as Britain Refuses to Return Documents to Germany," *The Guardian*, December 28, 2011, available at https://www.theguardian.com/world/2011/dec/28/stasi-files-row-britain-germany).

179. "Stasi Files: German Plan to Transfer Files Sparks Concern," September 27, 2019, at https://www.bbc.com/news/world-europe-49847900.

## EPILOGUE

1. The following is based on testimony of Perla Mark, wife of Rabbi Abraham Mark, at the Eichmann trial, session 48, May 23, 1961, available at https://collections.ushmm.org/search/catalog/irn1001582. Additional information from Yad Vashem's International Institute for the Study of the Holocaust, *Encyclopedia of the Ghettos*, entry for Czernowitz, at https://www.yadvashem.org/yv/he/research/ghettos_encyclopedia/ghetto_details.asp?cid=867.

2. Sanford Levinson, "Contemplating Torture: An Introduction," in *Torture: A Collection*, ed. Sanford Levinson (Oxford: Oxford University Press, 2004), 33.

3. James E. Mitchell, *Enhanced Interrogation: Inside the Minds and Motives of the Islamic Terrorists Trying to Destroy America* (New York: Crown Publishing, 2016), 150.

4. John W. Schiemann, *Does Torture Work?* (Oxford: Oxford University Press, 2016), 211. On competing arguments against torture and rhetorical coercion, see Frank Foley, "The Delegitimation of Torture: Rhetoric, Shaming and Narrative Contestation in Two British Cases," *European Journal of International Relations* 27, no.1 (2021): 102–26.

5. Tony Lagouranis, *Fear Up Harsh: An Army Interrogator's Dark Journey Through Iraq* (New York: New American Library, 2007), 244.

6. Darius Rejali, *Torture and Democracy* (Princeton: Princeton University Press, 2007), 465–66.

7. For criticisms of this absolutist Kantian view, like the claim that absolute rights are unjustifiable or that they clash with competing absolute rights, such as the right to self-defense, see Mirko Bagarig and Julie Clarke, "Not Enough Official Torture in the World? The Circumstances in Which Torture Is Morally Justifiable," *University of San Francisco Law Review* 39 (spring 2005): 601–2; Oren Gross, "The Prohibitions on Torture and the Limits of the Law," in Levinson, *Torture: A Collection*, 229–53; Charles Fried, *Right and Wrong* (Cambridge: Harvard University Press, 1978), 10; Jan Goldman, ed., *Ethics of Spying: A Reader for the Intelligence Professional* (Lanham, MD: Scarecrow Press, 2006); Robert D. Chapman, "A Review of Lies, Torture, and Humanity," *International Journal of Intelligence and Counterintelligence* 20, no.1 (2007): 188–94; Fritz Allhoff, *Terrorism, Ticking Time Bombs, and Torture* (Chicago: University of Chicago Press, 2012), 121; Eric Posner and Adrian Vermeule, "Should Coercive Interrogation Be Legal?" *Public Law and Theory Working Papers*, University of Chicago Law School, 2005, 5; and Louis Michael Seidman, "Torture's Truth," *University of Chicago Law Review* 72, no. 3 (2005): 895–97.

8. The most eloquent defense of this position appears in Elaine Scarry, *The Body in Pain: The Making and Unmaking of the World* (New York: Oxford University Press, 1985), especially 27–59. See also John W. Schiemann, *Does Torture Work?* (Oxford: Oxford University Press, 2016), 12.

9. Bagarig and Clarke, "Not Enough Official Torture in the World?" 599, citing Ronald Dworkin, *Taking Rights Seriously*, 4th ed. (London: Gerald Duckworth, 1978), 198; Charles Fried and Gregory Fried, *Because It Is Wrong: Torture, Privacy, and Presidential Power in the Age of Terror* (New York: W. W. Norton, 2010), 55.

10. David Sussman, "What's Wrong with Torture," *Philosophy and Public Affairs* 33 (2005): 4, 8, 21–29.

11. Seidman, "Torture's Truth," 905–7.

12. Henry Shue, "Torture," *Philosophy and Public Affairs* 7, no. 2 (winter 1978): 127–30; and Sussman, "What's Wrong with Torture," 6. For the contrary argument, that terrorists are not innocent and can escape torture by cooperating, see Miriam Gur-Arye, "Can the War against Terror Justify the Use of Force in Interrogation? Reflections in Light of the Israeli Experience," in Levinson, *Torture: A Collection*, 192; Sussman, "What's Wrong with Torture," 18; Bob Brecher, *Torture and the Ticking Bomb* (Malden, MA: Blackwell, 2007), 78, citing Jean Améry, "Torture," in Jean Amery, *At the Mind's Limit,* trans. S. Rosenfeld (Bloomington: University of Indiana Press, 1980).

13. David Luban, "Liberalism, Torture, and the Ticking Bomb," in *Intervention, Terrorism, and Torture*, ed. S. P. Lee (Springer: Netherlands, 2007), 249–62.

14. Levinson, *Torture: A Collection*, 172, citing Supreme Court of Israel, "Judgment Concerning the Legality of the General Security Service's Interrogation Methods" (September 6, 1999). On the stance of Israeli courts regarding torture, see also Assaf Meydani, "The Interrogation Policy of the Israeli General Security Service: Between Law and Politics," *International Journal of Intelligence and Counterintelligence* 21, no.1 (2008): 26–39; and Daphna Sharfman and Ephraim Kahana, "Combating Terrorism With Intelligence: The Normative Debate in Israel," *International Journal of Intelligence and Counterintelligence* 25, no. 3 (2012): 546–70.

15. Mary Ellen O'Connell, "Affirming the Ban on Harsh Interrogation," *Ohio State Law Journal* 66 (2005): 1256; Kira Vrist Ronn, "Intelligence Ethics: A Critical Review and Future Perspectives," *International Journal of Intelligence and Counterintelligence* 29, no. 4

(2016): 760–84; and Sir David Omand and Mark Phythian, "Ethics and Intelligence: A Debate," *International Journal of Intelligence and Counterintelligence*, 26, no. 1 (2013): 38–63.

16. Ron E. Hassner, "Persuasive and Unpersuasive Critiques of Torture," paper presented at the annual convention of the International Studies Association, April 2021.

17. M. Gregg Bloche, "Beyond Ethics on the Sly: The Behavioral Sciences and National-Security Interrogation," in Steven J. Barela, Mark Fallon, Gloria Gaggioli, and Jens David Ohlin, *Interrogation and Torture: Integrating Efficacy with Law and Morality* (Oxford: Oxford University Press, 2020), 279–318.

18. Aquinas did not comment on torture in his writing, though he must have been aware of the papal bull Ad Extirpanda (1252) that regulated inquisitorial torture in certain parts of Italy. Jordan Bishop, "Aquinas on Torture," *New Blackfriars* 87, no. 1009 (May 2006): 229–37.

19. This doctrine is expressed in *Summa Theologica* (II-II, Qu. 64, Art.7). For an analysis, see F. J. Connell, "Double Effect, Principle of," *New Catholic Encyclopedia* (New York: McGraw-Hill, 1967), 4:1020–22.

20. Mark Fallon and Susan E. Brandon, "The HIG Project: A Road to Scientific Research on Interrogation," in Steven J. Barela, Mark Fallon, Gloria Gaggioli, and Jens David Ohlin, *Interrogation and Torture: Integrating Efficacy with Law and Morality* (Oxford: Oxford University Press, 2020): 135.

21. Fallon and Brandon, "The HIG Project," 134.

22. Fallon and Brandon, "The HIG Project," 137.

23. Correspondence of July 18, 2018.

24. Correspondence of October 27, 2020.

# Index

Abu Ghraib prison, 127, 129–32
Acosta, Manuel de, 71
Acuña, Fernando de, 100
Afghanistan, 128–30, 136
Aguilar, 34–35
Aguilar, Isabel de, 78
Al-Baluchi, Ammar, 120
Al-Faruq, Omar, 124
Algeria, 4, 9–10, 124, 126, 132, 141
Alguazil, Felipe, 68
Al-Jaza<hamza>iri, Abu Yassir, 121
Al-Kuwaiti, Abu Ahmad, 120–21, 123
Alleg, Henri, 124–25
Al-Libi, Abu Faraj, 120
Al-Libi, Ibn al-Shaykh, 128
Almeida, Jorge de, 94, 96, 115
Al-Nashiri, Abd al-Rahim, 120
Alonso, Beatriz, 59–60
Al-Qaeda, 6–8, 10, 17, 20, 120, 122, 124, 128, 131, 135
Al-Qahtani, Muhammad, 123–24
Al-Shibh, Ramzi bin, 8, 120
Al-Tayyar, Jarar, 8
Álvarez, Jorge, 108, 111
Álvarez, Juan, 108
Álvarez, Leonor, 58–59
Álvarez, Manuel, 111
American Psychological Association, 150
Amnesty International, 141
Andalusia tribunal, 38, 41
Andrada, Leonor de, 83
Aquen, Luis, 69
Aquinas, Thomas, 149
Archivo Histórico Nacional, 67
Argentina, 73
Argüello, García de, 55
Armenderría, Guido de, 72
Army Field Manual (1992), 10, 121
Atiença, Mateo de, 74
Atta, Mohammad, 124
Aussaresses, Paul, 10
autos-da-fé, 20, 43, 45, 49, 82–83, 93, 95–97, 112, 114, 117
Avana, María de, 73

Báez Pinto, Francisco, 72
Bagram Air Force Base, 130
Bajo, Juan, 68
Bancroft Library (University of California, Berkeley), 23, 33, 83–84, 99, 101, 105–6
Beghal, James, 124
Beinart, Chaim, 14, 39–40, 140
Beza, Theodore, 72
Biderman, Albert, 9
Bigeard, Marcel, 10
Bin Attash, Khallad, 120
Bin Laden, Osama, 6–8, 120–21, 124, 127
Blair, Dennis, 133
Bloche, M. Gregg, 148–49
Bosque, Juan del, 72
Brennan, John, 7
Britain, 9, 132, 135
Bryson, Jennifer, 133
burnings at the stake, 42–43, 45, 48–49, 56, 63, 82, 103, 107, 112. *See also* autos-da-fé

Campo, Elvira de, 29–31
Camus, Albert, 133
Canary Islands tribunal, 18, 117, 139
Canete, Miguel, 76
Carle, Glenn, 136
Carvajal, Anica de, 82, 87, 89, 94, 111–12
Carvajal, Baltasar de, 87, 89–92, 94, 110
Carvajal, Catalina de, 82, 89–91, 93–95, 111
Carvajal, Francisca de, 82, 87–96, 105, 111
Carvajal, Francisca Núñez de, 86–89
Carvajal, Fray Gaspar de, 88–89, 91, 93
Carvajal, Guiomar de, 88
Carvajal, Isabel de, 82, 87–91, *92*, 93–95, 103, 105, 111, 115
Carvajal, Leonor de, 82, 89–91, 94–96, 98, 103, 105, 111
Carvajal, Luis de, 82–98, 100–103, 105, 107–8, 110–15
Carvajal, Maríana de, 82, 89–91, 93–94, 105, *111*, 112–13
Carvajal, Miguel de, 89
Carvajal y de la Cueva, Luis de, 85–87, 89, 91, 93